Professional Teaching Competency

Professional Teaching Competency

Edited by
Dr. G. VISVANATHAN
Professor, Department of Education,
Annamalai University, Tamil Nadu
and
Dr.S.K.PANNEER SELVAM
Assistant Professor, Department of Education
Bharathidasan University, Tamil Nadu

RANDOM PUBLICATIONS
NEW DELHI (INDIA)

Professional Teaching Competency

ISBN 978-93-5111-355-3

Published in 2014 in India by
RANDOM PUBLICATIONS
4376-A/4B, Gali Murari Lal, Ansari Road
New Delhi-110 002
Phone: +9111-43580356, 23289044
E-mail: randomexports@gmail.com; sales@randompublications.com; info@randompublications.com

Reprinted 2024

Type Setting by : Shah Computer Graphics, Delhi-110094
Digitally Printed at : Replika Press Pvt. Ltd.

Contents

1
Intelligence and Teaching Competence of Teacher Trainees

2
Review of Relaterd Literature 13

3
Methodlogy 28

2
Emotional Intelligence of Elementary School Teachers

4

Personality Disorder of College Students

1. Intelligence and Teaching Competence of Teacher Trainees

1

Problem and its Perspectives

INTRODUCTION

Teachers should be the living incarnation of the great trinity of truth, goodness and beauty. They must have a deep sense of reasoning, non-violence and objective outlook towards everything and they must appreciate beauty and orderliness. Teacher must have robust optimism and free from frustration and compassion; his personality will be dead wood without tender feelings for anybody. His vision of life must be based on love sympathy and affection for all in general and for the needy and deprived classes of the society in particular.

According to **Viswakavi Rabindranath Tagore** "A lamp never lights another lamp unless it continues to burn its own flame. A teacher can never truly teach unless he is still learning in himself"

IMPORTANCE OF EDUCATION

Education is an exclusively human activity. Man inherits his cultural heritage from his elders in society, through education. A person without education is really like a blind. In the words of Rousseau, "Plants are developed by cultivation and men by education" Education nourishes us like a mother. It directs us to the proper path like the father. It guides us to reach our destination like a teacher.

According to **John Dewey,** "True education comes through the stimulation of child's power by the demands of social stimulation in which he finds himself".

CONCEPT OF INTELLIGENCE

Intelligence is the general mental adaptability for new problems and new situations of life. It is the power within a person to analyze what to do and act accordingly. It also emphasis the ability to learn, that is one's intelligence is educable. It also emphasis on effective use of concept and symbols in dealing with situations. Intelligence is an inherited capacity of an individual. It is the capacity to improve upon native tendency in the light of past experiences. This is manifested through his ability to adopt and to reconstruct the factors of his environment in accordance with his group. Most psychologists accept the idea that learning capacity is an essential aspect of intelligence. There are instances of pupils who face special fields like art and mechanics. Intelligence is the general capacity of an individual to consciously adjust his thinking to new requirements

INTELLIGENCE

Intelligence is the capacities to acquire and apply knowledge. Intelligence is the general ability Intelligence is assumed to be basically a matter of relationships. Many psychologists observe the positive relationships between different types of performance. There are various definitions given by the psychologists as follows

According to **Colvin** "An individual possess intelligence in so far as he has learned or can learn to adjust himself to an environment".

Freeman states "An individual is intelligent in proportion as he is able to carry on abstract thinking".

Gates observes, "Intelligence is a composite organization of abilities to learn, to grasp broad and stable facts especially abstract facts with alertness accuracy, to exercise mental control and to display flexibility ingenuity in seeking the solutions to problems".

Rex Knight notes, "Intelligence is the ability to discover the relevant qualities and relations of the objects or ideas that are before us and to evoke relevant idea; in other words it is capacity of relational thinking, directed to the attainment of some end".

CHARACTERISTICS OF INTELLIGENCE

According to **Woodworth,** "An intelligent person makes use of his past experience to an immediate problem or seeks a goal. He can adopt himself to a novel situation and face to solve a new problem or master a complex situation. He tries to understand the cause of the problem before trying a solution for it. Thinks ahead of time, keeps a brooder outlook and tries to be different from others.

TYPES OF INTELLIGENCE

Intelligence is the aggregate or global capacity of the individual to act purposefully to think rationally and to deal effectively with his environment. Philosophers and psychologists developed various types with regard to nature of intelligence; they classified intelligence into various categories.

CONCRETE INTLLIGENCE

This type of intelligence is applicable when the individual is handling concrete objects or machines. The person uses this intelligence in the operation of tools and instruments. Engineers and mechanics generally have this type of intelligence.

ABSTRACT INTELLIGENCE

This type of intelligence is acquired after an intensive study of book and related literature. It is mostly literary in content. Mostly good teachers, lawyers, doctors and philosophers have this type of knowledge.

SOCIAL INTELLIGENCE

Persons having this type of intelligence have a dynamic personality. They know the art of winning friends and influencing them. They present their views in an attractive manner and generally seek the approval of their friends and associates. Leaders, ministers, members of the diplomatic sources and social workers have it.

It is difficult to say about the distribution of the above three types of intelligence. Some may have more of concrete intelligence though he may not be an engineer. It is also possible that an engineer may have more of abstract intelligence and less of concrete.

Howard Gardner classified the intelligence into nine types based on multiple intelligence theory, they are:

Naturalist Intelligence
Musical Intelligence
Logical Mathematical Intelligence
Existential Intelligence
Interpersonal Intelligence
Bodily-Kinesthetic Intelligence
Linguistic Intelligence
Intra-personal Intelligence
Spatial Intelligence

MEASUREMENT OF INTELLIGENCE

Some of the basic expressions for the measurement of intelligence are mental age, chronological age and intelligence quotient.

CHRONOLOGICAL AGE

Chronological age is the physical age of a person, counted from the date and time of his birth. It is counted in terms of years, month and date etc.

MENTAL AGE

Mental age is an index of intelligence rank. Mental age means that a given child's performance of a test is like the average performance on the same test of children of a given chorological age.

INTELLIGENCE QUOTIENT

Intelligence quotient is synonymous with intelligence. Intelligence quotient (I.Q) means a child's Mental Age (M.A) divided by his Chronological Age (C.A) multiplied by IQ = (MA/CA) 100.

INTELLIGENCE AND EDUCATIONAL IMPLICATION

Mental development is influenced by both heredity and environment. A very little change can be alone to change the influence of heredity. But the parents, the teachers and the school can provide a healthy and motivating intellectual environment for the child. In this regard, the combined efforts of the child, the family and the society can do a great deal of work. The cultural and social experiences, learning opportunities and discipline, which he receives in the learning environment contributes significantly towards his mental development in contrary to the notion that many students who fail in examination do have sufficient intelligence, but are unable to progress because of certain personality inadequacies, family problems and social factors.

TEACHNG COMPETENCE

The teacher has a major role in the educational development **Gandhiji** remarked that "no country can make any progress without good teachers" The quality and standard of education depends on the quality and standard of teachers. Teacher is the torch bearer of the race and guardian of the feature of the mankind.

According to **Humagun Kabir:** "Teachers are literally the architects of a nations destiny " **Mrs. Indira Gandhi** stated, "The nations well being depends upon the teachers well being our teachers are the 'custodians' of future. No society can afford to neglect them".

"Competency" ordinarily is defined as "Adequate for the purpose; suitable, sufficient, or as capable". In a sense it refers to adequate preparation to begin a professional career, and has a direct linkage to verification requirements.

Cooker (1976) defined "competence is seen as the ability to cope with a certain class of problems encountered on the job. A teacher who can deal with problems in certain area is said to be competent in that area a fully competent teacher is one who can cope successfully with any "propositional problem." Competency in teaching stems forms the capacity to reach out differing children and to create a rich and multidimensional environment for them **(Joyce** and **Well 1985).**

To study the effectiveness "competency based teacher training (CBTT) Strategy" for developing following basic teaching competencies among pre service teacher;

(1) Cognitive- based teaching competency

(2) Performance -based teaching competency

(3) Affective - based teaching competency

(4) Consequence - based teaching competency

(5) Managerial - based teaching competency

CONCEPTS OF TEACHING COMPETENCE

A competent teacher has good command of subject matter and solid core of teaching skills. They have excellent instructional strategies supported by methods of goal setting, instructional planning and classroom management. They know how to motivate, communicate and work effectively with students. The teachers play an important role in molding and shaping the attitudes, habits, and manners and above all, the character and personality of the students. The teacher with competency does the planning, organization, reading and controlling of teaching. He is free to perform various activities to provide a learning experience to the learners.

DEFINITIONS

In the words of **Murthy** and **Lulla,** "Competence based teacher education is that type of professional education of ãlassroom teachers that takes the pre-determined competence of teaching behaviors as the base of teacher education programs".

The Education Commission (1964-66) observed, "Of all the different factors, which influence its quality of education and its contribution to national development, the quality, competence and characters are undoubtedly the most significant".

COMPETENCIES TO BE DEVELOPED

Competence in the use of any methodology involves being able to choose intelligently with the knowledge, experience and skill to make chosen methods work effectively. This can only be acquired by experience, which requires confidence, risk taking and reflection on what happens, so the competencies that are to be developed among the teacher trainees are as follows.

1. Competence to understand the sight process of learning, including learning, learning by doing, learning to be, learning to do and learning to become.
2. Competence to devise dynamic methods in the day-to-day situations based on the needs and interests of children
3. Competence to organize the classroom in such a manner that different kinds of activities may be organized in it so that children may receive required guidance from teacher.

4. Competence to become an example of qualities that he/she wants to develop among his/ her students, realizing that example is superior to mere instruction and preaching.
5. Competence in regard to language, delivery of speech and other method of communication.
6. Competence in regard to the contents of the subject that he / she are supposed to teach. The teacher should be able to answer questions that belong to the immediate reason or even to some remotely related subject matter, which may occur in subsequent reason.
7. Competence to engage children in a meaningful manner so that children my develop capacity to ask question and may be inspired to find out the answers by themselves.
8. Competence to innovate so as to create proper environment in the classroom to enable children to develop wider horizons of perceptions.
9. Competence to develop among students a scientific temper, which is often confined to cultivation of various attitudes, includes objective observation, experimentation and consideration of every point of view relevant to the enquiry in a logical manner.

The competencies mentioned above suggest that the school teacher in the developing countries may inspire a change in the impulses of the pupils growing personality so as to have a balanced blending of knowledge, power, love and skills that are required for his/her development as a good individual and useful member of the society. The teacher has to develop competence to innovative methods oriented and learner's need based. The teachers may be apprised what they are supposed to teach.

COMPETENCY AREAS

National Council for Teacher Education **(NCTE)** has identified ten competency areas in teacher preparation:

(i) Contextual competencies including development of education in society and teacher's role in it.
(ii) Conceptual competencies comprising various concepts of education and learning and psychological, sociological and physiological aspects of education.

(iii) Curricula and content competencies relating different stages of education like primary, upper-primary and secondary.

(iv) Transitional competencies as regards general subject-wise and stage-wise dimensions.

(v) Competencies in other educational activities such as planning and organizing morning assembly, etc.

(vi) Competencies relating to teaching-learning materials

(vii) Evaluation competencies including preparation, selection, use of tools, justice etc.

(viii) Management competencies including organization of classroom, school and community activities.

(ix) Competencies related to working with parents understand the role; discuss the problems; active co-operation; organize parent teacher meetings; explore and utilize educational resources etc.,

(x) Competencies related to working with the community and other agencies through understand the importance; contribute for improvement; realize the objectives; develop wholesome relationship; explore and exploit community educational resources activities etc.

A TO Z OF TEACHING COMPETENCIES

Teaching is an interactive process involving many aspects of teacher, student, learning process and learning situations. So in order to be a competent teacher one must have competent in the following dispositions.

'A' is for alertness.

'B' is for business like attitude to keep busy in worthwhile tasks.

'C' is for clarity and co-operative teaching learning.

'D' is for devotion and discovery.

'E' is for enthusiasm, expecting children to learn and evaluation.

'F' is for feedback for the guidance of the learner and evaluation

'G' is for goal setting and achieving.

'H' is for hard work, honest work, humility and humor.

'I' is for involvement of children.

'J' is for judicious attitude and just action.

'K' is for knowledge of the students, subject-mater of oneself.

'L' is for linking learning with daily experiences and life.

'M' is for motivation.

'N' is for need-based learning.

'O' is for objectivity and providing out of classroom learning experiences.

'P' is for practice and praising children when needed.

'Q' is for quiz organizing for monitoring learning progress

'R' is for relationships and review.

'S' is for stimulation.

'T' is for tolerance and the technology of teaching learning.

'U' is for unbiased attitude and unexpected encounters and situations.

'V' is for a variety of learning experience.

'W' is for warmth and wisdom.

'X' is for x-ray of the learning process.

'Y' is for yearning and eagerness.

'Z' is for zeal.

ESSENTIAL QUALITIES OF A COMPETENT TEACHER

In order to be a competent teacher, he must possess certain special qualities such as

(1) Qualities relating to professional requirements

(2) Qualities relating to character and personality.

(3) Qualities relating to human relationship.

(4) Qualifications relation to professional educational/ training

SIGNIFICANCE OF THE STUDY

Intelligence is the important aspect of an individual. Through intelligence one can know his abilities and capabilities. Intelligence test is used to categories people into different group. Person having intelligence is capable of doing all things. Teaching is an interactive process, involving four aspects teacher, student, learning process and learning situation. A competent teacher possesses all the necessary qualities to interact with the school and community. Teacher with intelligence will be able to teach students with all capabilities. So the present study has been conducted to verify how intelligence is correlated with the teaching competency of the B.Ed teacher trainees. It is must that every teacher trainee should have minimum intelligence to be perfect in his teaching competency. Hence this study has been conducted to verify these interesting aspects.

CONCLUSION

The first chapter is chiefly concerned with the conceptual framework of the problem chosen for the present study. The descriptions on teaching competence and intelligence among the teacher trainees have been presented to highlight the conceptual position with which this study has been planned and conducted.

2

Review of Relaterd Literature

INTRODUCTION

The key to the vast store house of the published literature may open door to source of significant problems and exclamatory hypotheses and provide helpful orientation for definition of the problem, background for selection of procedure and comparative data for interpretation of results. In order to be truly creative and original one must read extensively and critically as stimulus to thinking good (1959)

Review of related literature gives a broad idea to the investigator to carry out his research work in a successful manner. It also helps him get thorough knowledge in his research work. Review tells the researcher what has been done and what needs to be done in a particular topic.

The related literature available on the proposed study is presented in this chapter under the following heads.

1. Studies related to intelligence.
2. Studies related to teaching competence.
3. Studies on intelligence and teaching competence.

FOREIGN STUDIES ON INTELLLIGENCE

Ann (2000) conducted an investigation on, "The influence of preference for novelty and gender on intelligence." The purpose of this research was to further investigate the link between preference for novelty and intelligence. A total sample of 86 children in grade V was selected. The result showed positive effect of cognitive novelty preference on intelligence.

Asthana (2000) made an attempt to assess the differences in some cognitive variables of general intelligence in rural and urban children. The study was conducted on 60 rural and 60 urban primary school children. Alexander along pass Test was used of measure general intelligence. The findings of the study showed that the rural children were to less intelligence into comparison to the urban primary schools children.

Hoenig (2002) conducted a study on the relation between memory and intelligence in children with learning disabilities. Memory of the ability to retain information was evaluated using the Test of Memory and Learning, a recently released test that gives a comprehensive measure of global memory functioning. Winchester's intelligence Scale for children used to assess intelligence. The tests to 80 students (aged 6-12 years) with learning disabilities. The correlation between global measure of memory and global measure of intelligence was significant indicating that the memory should be viewed as an important component when evaluating children with learning disabilities.

De. Smedt (2003) conducted a research on pre-academic and early-academic achievement in children with relocardio facial syndrome of borderline or normal intelligence. The study focused on pre-academic and early -academic skills in borderline to normal intelligent children within the last year of kindergarten and first grade of a primary school in Flanders. In the Kindergarten group, meta-linguistic awareness and counting skills were examined. In the group of first graders, children were tested on reading, spelling and mathematics. 13 children participated in this study. There were no differences in intelligence and academic outcomes between boys and girls, and no differences in IQ and academic achievement between children with cardiac defects or severe velopharyngeal insufficiency (IPI) and children without these deficits. With regard to pre-academic achievement in general, a characteristic profile with clearly better results for meta-linguistic awareness in comparison with counting skill was found, but this difference was not statistically significant. However, at an individual level –especially within the domain of counting skills and mathematics, there is wide variability, with some children showing remarkable learning difficulties already at an early age.

Demethiou (2003) conducted research on, "The Missing link in the relations between intelligence and personality". The researcher studied relationship between performance tasks representing five cognitive domains (quantitative, categorical, spatial, causal and prepositional reasoning) and self-attribution of ability in regard to them and also in regard to four general cognitive functions (processing speed, working memory, self-monitoring and self-regulation), and the big five factors of personality (extraversion, agreeableness, conscientiousness, neuroticism and openness to experience) on students in the age group of 12-17 years. Structural equations modeling showed that self-attribution of ability are to some extent, dependent on cognitive performance. Cognitive performance is weakly related only to two of the five factors (openness and conscientiousness) of personality Self-attribution of ability is substantially related to all but the neuroticism factor differs. Apart from openness to experience, the dependence of personality dimensions on the dimensions of cognitive self-representation tends to weaken with age. It is concluded that influence of cognitive abilities on personality can be mediated by self-awareness about them.

Garlick (2003) conducted a research on "integrating brain science research with intelligence research" and he says that the possible cause of differences unintelligence is crucial to children who are to achieve their full potential. Such understanding has been hampered until recently, however, because researchers who study intelligence have neglected recent findings in the brain sciences suggesting that the brain develops in response to environmental stimulation. These findings contradict intelligence research, which suggests that intelligence abilities are inherited. However the findings from intelligence research and the brain sciences can be integrated if it is accepted that there are individual differences in the process by which the brain adapts to the environment, such that some peoples' brains are better at adapting than others. The findings obtained from intelligence research are consistent with this integrated model. Such integration has implications for better understanding of the nature of intelligence.

Kinlaw (2003) conducted a research on "The Development of children's beliefs about intelligence." Research was focused on the development of children's beliefs about intelligence and proposed that this development requires simultaneous processes of concept acquisition and theory building. Research in beliefs about the nature of intelligence has focused on children's definitions of intelligence, beliefs about the component structure of intelligence and the criteria, children use to evaluate ability. Children's beliefs about the stability of intelligence have been examined in terms of constancy, controllability, capacity and the origins of intelligence and mechanisms of change. It was found that intelligence and achievement are positively related.

Meullum (2003) conducted a research on comprehensive test of nonverbal intelligence. It discuss the apprehensive test of nonverbal intelligence, which was designed to provide an estimate of the intelligence of individuals who are not proficient in English, or who are deaf, disadvantaged, language disordered, or motor impaired. The test formats and items were selected on the basis of statistical analysis. The results showed that items contained little gender or no ethnic bias

Petrill (2003) conducted a research on, "The development intelligence behavioral genetic approaches". The purpose was to outline the behavioral genetic literature on the development of intelligence in childhood, adolescence and adulthood; to describe the implications of these findings for neuroscience and to search for genetic makers and evil factors influencing intelligence. Behavioral genetic research suggests that genetic influences relating to intelligence becomes the greatest across development stages.

Rushton (2003) conducted a research on African white IQ differences from Zimbabwe on the Weshsler's Intelligence Scale for children revised, mainly in the 'g' factor. It was noted that African white differences on the sub tests of the Weschler's Intelligence Scale in Zimbabwe were like the black white, differences in the US being positively associated with the sub tests. 12-14 years old Zimbabweans in Canada in the ten sub-tests were compared against white Americans.

Junhi (2004) conducted a research on "Low intelligence and levels of lead and cadmium in children. The researcher studied the influence levels of lead and Cadmium in the bodies of children on their intelligence. 112 children with low intelligence and 80 children with high intelligence were selected from 3,700 elementary schools (7-12 years) by using an intelligence test peripheral blood and first urine of both the groups were collected in the morning to measure the levels of lead and Cadmium. The results showed that there was significant difference in the level of lead in the blood between the two groups

INDIAN STUDIES ON INTELLIGENCE:

Sinha and Vibha (1998) studied the relationship between level of bed exposure and intelligence and vigilance performance in a sample of 960 school going children of Agra. Biological monitoring of lead through nadir analysis was done to assess the level of lcad cxposure. The tool used for intelligence and vigilance was Whechster Intelligence Scale for children. It was found that increased level of lead in the hair caused a decrease in intelligence and vigilance test scores.

Archana (1998), made an investigation on intelligence to find out whether there is any relationship between intelligence, gender, religion and socioeconomic status. The study was done on 480 students. The tools were Mohsin Gender Intelligence test and Socio-economic Status scale by Kuppuswamy. The study revealed the following: General does not exercise any significant influence on the intelligence level. Socio-economic status has significant effect on the subjects. Religion and socio-economic status, independently as well as internationally are significant factors in the determination of IQ. She explored the independent as well as interactions effect of religion on intelligence. Two religious groups –Hindus and Muslims with an incidental sample of 480 college students, were administered using Mohsin General Intelligence Test. A three way ANOVA revealed that religion had significant impact on intelligence level religions interacting with socio-economic status creates significant difference in intelligence scores.

Agarwal (1999) made and attempt to compare the failed and passed students on the basis of their intelligence, family relations, socio-economic status and adjustment. The sample size was 200, who were selected from the higher secondary schools of Uttar Pradesh. The tool used was Jalotai Group Test of General Ability, Bharadwaj, Gupta and Chauhan's Socio-Economic Scale and Sherry and Sinha's Adjustment Inventory for school students. The major findings intelligence, family relations and socio-economic status are permanent factors related to the scholastic achievement of high school students. Intelligence is innate and cannot be increased beyond limit.

Tyagi (1999) made a study to compare the acoustic behavior of boys and girls as a function of intelligence. A Stratified random sample of 480 boys and 480 girls was administered using the Mental Ability Test (Joshi) and Altruism Scale (Tyagi). The results revealed that girls were more intelligent and altruistic than boys. Altruism correlated with intelligence.

Sharma and **Kumar (1999)** made an attempt to compare the intelligence of the first born child The sample consisted of 120 children and tools used were: For the children of 5-11 years of age, Raven's Colored Progressive Matrices. For the children above 11 years of age, Raven's Advanced Progressive Matrices. The major findings were that there was no significant difference in intelligence of the first –born and the second born child, and no significant difference in intelligence of the first-born and the third born child.

Prabha and **Monika (2000)** examined the role of sex, intelligence and socio-economic status in the achievement of computer education. The sample size was 223. The tools were the Group Test of Intelligence (Ahuja) and Socio-Economic Status Scale by Bharadwawj. The examination marks scored in computer education were used as an index for computer achievement scores. The study showed that intelligence and computer education are positively and significantly correlated.

Gupta (2000) explored the effect of prolonged deprivation on intelligence and attainment of academic achievement of students. The sample consisted of 1453 students of grade 10. The Bengali version of Prolonged Deprivation Scale (PDS) by Misra and Tripathi and Raven's Progressive Matrices were administered to the subjects. Examination marks were taken as academic achievement score. The main findings were: Boys scored higher on the measures of both the intelligence and academic achievement than girls. There is a positive correlation between intelligence and academic achievement. Prolonged deprivation adversely affects the intelligence of boys and girls.

Deshmukh (2000) designed his study to compare high and low self-concept groups of junior college students with intelligence. The sample consisted of 832 students ranging in the age group of 16-20 years, studying in XII standard. The main finding was that high and low self-concept groups of junior college students differ significantly on intelligence.

Varma and **Varma (2000)** examined the relationship between academic achievement and intelligence, parental involvement, subject's motivational resources and assessed father and mother's contribution. Samples of 206 secondary school girls were administered using the tests. Analysis of the results. Control shows the understanding; perceived competence and self-regulation were more powerful than intelligence in academic achievement. Intelligence affect directly and indirectly by influencing motivational variables. Intelligence is not the only factor, which affect academic achievement.

Sangwan (2001) examined the relationship between intelligence and ecological factors in a Sample of 42 slow learn, with an IQ range of 90-110. The Stanford Binet Intelligence Scale was administered to assess the IQ of these children and an Interview Schedule was used to obtain the information on ecological factors like birth order, type of family, school environment, parent's education and occupation. The study revealed that these entire factors except birth order play an unimportant role in children's cognitive development and IQ.

Aswal (2001) made and attempt to examine the relationship between intelligence and achievement in Mathematics across different socio-economic status levels. A Sample of 200 students of grade 11 was administered. Group Test, and the Socio-Economic Status Scale and marks in Mathematics, scored in the high school board examination, were used as indices of Mathematics achievement. The major findings were: there is a significant correlation between intelligence and achievement in Mathematics. The relation between intelligence and achievement is significant across high, average and low socio-economic status. According to this study, intelligence, achievement and socio-economic status are interrelated.

Himain and **Asha (2001**) examined the relationship of Piaget stages of cognitive development and intelligence and creative thinking potential of female primary school students. The tools used were Culture Fair Test of Intelligence of 'g' and Piaget tasks, Verbal and Figural form of Torrance Test of Creative Thinking. The findings were: There is significant difference in the creative thinking at different stages of Piaget's stages of development and IQ is significant for all the subjects.

Lakxmi Thakur (2001) designed her study to see the effect of the different factors of home (conformity, reward, deprivation, permissiveness) that influence intelligence and educational aspirations.

The sample for the study was selected randomly. In the total sample 50% students were males and 50% were females. The findings of the study were: intelligence and educational aspirations positively correlated with each other, which indicate a linear incremental relationship between them. Conformity plays positive role intelligence. Reward is positively correlated with intelligence. Deprivation always has an effect on intelligence. Permissiveness has positive but non-significant correlation with intelligence.

Malini (2003) investigated on the main effect and interactive effect of non-verbal intelligence and mastery learning strategy on achievement in mathematics. Non-equivalent parallel group experimental design was used for the study. Tow variations of mastery learning strategy were tried on two experimental groups. The sample size was 46 drawn from standard IX Students. The major findings were: The main effect t due to non-verbal intelligence is found to be significant. The interaction between non-verbal intelligence on achievement and mastery learning strategy on achievement in mathematics were significant.

Raina (2003) made a study entitled, "Does preference for sons have a differential impact on the intelligence of boys and girls?" The study examined impact of son preference on the intelligence of boys and girls from a developing country. It was hypothesized that preference for sons enhances the intelligence among boys whereas it hampers the intelligence of girls. About 204 boys and 213 girls studying in grade VI to VII in an urban center of the state of Himachal Pradesh was taken as the sample.

FOREIGN STUDIES ON TEACHING COMPETENCE

Gregrersen and **Traves (1968)** used the projective technique for making a study of the child concept of the teachers. They made use of drawing of children, environment, which have special significance for them. Choeng and Devault at university of Wisconsin also made similar study in 1966.

Richard M. Galger and **Tom. D. Freyo (1974) i**nvestigated to two research questions (a) would rewarding items on a questionnaire for evaluating faculty teaching effectiveness substantially affect student's ratings (b) Would students ratings of professors teaching quality be totally consistent with their ratings of benefits derived from courses? Results shows that students' ratings were affected very little by a major rewarding of items and that a substantial degree of linear independence existed between students perception of the quality benefited from the instructional process.

Garrett and **George, W. (1978)** studied the teachers perception of selected factors affecting the success of teaching process. A study sought to determine how various groups of teachers rated selected factors in teaching success. A review of literature of the topic indicated that both teachers and non–teacher was conducted to collect data from teachers of 64 elementary and secondary schools that were part of the test.

Lawrenz, Frances (1987) studied the gender effects for students' perception of the classroom psycho-social environment. This study compared to classroom environments as perceived by fourth grade, seventh grade and high school boys and girls in classes taught by males and females to determine if any perceptual differences existed. The analyses showed no difference for fourth grade students, one for seventh grade students, and three for high school students.

Brosious Janice A. and **Smith R. Lyle (1990)** studied the impact of Teachers Attractiveness and Gender on Students Perception of the Teacher's Ability. A group of seventh grade maths students (N=28) was chosen for the experiment, the students rated photograph of teachers in the area of organization, classroom management, motivation, communication, sensitivity, imagination, and competence. The results of this analysis revealed a significant main effect of student perceptions due to the attractiveness of the teacher in the area of organization, classroom significant main effect on student's perceptions due to the gender of the teacher. The students rated the female photographs higher than male photographs in the area of organization. Finally, there was a significant interaction between the attractiveness of the teacher and gender of teacher in the areas of organization, sensitivity and imagination. Overall, females rated higher than males and teachers considered attractive were given higher ratings than teachers considered average and unattractive.

Ocepek, Linda Jeanne (1993) tested some "Selected elements of effective teaching: A study of perception of high school teachers in Illinois, Indian and Ohio." This study utilized an export co-relational design. A 42 item Value Rating Scale (VRS) was mailed to a stratified random sample of 384 public high school teachers in Illinois, India and Ohio. The teachers rated 42 indicator behaviors subsumed under the six elements of effective teaching.

Kim Keyng Suk (1999), studied "Teacher's perceptions of competencies needed for working inclusive early childhood education programs". A survey using five-point Likert scales included 7 teacher competency domains, each with a set of competency statements, and 12 teachers roles needed for working in inclusive pre-school program. 23 ECE teachers and 52 ECSE teachers in non-inclusive programs and 39ECE teacher and 25 ECSE teachers inclusive program participated in this study. To determine the early childhood education (ECE) and Early Childhood. Special Education (ECSE) teacher's perceptions of importance teacher competencies, current levels of these competencies and appropriate teacher roles for working in inclusive early childhood programme. They found the ECSE teacher had significantly higher perceptions than the ECE teachers of their self-proficiency of competencies related to child development, curriculum and instruction, assessment procedures, working with other adults, and professionalism.

Kastair, Jamal (1999) carried out a study on "An evaluation of professional teaching competency of the instructors of the institute of Agriculture Sabah, Malaysia." A survey was carried out at the institute involving the instructors, the principal and the first and second year students as respondents. Each instructor and the principal completed questionnaires containing 40 competency items of 7 categories, while each of the first and the second year students completed a questionnaire containing 33 competency items on 5 categories. The respondents were asked to assess the competence level of the instructors based on a five point Likert type scales. Evaluation by the professional teaching competency of the instructors of the Institute of Agriculture Sabah, Malaysia. They found that instructors' competence level was relatively high with respect to personal characteristics / attribute category, and lower with respect to planning and application of the principles of teaching-learning process.

INDIAN STUDIES ON TEACHING COMPETENCE

Chatter Jee, B.B *et al.* (1965) studied about the predication of teaching competency as a function of sharing a common frame of reference. The major findings were: The range of the scaled teaching competency scores given by the staff judges increased in the post-presentation assessments as compared to the pre-presentation predication, while the post-presentation scaled scores of teaching competency given by the instructors themselves were found to have low range compared two scores distributions obtained from the staff judges.

Saraswathi, L.S (1973) conducted a study about the jobs held by home scientists and the competencies needed on the jobs held as perceived by the employed home scientists and their employers in the District. The Major Findings were; The high competency perception proportion indicated that majority of the items included in the competency tests were perceived by the two sets of respondents (Teachcrs and research workers and those on miscellaneous jobs) as required as the job with an exception of those of the jobs of the assistant lecturers in colleges and teachers in secondary schools.

Nair, S.R (1974) reported about and impact of certain sociological factors on teaching ability in the classroom of government training college in Tiruchur. The major finding of this work was that private school teachers in general were found to have better teaching ability than the government school Teachers. Sex was not found to be affecting teaching ability. A positive relationship existed between ages and teaching ability. Caste and religion were not found to be affecting teaching ability.

Sharma, S.K (1981) analyzed the various relationship of teaching effectiveness in terms of competency. The study was carried out at three different stages. In the final study 220 classrooms teaching learning situations were observed. The major findings were: There were no significant relationship between the ages of Hindi teachers, their attitude, interest and intelligence and their teaching competency. Male and female Hindi teachers did not differ significantly in their teaching competency. There was significant negative correlation between the self-perception of Hindi teachers teaching at higher secondary level and their teaching competency. There was a significant positive correlation bctween the teaching competency of teachers at higher secondary level and academic achievement of their pupil of grade XI in Hindi. The teaching competencies identified were: giving assignments, loud reading, asking questions, introducing lessons, pacing, managing the classroom, presenting verbal mode, clarification, using the black board, using appropriate reinforcement, achieving closure, probing question, creation interest and improving pupils reading behavior.

Rajan, S. Sathyagiri (1985) conducted a study about the competency, personality, motivation, perception and profession of college teachers. The major findings wer:; Teacher competency was related to intelligence, emotional stability, conscientcasness, tender mindedness, trusted nature, and placed nature, self-sufficiency, and placed nature, self-sufficiency and relaxedness factors of Cattell's 16PF questionnaires. It was significantly related to creativity, dynamism, organized demeanors and warmth and acceptance, self-actualization and professional perception of teachers. The more competent teachers significantly differed from the less competent teachers in all the above variables. Those variables that correlated significantly with teacher competence inter correlated with one another significantly.

Das, B.C (1993) conducted a study about the effectiveness of concept attainment model in terms of teaching competency of pre-service student teachers. It was found that concept attainment model effectively developed the teaching competency of pre-service students teachers.

Naseema, C. (1994) reported about a teaching competence of secondary schools physical science teachers in relation to satisfaction of teaching physical science. The major findings were: It was found that 30.92 percent of physical science teachers differed in perceived teaching competence which can be attributed to work (0.01) rewards (1.73), context of work (o.87), self (0.61), others (0.56); 26.89 percent of physical science teachers differed in observed teaching competence which can be attributed to work (0.86), reward (0.002) context of work (1.5), self (2.32), others (1.91).

Kukreti, B.R. (1994) reported about a correlation study between job motivation and teaching competency. The major findings were: the competent teachers had joined the teaching profession because they regarded teaching 0as a prestigious job. They believed that the teaching profession provided them reasonable salary, security, opportunity of social service, to establish human relation and enhance their knowledge. Incompetent teachers entered the teaching profession because they thought that their profession would get fame, personal freedom, influencing opportunity and enough leisure with little burden of work.

Thigarajan, A. *et.al.* (1995) conducted a study about the teaching competency and achievement. The major findings were; The teaching competency and achievement of boys had significant relationship. The relationship between teaching competency and achievement of boys and girls differed significantly.

Panda, S.C, (1996), Conducted a study about the effect of competency-based instruction in achieving MLL competencies in grade IV Oriya medium schools. The major findings were: There was remarkable difference in the achievement of both the groups. The competency-based instruction yielded significantly better results than the traditional method of teaching.

Shamala, S.K. (1997) reported about enhancing teaching competency through integration of art education for effective language teaching at the primary stage. The major findings were: Prior the implementation of MLL based curriculum, it was highly essential to orient the primary school teachers to know how to develop local specific competencies based different activities. There was a positive impact of module to empower primary school teachers in developing competency based local specific curriculum. The main Objective are: To determine the value of high school teachers place on these elements: classroom climate, questioning, set induction, stimulus variation, reinforcement and closure. In this study classroom climate, questioning, set induction, stimulus variation, reinforcement and closure are sported as a set of selected elements for improving instruction.

Thamilmani, P.(2000) conducted a study on teacher competency, teacher personality and teacher attitude on student achievement in science in high schools. The study included a sample of 100 teachers (58 male, 42 female teaching science and 300 students X studying under those teachers). The tools used were: Teacher Competency – Student Rating Scale, Teacher personality and teacher attitude of science teachers are related to the academic achievement of X standard students in science. They revealed male and female teachers differed significantly in their personality traits and attitude towards teaching.

Palaniyandi, R (2001) investigated the competency needs of pre-serve teacher trainees. The teacher educators and student teachers from six DIETs constituting 273 pre-service Teacher trainees 106 teacher educators and 462 practicing teachers working in these districts were the samples for the study. To identify the competency needs of pre-service teacher trainees as perceived by the pre-service trainees. They revealed learning process related competencies emerged as a group having the highest number of competencies.

Manjula P. Rao (2002) studied Teacher Competencies and learners' achievement in Tribal areas of Karnataka. Twenty schools belonging to

3 taluks, 261 students of third standard and 31 teachers teaching the same students constituted the sample of this study. The research tool used in this study are: The achievement test developed based on the competencies specified for class III in Language, Mathematics, EVS – I and EVS-II to assess teachers' competence in subject areas. To study the relationship between teachers' competency and students achievement: in language, Mathematics, EVS -I and II. They found that majority of the teachers do not have to knowledge competencies in EVS- I (66.5%) and EVS-II (89.9%).

Amaladoss Xavirer, S and Amalraj, A. (2002), conducted a correlative study on teaching competency and its dimensions in post - graduate chemistry teachers. The study included data from 89 postgraduate chemistry teachers of higher secondary schools in Kanyakumari District in Tamil Nadu. A Teaching Competency Rating Scale was used to assess the teaching competency of chemistry teachers. They revealed that there exists significant relationship between the low-level of post- graduate chemistry teachers with regard to the teaching competency dimensions: content, organization, knowledge, clarity, communication, rapport, audio-visual aids and personality.

Jayakanthan, S. (2003) conducted a study of general teaching competency of secondary school teachers in relation to their attitude in teaching. The study included samples of 3000 teacher from 14 schools. The General Teaching Competency Scale of Passi *et al*, and Teacher Attitude Scale of Ahulwalia were used to carry out the study found that Government and aided school teachers differed significantly in general teaching competency. Male and female teachers differed significantly in teaching competency.

Krishna Prasad, B. and Mthiah, P.N.(2003). carried out a study on teacher effectiveness and temperament variables of secondary school teacher. The study was carried out to a sample of 300 teachers of various secondary schools in Thirunelveli District in Tamil Nadu. MTA-test of Personality for measuring the variables of Temperament, Checklist on Teacher Effectiveness developed and validated by the investigators, and a Personal Information Schedule were used. They found that there exist significant differences among high, average and low effective teachers in five variables (inferiority, self sufficiency, sociability, stability, objectivity) of temperament.

Laxmidhar Bhara (2004) made an attempt to find out the performance of B.Ed trainees. of IASEs and CTEs. Six fifty student-teachers (259 male and 391 female) drew purposively from tow CTEs and one IASE of Orissa in two consecutive sessions 1995-96 and 1996-97. The Major findings were: that women student teachers excel their male counter parts in their aggregate (theory and practical) performance.**Jeba A., (2005)** studied the teaching competency and mental health of student teachers in DIETs. The size of the sample was 300 student-teachers in a DIET undergoing D. Ed.. Elementary Teachers Training course. Tools used in this study are: Mental Health status scale constructed by M. Abraham and K.C.B. Praszanna. Teaching Competency Scale the study was conducted to find out gender and group (Arts, science) difference in teaching competency and mental health status, the relationship between teaching competency and mental health status of student teachers in DIET. Major findings were that there is no significant difference between man and women student teacher.

CONCLUSION

In this chapter, the related literature with regard to the variables, intelligence and teaching competence have been reviewed so as to get proper theoretical orientation of the problem and the design of the study is followed in the next chapter.

3

Methodlogy

INTRODUCTION

This chapter gives an overall view of the design of the study, research tools used in the study, nature and selection of the sample and a brief description of the procedure adopted for collection of data.

METHODOLOGY

NEED AND SIGNIFICANCE OF THE STUDY

Teachers play a vital role in the development of future citizens. Teaching is an interactive process, involving four aspects teacher, student, learning process and learning situation. A competent teacher possesses all the necessary qualities to interact with the school and community. Intelligence is the important aspect of an individual, through intelligence tone can know his abilities and capabilities. Intelligence test is used to categories people into different group. Intelligence helps a person to understand the concept and to interpret on it. So, the present study has been conducted to evaluate the level of intelligence and its influence on the teaching competence of the B.Ed teacher trainees.

STATEMENT OF THE PROBLEM

The problem for the present study is titled as, *"Intelligence and Teaching competence among the B.Ed teacher trainees"*.

OPERATIONAL DEFINITION OF KEY TERMS

INTELLIGENCE

In this study, intelligence was assessed by the **Standard Progressive Matrices,** developed and standardized by **Raven**. The score obtained by the subject in the test indicate the level of intelligence.

TEACHING COMPETENCE

Teaching competence of the teacher trainees indicates the score obtained by the subjects on the basis of the assessment made by their subject teachers, to know the level of teaching competence of the teacher trainees, the investigator adapted the **Teaching Competence Rating Scale (TCRS)** developed and standardized by **S. Mani (2005).**

B.Ed Teacher Trainees

In this investigation the teacher trainees refer to the trainees with minimum qualification of graduation who pursue pre serviced teacher education in course of study to acquire a general B.Ed degree during the academic year 2006-2007 in College of Education.

OBJECTIVES OF THE STUDY

The following objectives are set in the present study;

(1) To assess the level of intelligence of B. Ed. teacher trainees.

(2) To find out the level of teaching competence of B.Ed teacher trainees.

(3) To find out whether there is significant difference between overall scores on intelligence of B. Ed teacher trainees with respect to:

Gender

Educational Qualification

Optional Subject

Types of Management of Colleges

Medium of Instruction

Location of the College

Parental Occupation

Parental Qualification

4) To find out whether there is any significant difference between the overall score on teaching competence of B. Ed teacher trainees with respect to:

   Gender

   Educational Qualification

   Optional Subject

   Types of Management of Colleges

   Medium of Instruction

   Location of the Colleges

   Parental Occupation

   Parental Educational Qualification:

(5) To find out whether there is significant association between intelligence and teaching competence of B. Ed teacher trainees.

(6) To find out the relation between intelligence and teaching competence of B.Ed., teacher trainees.

HYPOTHESES

1. The B.Ed., teacher trainees have above average level of intelligence.
2. The B.Ed., teacher trainees are competent in teaching.
3. There is no significant difference between the overall scores on intelligence of the B. Ed teacher trainees with respect to;

   Gender

   Educational Qualification

   Optional Subject

   Types of Management of Colleges

   Medium of Instruction

   Location of the Colleges

   Parental Occupation

   Parental Educational Qualification.

4. There is no significant difference between the overall scores on teaching competency of B. Ed teacher trainees with respect to:

   Gender

   Educational Qualification

   Optional Subject

   Types of Management of Colleges

   Medium of Instruction

   Location of the Colleges

   Parental Occupation

   Parental Educational Qualification:

5. There is no significant association between intelligence and teaching competence of B. Ed teacher trainees.
6. There is no significant relation between intelligence and teaching competence of B.Ed., teacher trainees.

METHOD OF STUDY

In the present study survey method is employed. This method is used to describe and interpret, what exist at present. It is concerned with the condition of relationships that exist, practices that prevails, beliefs, points of view or attitudes that are held, processes that are going on and effects that are being felt.

VARIABLES OF THE STUDY

RESEARCH VARIABLES

(1) Intelligence

(2) Teaching competence

PERSONAL VARIABLES

(1) Gender

(2) Educational Qualification

(3) Optional subject

(4) Parental Occupation

(5) Parental Educational Qualification

INSTITUTION RELATED VARIABLES

(1) Types of the management of collage.

(2) Medium of Instruction

(3) Location of the Colleges

TOOLS USED IN THE STUDY

(1) Personal Data Sheet developed by the Investigator. (Appendix i)

(2) Standard Progressive matrices developed and standardized by Raven. (Appendix II)

(3) Teaching Competence Rating Scale(TCQS) developed and standardized by S. Mani (appendix III)

PERSONAL DATA SHEET

The personal data sheet was prepared to collect information on personal and institutional related details, such as gender, educational qualification, and medium of instruction, types of management, locality, parental annual income, parental educational qualification and parental occupation.

INTELLIGENCE

DESCRIPTION

Raven's Progressive Matrices Test was used to measures the intelligence of the B.Ed teacher trainees, as the purpose of the study is to find out the relationship between intelligence and teaching competence. Intelligence questionnaires consist of 60 questions, which were divided into 5 sets (A, B, C, D and E) of 12 each. In each set, the first problem is as nearly as possible self-evident. The problems, which follow, become progressively more difficult. The order of the tests provides the standard training in the method of working. The five sets provide five opportunities for grasping the method and five progressive assessments of a person's capacity for intellectual activity.

ADMINISTRATION

The investigator with the help of respective school teachers did the administration of the test. The investigator met the students and explained the instructions to them on how to answer the test. The students were asked to answer all the questions without fail and they were given only 30 minutes to answer.

SCORING PROCEDURE

Each item carried one mark. Adding the total marks obtained by the B.Ed. teacher trainees in 5 sets of test was done. By taking the total marks obtained by the students further calculations were done and they were clarified into intelligence average, above average superior.

TEACHING COMPENTENCY - DESCRIPTION

To find the level of teaching competency among the teacher trainees Teaching Competency Rating Scale was used. The tool consists of 3 dimensions and 8 components in classroom teaching.

The Dimensions and the Components are:

A. Planning Preparation and Organization.
   1. Planning
   2. Preparation
   3. Organization

B. Knowledge of the Subject –Matter
   1. Mastery in Subject

C. Presentation and Classroom Management
   1. Motivation
   2. Communication
   3. Interaction
   4. Evaluation and Closure

The items are rated in 5 point scale as follows

Options	**Scores**
Very poor	1
Poor	2
Average	3
Good	4
Very good	5

ADMINISTRATION

The Teaching Competence Rating Scale (TCRS) meant to assess teaching competence of teacher trainees were given to the respective optional subject teachers (supervisors/teacher educators). They were requested to rate the teaching competence of their students only after the completion of the intensive teaching practice. The supervisors/ teacher educators were asked to encircle only one numerical value for each component of all the three dimensions with the help of the indicators given in the tool. Time limit was not prescribed to finish the rating.

SCORING

The maximum score for all the three dimensions would be 40 and minimum 8. On the basis of the overall score, the teacher-trainees were classified into less competent, competent and more competent by using the m $\pm 1\sigma$ procedure.

PILOT STUDY

Pilot study was carried out to test the suitability of the time required to administer to test, and to establish the validity and reliability of the tool. The test was administered to a group of 50 B. Ed. teacher trainees in the month of September 2006

ESTABLISHING RELIABILITY AND VALIDITY OF THE TOOLS

Reliability of Intelligence Test

In the present study reliability of this tool Standard Progressive Matrices has been established by odd even method on 50 B. Ed. teacher trainees selected for the pilot study. The reliability of this tool has been found as 0.64

Validity of Intelligence Test

The validity is computed as the square root of reliability and this works out to be 0.8.

Reliability of Teaching Competence Rating Scale

Test-retest technique was used to establish the reliability of the tool and it was found to be 0.87.

Validity of Teaching Competence Rating Scale

The validity is computed as the square root of reliability and this works out to be 0.93.

MAIN STUDY

The validated tools were used for the main study to collect the necessary data. The study was carried out in the month of November 2006 in six B.Ed colleges in and around Chennai, which are affiliated to University of Madras in the state of Tamil Nadu.

SAMPLE OF THE STUDY

The present study is mainly concerned with 220 B. Ed. teacher trainees of six B.Ed colleges in and around Chennai, which are affiliated to University of Madras, Tamil Nadu.

Category wise distribution of the sample

Variables	Category	Total (220)	Percentage
Gender	Male	104	47.27
	Female	116	52.73
EducationalQualification	U.G.	94	43.52
	P.G.	122	56.48
Optional subjects	Language	59	26.82
	Arts	47	21.36
	Science	114	51.82
Types of management of colleges	Government	81	36.82
	Aided	60	27.27
	Self-financed	79	35.91
Medium of Instruction	Tamil	81	36.82
	English	139	63.18
Location	Urban	141	64.09
	Rural	79	35.91
Father's Occupation	Employed	110	50
	Unemployed	41	18.64
	Self-employed	69	31.36
Mother's Occupation	Employed	42	19.09
	Unemployed	140	63.64
	Self-employed	38	17.27
Father's Education	Illiterate	18	8.18
	School level	128	58.18
	College level	74	33.64
Mother's Education	Illiterate	49	22.27
	School level	141	64.09
	College level	30	13.64

COLLECTION OF DATA

Necessary permission was obtained from the head of the institutions to administrate the tools. Data are collected from six B.Ed colleges, and five students from each department are selected for the study. In addition to this the optional teachers co-operation was also sought to assess the teaching competency of the B.Ed teacher trainees.

DELIMITATION

1) The sample for the present study has been restricted to 220 B. Ed. teacher trainees as stratified random sample selecting only 5 samples from each optional subject.
2) The study was restricted to in and around Chennai City only.
3) The age of the sample was restricted to 20-25 years only.
4) The teaching competence assessment was done only by the teacher educator and not by the investigator.

STATISTICAL TECHNIQUES USED

Descriptive and inferential statistical techniques are used in the interpretation of the data to draw out a meaningful picture of results from the obtained data. In the present study the following statistical techniques are used

- Percentile
- Differential (Mean, Standard deviation, t-test and ANOVA)
- Correlation (correlation co-efficient and Chi-square)

CONCLUSION

This chapter outlines the design of the present study. The procedure followed and the nature of the sample. It describes the hypotheses to be tested, the tools used and the methods of administration and scoring. Adopting the methods and procedures discussed earlier in this chapter, tests were administered and information was gathered. The obtained data were then analyzed using appropriate statistical techniques described above and its results are presented in the next chapter.

4

Analysis and Interpretation of the Data

INTRODUCTION

This chapter presents the results obtained from the analysis of data collected from six different educational colleges based on two variables viz., intelligence and teaching competence. The data has been subjected to various descriptive and inferential statistics correlation among the different variables was computed.

Hypothesis 1

The B.Ed., teacher trainees have above average level of intelligence.

Table 1

The level of intelligence of B.Ed., teacher trainees

Groups	Number of Students (N = 220)	Percentage %
Average	63	28.6
Above average	139	63.2
Superior	18	8.2

It is observed from the above table (1) that the intelligence of B.Ed teacher trainees is above average. Hence, hypothesis is accepted.

Hypothesis 2

The B.Ed., teacher trainees are competent in teaching.

Table 2

The level of teaching competence of B.Ed., teacher trainees

Classification	Score	Number of Students (n = 220)	Percentage %
Low Competent	Below 90	57	25.9
Competent	90 to 160	86	39.1
More Competent	Above 160	77	35.0

It is observed from table (2) that B.Ed teacher trainees are competent in teaching. Hence the hypothesis is accepted.

Hypothesis 3 a

There is no significant difference between the overall scores of Intelligence of B.Ed teacher trainees with respect to gender

Table 3

Significant difference between the mean scores of Intelligence of B.Ed teacher trainees with respect to gender

Variables	Gender				t - value	L S
	Male		Female			
	Mean	SD	Mean	SD		
OVERALLINTEL-LIGENCE SCORE	45.87	7.41	46.95	6.35	1.17	NS

As the calculated value (1.17) is less than the table value (1.96), it is concluded that there is no significance difference between mean scores of intelligence of B.Ed teacher trainees Hence, the hypothesis is accepted.

pothesis 3 b

There is no significant difference between the overall scores of Intelligence of B.Ed teacher trainees with respect to their Education qualification.

Table 4

Significant difference between the mean scores of Intelligence of B. Ed teacher trainees with respect to their Education Qualification.

Variable	Educational Qualification				t-value	LS
	UG		PG			
	Mean	SD	Mean	SD		
INTELLIGENCE SCORE	47.12	6.69	45.84	7.08	1.34	NS

As the calculated value of the above table (4) is less than the table value (1.96), it is concluded that there is no significant difference between the Intelligence mean scores of B.Ed teacher trainees with respect to their educational qualification. Hence the hypothesis is accepted.

Hypothesis 3 c

There is no significant difference between the overall scores of Intelligence of B.Ed teacher trainees with respect to the Medium of Instruction.

Table 5

Significant difference between the mean scores of Intelligence of B.Ed teacher trainees with respect to the Medium of Instruction.

Variable	Medium of Instruction				t-value	LS
	English		Tamil			
	Mean	SD	Mean	SD		
INTELLIGENCE SCORE	45.95	6.29	47.27	7.74	1.38	NS

Since the calculated value (1.38) is less than the table value (1.96), it is concluded that there is no significant difference between the intelligence mean scores of B.Ed teacher trainees with respect to the medium of instruction. Hence, the hypothesis is accepted.

Hypothesis 3 d

There is no significant difference between the overall mean scores of Intelligence of B.Ed teacher trainees with respect to the location of colleges.

Table 6

Significant difference between the mean scores of Intelligence of B.Ed teacher trainees with respect to the location of colleges.

Variable	Location				t-value	LS
	Urban		Rural			
	Mean	SD	Mean	SD		
INTELLIGENCE SCORE	46.05	7.92	47.13	4.38	1.12	NS

As the calculated value (1.12) of the above table is less than the table value (1.96), no significant difference between is found the intelligence mean scores of B.Ed teacher trainees with respect to the location of the colleges. Hence, the hypothesis is accepted.

Hypothesis 3 e

There is no significant difference between the overall mean scores of Intelligence of B.Ed teacher trainees with respect to their Optional subject.

Table 7

Significant difference between the mean scores of optional Subject on Intelligence

Sources	df	Sum of squares	Mean sum of squares	F-ratio	LS
Between group	2	106.617	53.39		
Within the group	217	10243.491	47.21	1.129	NS
Total	219	10350.109			

From the above table, it is noticed that the calculated table value (1.13) is less than the table value (1.96). So it is concluded that there is no significant difference between the mean scores of Intelligence of B.Ed teacher trainees with respect to their optional subject. Hence, the hypothesis is accepted.

Hypothesis 3 f

There is no significant difference between the overall mean scores of Intelligence of B.Ed teacher trainees with respect to the types of management of college.

Table 8

Significant difference between the mean scores of Types of management of colleges.

Sources	df	Sum of squares	Mean sum of squares	F-ratio	LS
Between group	2	342.950	171.475		
Within the group	217	10007.158	46.116	3.718	0.05
Total	219	10350.109			

As the calculated value (3.72) is greater than the table value (1.96) at 0.05 levels in the table 4.08, it is concluded that there is significant difference in the mean scores of Intelligence of B.Ed teacher trainees with respect to the types of management of colleges.

Therefore, further analysis of multiple comparisons of the significant difference of the mean scores of Intelligence among the types of management of colleges have been computed, the details of which are presented in table 9.

Table 9

Multiple comparison of significant difference between the mean scores on Intelligence of B.Ed teacher trainees with respect to The management of colleges.

Groups	Mean	SD	SE of Mean	t-value	LS
Government vs	47.27	7.74	0.86	2.15	0.05
Aided	44.40	7.93	1.02		
Government vs	47.27	7.74	0.86	0.15	NS
Self-financed	47.12	4.28	0.49		
Aided vs	44.40	7.93	1.02	2.58	0.05
Self-financed	47.12	4.28	0.49		

From the above table, in the first comparison as the calculated table value (2.15) is greater than table value (1.96) Significant difference is found on the mean scores of intelligence of B.Ed. teacher trainees with respect to the types of management of college.

In the second comparison, no significant difference is found between the mean scores of intelligence among the B.Ed teacher trainees with respect to the types of management of college.

In the third comparison, as the calculated table value (2.58) is greater than table value (1.96), significant difference is found between the mean scores on intelligence of B. Ed. teacher trainees with respect to the types of management of colleges. Hence, the hypothesis is partially accepted.

Hypothesis 3 g

There is no significant difference between the overall mean scores of intelligence of B.Ed teacher trainees with respect to their parental occupation.

Table 10

Significant difference between the mean scores of Fathers' occupation on intelligence of B.Ed teacher trainees.

Sources	df	Sum of squares	Mean sum of squares	F-ratio	LS
Between group	2	173.283	86.641		
Within the group	217	10176.826	46.987	1.848	0.05
Total	219	10350.109			

Table 11

Significant difference between the mean scores of Mothers' occupation on intelligence of B.Ed teacher trainees.

Sources	df	Sum of squares	Mean sum of squares	F-ratio	LS
Between group	2	39.722	19.861		
Within the group	217	10310.388	47.513	0.418	NS
Total	219	10350.109			

As the calculated values are less than (1.848,0.418) table value(1.96), no significant difference is found between the means scores on intelligence of B.Ed teacher trainees with respect to their parental(Father&Mother) occupation, Hence, the hypothesis in accepted.

Table 12

Significant difference between the mean scores of Intelligence of B.Ed teacher trainees with respect to their Fathers' Educational Qualification.

Sources	df	Sum of squares	Mean sum of squares	F-ratio	LS
Between group	2	12.617	6.308		
Within the group	217	2571.069	11.848	0.532	NS
Total	219	2583.686			

Hypothesis 3 h

There is no significant difference between the overall mean scores of Intelligence of B.Ed teacher trainees with respect to parental educational qualification.

Table 13

Significant difference between the mean scores of Intelligence of B.Ed teacher trainees with respect to Mothers' Educational Qualification.

Sources	df	Sum of squares	Mean sum of squares	F-ratio	LS
Between group	2	61.175	30.587		
Within the group	217	10288.934	47.414	0.645	NS
Total	219	10350.109			

As the calculated table values (0.532, 0.645) is less than table value (1.96) it is concluded that there is no significant difference between the means scores of intelligence of B.Ed teacher trainees with respect to their Parental education qualification. Hence, the hypothesis in accepted.

Hypothesis 4.a

There is no significant difference between the overall mean scores of teaching competence of B.Ed teacher trainees with respect to gender.

Table 14

Showing the significant difference between the mean scores of Teaching competence of B.Ed teacher trainees with respect to gender

Variable	Gender				t-value	LS
	Male		Female			
	Mean	SD	Mean	SD		
TEACHING COMPETENCY	29.25	3.96	29.58	2.89	0.71	NS

From the above table (14) no significant difference is found between the mean scores on the teaching competence of B.Ed teacher trainees. Hence, the hypothesis is accepted.

Hypothesis4 b

There is no significant difference between the overall mean scores of teaching competence of B.Ed teacher trainees with respect to their education qualification.

Table 15

Significant difference between the mean scores of teaching competence of B.Ed teacher trainees with respect to their education qualification.

Variable	Educational Qualification				t-value	LS
	UG		PG			
	Mean	SD	Mean	SD		
TEACHING COMPETENCY	29.54	3.36	29.33	3.55	0.45	NS

As the calculated table value (0.45) is less than the table value (1.96), no significant difference is found between the mean scores of teaching competence of B.Ed teacher trainees with respect to their educational qualification. Hence the hypothesis is accepted.

Hypothesis 4 c

There is no significant difference between the overall man scores of teaching competence of B.Ed teacher trainees with respect to their Medium of Instruction.

Table 16

Significant difference between the mean scores of teaching competence of B.Ed teacher trainees with respect to their Medium of instruction

Variable	Medium Of Instruction				t-value	LS
	English		Tamil			
	Mean	SD	Mean	SD		
TEACHING COMPETENCY	29.04	3.79	30.07	2.61	2.17	0.05

In the above table the calculated value (2.17) is greater than the table value (1.96) at 0.05 level, significant difference is found between the mean scores on teaching competence of B.Ed teacher trainees with respect to the medium of instruction. Hence, the hypothesis is rejected.

Hypothesis 4 d

There is no significant difference between the overall mean scores of teaching competence of B.Ed teacher trainees with respect to the location of college

Table 17

Significant difference between the mean scores of teaching competence with respect to the location of colleges.

Variable	Location				t-value	L.S.
	Urban		Rural			
	Mean	SD	Mean	SD		
TEACHING COMPETENCY	29.26	3.66	29.71	2.99	0.92	NS

In the above table, the calculated value (0.92) is less than the table value (1.96), no significant difference is found between teaching competences of B.Ed teacher trainees with respect to the location of colleges. Hence, the hypothesis is accepted.

Hypothesis 4 e

There is no significant difference between the overall mean scores of teaching competence of B.Ed teacher trainees with respect to their optional subject.

Table 18

Significant difference between the mean scores of optional subject on teaching competence.

Sources	df	Sum of squares	Mean sum of squares	F-ratio	LS
Between group	2	44.498	22.249		
Within the group	217	2539.188	11.701	1.90	NS
Total	219	2583.686			

From the above table (4.07), the calculated tablc value (1.90) is less than table value (1.96), no significant difference is found between the mean scores of teaching competence of teacher trainees with respect to their optional subject. Hence, the hypothesis is accepted.

Hypothesis 4 f

There is no significant difference between the overall mean scores of teaching competence of B.Ed teacher trainees with respect to the types of management of colleges

Table 19

Significant difference between the mean scores of teaching competence of B.Ed teacher trainees the types of management of college.

Sources	df	Sum of squares	Mean sum of squares	F-ratio	LS
Between group	2	135.493	67.746		
Within the group	217	2448.193	11.282	6.005	0.01
Total	219	2583.686			

In the above table(19) as the calculated value (6.005) is greater than the table value (2.58) at 0.01 level, significant different is observed between the mean scores of teaching competence of B.Ed teacher trainees with respect to the types of management of colleges

Therefore further analysis of multiple comparison of the significant difference of the mean scores of teaching competence among the three types of management of colleges have been computed, the details of which are presented in table (20).

Table 20

Multiple comparison of significant difference between the mean scores of teaching competence of B.Ed teacher trainees with respect to the types of management of colleges.

Variables	Mean	SD	SE of Mean	t-value	LS
Government Vs	30.07	2.61	0.290	3.16	0.01
Aided	28.17	4.52	0.583		
Government Vs	30.07	2.61	0.290	0.82	NS
Self-financed	29.71	2.99	0.337		
Aided Vs	28.17	4.52	0.583	2.42	0.05
Self-financed	29.71	2.99	0.337		

From the above table, in the first comparison the calculated table value (3.16) is greater than table value (2.56), which shows the significant difference is found at 0.01 level, between the men scores of teaching competence of B. Ed. teacher trainees. It is also noted that the teacher trainees of government colleges got higher mean value (30.07) than the teacher trainees of aided colleges.

In the second comparison, no significant difference is observed between the mean scores of B. Ed teacher trainees teaching competence with respect the types of management of college.

In the third comparison, the calculated table value (2.42) is greater than table value (1.96) at 0.05 level, which indicates the significant difference between the mean scores of teaching competence of B.Ed teacher trainees with respect to Aided and Self-finance colleges.

Therefore, the hypothesis is partially accepted.

Hypothesis 4 g

There is no significant difference between the overall mean scores of teaching competence of B.Ed teacher trainees with respect to their parental occupation.

Table 21

Significant difference between the teaching competences means scores of B.Ed teacher trainees of with respect to their fathers' occupation.

Sources	df	Sum of squares	Mean sum of squares	F-ratio	LS
Between group	2	8.595	4.297		
Within the group	217	2575.091	11.867	0.362	NS
Total	219	2583.686			

Table 4.22

Significant difference between the teaching competences means scores of B.Ed teacher trainees with respect to their Mothers' occupation.

Sources	df	Sum of squares	Mean sum of squares	F-ratio	LS
Between group	2	13.969	6.985		
Within the group	217	2528.716	11.842	0.589	NS
Total	219	2583.687			

From the above tables (21,22) it is observed that the calculated table (0.362,0.589) value is less than the table value no significant difference are observed between the means scores of teaching competence of B. Ed teacher trainees with respect to their parental occupation, Hence, the hypothesis is accepted.

Hypothesis 4 h

There is no significant difference between the overall mean scores of teaching competence of B.Ed teacher trainees with respect to their parents educational qualification

Table 23

Significant difference between the teaching competences means scores of B.Ed teacher trainees with respect to their Fathers' educational qualification

Sources	df	Sum of squares	Mean sum of squares	F-ratio	LS
Between group	2	9.574	4.787		
Within the group	217	1274.808	5.875	0.815	NS
Total	219	1284.382			

From table (23) it is noticed that the calculated value (0.815) is less than the table value (1.96), no significant difference is found between the mean scores of teaching competence of B.Ed teacher trainees with respect to their fathers' educational qualification.

Table 24

Significant difference between the teaching competences means scores of B.Ed teacher trainees with respect to their Mothers' educational qualification

Sources	df	Sum of squares	Mean sum of squares	F-ratio	LS
Between group	2	90.238	45.119		
Within the group	217	2493.448	11.490	3.926	0.05
Total	219	2583.686			

From table (24) it is noticed that the calculated value (3.926) is greater than the table value (1.96) at 0.05 level, significant difference is found between mean scores of teaching competence of B.Ed teacher trainees with respect to their mothers' educational qualification.

Hence, further analysis of multiple comparisons of the significant difference of the scores of teaching competence among the parental education qualification have been computed, the details of which are presented below.

Table 25

Multiple comparison of significant difference between the mean scores of teaching competence of B.Ed teacher trainees with respect to parental education qualification

Source of variation	Mean	SD	SE of Mean	t-value	LS
Illiterate Vs	29.59	3.47	0.496	0.98	NS
School level	29.04	3.37	0.284		
Illiterate Vs	29.59	3.47	0.496	1.69	NS
College level	30.92	3.36	0.614		
School level Vs	29.04	3.37	0.284	2.79	0.01
College level	30.92	3.36	0.614.		

From the above table, in the first and second comparison, there no significant difference is found between the mean scores of teaching competence of B.Ed teacher trainees with respect to their parental educational qualification.

But in the third comparison, the calculated value (2.79) is greater than table value (2.56) at 0.01 level, significant difference is observed between the mean scores of teaching competence of B.Ed teacher trainees with respect to their mothers' educational qualification Hence, the hypothesis is partially accepted.

Hypothesis 5

There is no significant association between intelligence and teaching competence of B.Ed teacher trainees.

Table 26

Significant association between Intelligence and t teaching competence of B. Ed teacher trainees.

Intelligence	Teaching Competence			Total
	Less competent	Competent	More competent	
Average	25 (16.3)	25 (24.6)	13 (22.1)	63 (28.6)
Above average	32 (36)	51 (54.3)	56 (48.7)	139 (63.2)
Superior	0 (4.7)	10 (7)	8 (6.3)	18 (8.2)
Total (%)	57 (25.9)	86 (39.1)	77 (35)	220 (100)

Chi-square value 16.466 df-4 LS - 0.01

From the above table, the Chi-square value (16.466) is greater than the table value (13.28) for df 4 it is concluded that there exit significant association between intelligence and teaching competence of B. Ed. teacher trainees. Hence, the hypothesis is rejected.

Hypothesis 6

There is no significant relation between intelligence and teaching competence of B. Ed teacher trainee.

Table 27

Significant relation between the overall scores of and Intelligence and teaching competence of B. Ed. teacher trainees

Variables	Intelligence	LS
TEACHING COMPETENCY	0.2878	0.01

df =219

In the above table as the correlation co-efficient value (0.2878) is greater than the table value (0.273). it is concluded that there exist significance positive correlation between intelligence and teaching competence of B. Ed. teacher trainees. Hence, the hypothesis is rejected.

MAJOR FINDINGS

- The B.Ed., teacher trainees have above average level of intelligence.
- The B.Ed., teacher trainees are competent in teaching.
- No significant difference is found between male and female B.Ed., teacher trainees in intelligence.
- No significant difference is found in intelligence between the U.G. and P.G. qualified B.Ed., teacher trainees.
- No significant difference is found in intelligence between the English and Tamil medium B.Ed., teacher trainees.
- No significant difference is found in intelligence between the Urban and Rural B.Ed., college teacher trainees.
- No significant difference is found in intelligence of different optional subject B.Ed., teacher trainees.
- Significant difference is found in intelligence among the B.Ed., teacher trainees studying in different types of management of colleges (Government vs aided, Aided vs Self-Finance).

- o Parents' Occupation does not influence the intelligence of B.Ed., teacher trainees.
- o Parental Educational Qualification does not influence the intelligence of B.Ed., teacher trainees.
- o Gender does not influence the teaching competence of B.Ed., teacher trainees.
- o Educational qualifications of B.Ed., teacher trainees do not have bearing on the teaching competence.
- o Medium of instructions in B.Ed., colleges influences the teaching competence of B.Ed., teacher trainees.
- o No significant difference is found between urban and rural colleges B.Ed., teacher trainees teaching competence.
- o No significant difference is found between the different optional subjects B.Ed., teacher trainees teaching competence.
- o Significant difference is found in teaching competence of B.Ed., teacher trainees studying in different types of management of colleges (Government vs aided, aided vs self-finance).
- o Parental Occupations do not influence the teaching competence of B.Ed., teacher trainees.
- o Parental Educational Qualifications (Mothers') significantly influence the teaching competence of B.Ed., teacher trainees (Mothers' school level vs college level education).
- o Significant positive correlation is found between intelligence and teaching competence of B.Ed., teacher trainees.
- o Significant association is found between intelligence and teaching competence of B.Ed., teacher trainees.

CONCLUSION

This chapter analyses the hypotheses of the study. The finding and conclusions thus obtained from the analyses of this chapter have been summarized and presented along with a brief report of the research study and implications of the study in the following chapter.

5

Summary and Conclusion

INTRODUCTION

The present chapter provides a brief summary of the entire study and it also gives the statistical analysis of data presented in the previous chapter. The implications along with suggestions for replicating the study or for investigation at other closely related problems in other settings and with different samples and tools are also presented.

REVIEW OF THE RELATED LITERATURE

Review of related literature gives a broad idea to the investigator to carry out his research work in a successful manner. It also helps him get thorough knowledge in his research work reviews tells the researcher what has been done and what needs to be done particular topic.

METHODOLOGY

NEED AND SIGNIFICANCE OF THE STUDY

Teachers play a vital role in the development of future citizens. Teaching is an interactive process, involving four aspects teacher, student, learning process and learning situation. A competent teacher possesses all the necessary qualities to interact with the school and community. Intelligence is the important aspect of an individual, through intelligence tone can know his abilities and capabilities. Intelligence test is used to categories people into different group. Intelligence helps a person to understand the concept and to interpret on it. So, the present study has been conducted to evaluate the level of intelligence and its influence on the teaching competence of the B.Ed teacher trainees.

STATEMENT OF THE PROBLEM

The problem for the present study is titled as, *"Intelligence and Teaching competence among the B.Ed teacher trainees"*.

OPERATIONAL DEFINITAIONS OF KEY TERMS:

INTELLIGENCE

In this study, the intelligence was assessed by the Standard Progressive Matrices, which was developed and standardized by **Raven**. The score obtained by the subject in the test indicate the level of intelligence.

TEACHING COMPETENCE

Teaching competence of the teacher trainees indicates the score obtained by the subjects on the basis of the assessment made by their subject teachers, for the purpose the investigator adapted the **Teaching Competence Rating Scale** developed and standardized by **Dr.S. Mani (2005).**

B.Ed Teacher trainers

In this investigation the teacher trainees refer to the trainees with minimum qualification of graduation who pursue pre serviced teacher education in course of study to acquire a general B.Ed degree during the academic year 2006-2007.

OBJECTIVES OF THE STUDY

The following objectives are set in the present study;

1) To assess the level of intelligence of B. Ed. teacher trainees.
2) To assess the level of teaching competence of B.Ed teacher trainees.

3) To find out whether there is significant difference between overall scores on intelligence of B. Ed teacher trainees with respect to:

   Gender

   Educational Qualification

   Optional Subject

   Types of Management of Colleges

   Medium of Instruction

   Location of the College

   Parental Occupation

   Parental Educational Qualification

4) To find out whether there is any significant difference between

   a. the overall score on teaching competence of B. Ed teacher trainees with respect to:

      Gender

      Educational Qualification

      Optional Subject

      Types of Management of Colleges

      Medium of Instruction

      Location of the Colleges

      Parental Occupation

      Parental Educational Qualification:

5) To find out whether there is significant association between intelligence and teaching competence of B.Ed teacher trainees.

HYPOTHESES

1) The B.Ed., teacher trainees have above average level of intelligence.
2) The B.Ed., teacher trainees are competent in teaching.
3) There is no significant difference between the overall mean scores on intelligence of the B. Ed teacher trainees with respect to;

   Gender

   Educational Qualification

Optional Subject

Types of Management of Colleges

Medium of Instruction

Location of the Colleges

Parental Occupation

Parental Educational Qualification.

4) There is no significant difference between the overall mean scores on teaching competency of B. Ed teacher trainees with respect to:

Gender

Educational Qualification

Optional Subject

Types of Management of Colleges

Medium of Instruction

Location of the Colleges

Parental Occupation

Parental Educational Qualification:

5) To find out the relation between intelligence and teaching competence of B.Ed., teacher trainees.

6) There is no significant association between intelligence and teaching competence of B. Ed teacher trainees.

METHOD OF STUDY

In the present study survey method is employed. This method is used to describe and interpret, what exist at present. It is concerned with the condition of relationships that exist, practices that prevails, beliefs, points of view or attitudes that are held, processes that are going on and effects that are being felt.

VARIABLES OF THE STUDY

RESEARCH VARIABLES

1) Intelligence
2) Teaching competence

PERSONAL VARIABLES

1) Gender
2) Educational Qualification
3) Optional subject
4) Parental Occupation
5) Parental Qualification

INSTITUTIONAL RELATED VARIABLES

1) Types of the management of collage.
2) Medium of Instruction
3) Location of the Colleges

TOOLS USED IN THE STUDY

1) Personal data sheet developed by the investigator.
2) Standard Progressive matrices developed and standardized by Raven.
3) Teaching Competence Rating Scale developed and standardized by S. Mani (Appendix III)

PERSONAL DATA SHEET

The personal data sheet was prepared to collect information on personal and institutional related details, such as gender, educational qualification, and medium of instruction, types of management, locality, parental annual income, parental educational qualification and parental occupation.

SAMPLE OF THE STUDY

The present study is mainly concerned with 220 B. Ed. teacher trainees of six B.Ed colleges in and around Chennai, which are affiliated to University of Madras, Tamil Nadu.

COLLECTION OF DATA

Necessary permission was obtained from the head of the institutions to administrate the tools. Data are collected from six B.Ed colleges, and five students from each department are selected for the study. In addition to this the optional teachers co-operation was also sought to assess the teaching competency of the B.Ed teacher trainees.

DELIMITATION

1) The sample for the present study has been restricted to 220 B. Ed. teacher trainees as stratified random sample selecting only 5 samples from each optional subject.
2) The study was restricted to in and around Chennai City only.
3) The age of the sample was restricted to 20-25 years only.
4) The teaching competence assessment was done only by the teacher educator and not by the investigator.

STATISTICAL TECHNIQUES USED

Descriptive and inferential statistical techniques are used in the interpretation of the data to draw out a meaningful picture of results from the obtained data. In the present study the following statistical techniques are used

- Percentile
- Differential (Mean, Standard deviation, t-test and ANOVA)
- Correlation (correlation co-efficient and Chi-square)

MAJOR FINDINGS

- The B.Ed., teacher trainees have above average level of intelligence.
- The B.Ed., teacher trainees are competent in teaching.
- No significant difference is found between male and female B.Ed., teacher trainees in intelligence.
- No significant difference is found in intelligence between the U.G. and P.G. qualified B.Ed., teacher trainees.
- No significant difference is found in intelligence between the English and Tamil medium B.Ed., teacher trainees.
- No significant difference is found in intelligence between the Urban and Rural B.Ed., college teacher trainees.
- No significant difference is found in intelligence of different optional subject B.Ed., teacher trainees.
- Significant difference is found in intelligence among the B.Ed., teacher trainees studying in different types of management of colleges (Government vs aided, Aided vs Self-Finance).

- Parents' Occupation does not influence the intelligence of B.Ed., teacher trainees.
- Parental Educational Qualification does not influence the intelligence of B.Ed., teacher trainees.
- Gender does not influence the teaching competence of B.Ed., teacher trainees.
- Educational qualifications of B.Ed., teacher trainees do not have bearing on the teaching competence.
- Medium of instructions in B.Ed., colleges influences the teaching competence of B.Ed., teacher trainees.
- No significant difference is found between urban and rural colleges B.Ed., teacher trainees teaching competence.
- No significant difference is found between the different optional subjects B.Ed., teacher trainees teaching competence.
- Significant difference is found in teaching competence of B.Ed., teacher trainees studying in different types of management of colleges (Government vs aided, aided vs self-finance).
- Parental Occupations do not influence the teaching competence of B.Ed., teacher trainees.
- Parental Educational Qualifications (Mothers') significantly influence the teaching competence of B.Ed., teacher trainees (Mothers' school level vs college level education).
- Significant positive correlation is found between intelligence and teaching competence of B.Ed., teacher trainees.
- Significant association is found between intelligence and teaching competence of B.Ed., teacher trainees.
- The B.Ed., teacher trainees have above average level of intelligence.
- The B.Ed., teacher trainees are competent in teaching.
- No significant difference is found between male and female B.Ed., teacher trainees in intelligence.
- No significant difference is found in intelligence between the U.G. and P.G. qualified B.Ed., teacher trainees.
- No significant difference is found in intelligence between the English and Tamil medium B.Ed., teacher trainees.

- No significant difference is found in intelligence between the Urban and Rural B.Ed., college teacher trainees.
- No significant difference is found in intelligence of different optional subject B.Ed., teacher trainees.
- Significant difference is found in intelligence among the B.Ed., teacher trainees studying in different types of management of colleges (Government vs aided, Aided vs Self-Finance).
- Parents' Occupation does not influence the intelligence of B.Ed., teacher trainees.
- Parental Educational Qualification does not influence the intelligence of B.Ed., teacher trainees.
- Gender does not influence the teaching competence of B.Ed., teacher trainees.
- Educational qualifications of B.Ed., teacher trainees do not have bearing on the teaching competence.
- Medium of instructions in B.Ed., colleges influences the teaching competence of B.Ed., teacher trainees.
- No significant difference is found between urban and rural colleges B.Ed., teacher trainees teaching competence.
- No significant difference is found between the different optional subjects B.Ed., teacher trainees teaching competence.
- Significant difference is found in teaching competence of B.Ed., teacher trainees studying in different types of management of colleges (Government vs aided, aided vs self-finance).
- Parental Occupations do not influence the teaching competence of B.Ed., teacher trainees.
- Parental Educational Qualifications (Mothers') significantly influence the teaching competence of B.Ed., teacher trainees (Mothers' school level vs college level education).
- Significant positive correlation is found between intelligence and teaching competence of B.Ed., teacher trainees.
- Significant association is found between intelligence and teaching competence of B.Ed., teacher trainees.

EDUCATIONAL IMPLICATION

1) Necessary facilities and opportunities need to be provided to teacher trainees to acquire and develop the essential competences that are required in teaching profession.
2) Selection of teacher trainees should be made on certain criteria like testing their oral expressions and presence of mind, testing the depth knowledge of the subject and interpersonal relationships.
3) Entry behaviour of teacher trainees needs to assess and necessary supportive programme need to be organized to develop competences required for the teaching profession.

SUGGESSTION FOR FURTHER STUDY

The study also may be extended to school teachers and college teachers.

1) This study can also be done tithe DIET teacher trainees.
2) This inquiry can also be carried out to teacher trainees and teachers in other districts of Tamil Nadu.
3) A comparative study of gender difference among the teachers with respect to teaching competence and intelligence can also be done.
4) A study on the teaching competence and psychological factors of the different subject teachers can be taken up.

CONCLUSION

The quality of the teacher is determined by many factors and intelligence is the most vital factor among them. The present study indicates the close relationship between intelligence and teaching competence. Further it is also ensured in this present study that there is positive correlation between intelligence and teaching competence. The significant aspect, the types of management of college greatly influences not only the intelligence of the teacher trainees but also their teaching competence. However quality in education is possible only by preparing competent teacher.

BIBLIOGRAPHY

1. **Arachana (1998).**"Intelligence as a function of Religion Gender and socioeconomic status". *Indian Psychological Review*. 3:153-157.
2. **Asheval. G.G (2001).** "intelligence as a correlate of achievement in mathematics across Different levels of socio-economic status". *Indian Psychological Abstracts and Reviews* X(1):186.
3. **Asthana. M. (2000).** " General intelligence visual motor perception and memory in rural and urban children. *Indian Education Review*..54(1&2): 94-99.
4. **Das, B.C. (1993).** "Effectiveness of concept attainment model in terms of teaching competency of pre-service student teachers [perspectives in Education. *Indian Educational Abstracts* (Issue-4) 9(1): 34-35.
5. **Das, R.C. *et al* (1976)**. A study of effectiveness of micro teaching of teachers dept of teachers education. NCERT. New Delhi (Abridged Report).
6. **Kukreti (1994)**. Job motivation and teacher competency. A correlation and study. Experiments in education. Indian Educational Abstract Issue-2. 22(1): 10-14.
7. **Laxmi Thakur (2001).**"Effect of Home environment on intelligence and educational aspirations". *Journal of Education and Psychology*. 59(4):8-15.
8. **Maline, P.M. (2003).** " Effect of Intelligence and Mastery learning strategy of instruction of IX standard Pupils". *Experiment in Education*. XXXI(8):149-153.
9. **Panda, S.C. (1996)**. Effect of competency based instruction in achieving MLL competencies in Grade IV. National council of educational research. *Educational Abstract Issue*-6.
10. **Prabha, I . and Gupta, Monika(2000).**"Effect of sex, Intelligence and socioeconomic status on the achievement of students in Computer Education". *India Psychological Abstracts and Reviews*. III(2).
11. **Renuga. N (2003)**. A study on intelligence and creativity among XI standard Arts and Science Students in chennai city " M. Ed Thesis, Madras University

12. **Sadhya Giri Rajan (1985).** Competency and personality. Motivation and profession perception of college teachers. Fourth serve of research in education 1983-1988. Volume-11.

13. **Shamala, S.K. (1998).** Enhancing teaching competency through integration of arts education for effective language teaching at the primary stage. National council of educational research and training. *Indian educational Abstract Issue*-5.

14. **Sharma. A and Kumar, H (1999).** Birth order and intelligence", *Indian Psychological Review.* 52(6): 85-93.

15. **Singhal (1996)**. Teacher's self-efficacy and competency for improving quality of primary school. National council of educational research and training. *Indian Educational Abstracts* Issue-6.

16. **Sinha, S.P and Bvibha (1998)**. "Intelligence and Vigilance Performance as related to lead Exposure among children", *Indian Psychological Abstracts and Reviews.* VIII(1):183.

17. **Srivastsa.R.k (1999).** A correlation study of intelligence and academic achievement of High School pupils. *The Progress of education.* XXI(10):218.

18. **Thamilmani. P. (1990).** Teacher competency and teacher personality in relation to Achievement of High School. Students in science V *Survey of Educational Research* 11:19-26.

2. Emotional Intelligence of Elementary School Teachers

1

Confluent Education

INTRODUCTION

Confluent Education may be defined as the integration of cognitive, affective and behavioural dimensions of learning across intrapersonal, interpersonal and social contexts, 'Confluent' refers to the process of holistic learning involving body, mind, emotion and spirit. In educational settings, the term is used to describe methods for teaching traditional subjects such as languages, maths, science, social studies, physical education, and fine arts by applying affective, introspective, intuitive body / mind, movement and kinesthetic type of activities to the lessons being taught. The concept 'confluent education' attempts to restate the core components of Gandhiji's Basic Education. He criticized the overemphasis on knowledge acquisition alone. "Unless the development of the mind and body goes hand in hand with a corresponding awakening of the soul, the former alone would prove to be a poor lop-sided affair". To him, briefly, education means, "all round – drawing out of the best in child and man – body, mind and spirit". Revisiting the educational ideas of Swami Vivekananda echoes the similar man making, character-building education for India.

Educators and police makers today are becoming aware of the importance of providing all children with educational opportunities that develop their body, mind, emotion and spirit. They should enhance their emotional and social competence. Effective efforts to address children's responsible citizenship, as strongly advocated by Secondary Education Commission (1952). Ultimately this harmonious blending of cognitive, affective and behavioural dimensions of education will surely result in the wholesome development of personality of children.

National Curriculum Framework for School Education (2000) has strongly emphasized the importance of affective education in schools. "Education must facilitate learner's personal growth and psychologically equip them to cope with the rapid changes taking place in all spheres of life. Thus the focus of education is moving away from providing mere cognitive skills (the traditional 3 Rs.) to fostering inter-personal and intra - personal development. Nurturance of emotional intelligence, therefore, becomes a prime concern for schools and curriculum developers".

Teachers play the most essential role in developing a child's emotional intelligence (EI). They need to provide opportunities where a child can express and deal with his / her emotions. They should be willing to listen to them, have realistic expectations and not compare them, to other children. Teachers should not only encourage the child's abilities and interactions but also their sensibility. They should model social behaviours appropriately because children need adults as role models. These roles can be played equally well by parents as well as teachers. But majority of families have shrunk from an extended community to nuclear family. Children spend much less time in the family than in school. Parents are not always in a position to cope with or dispense such emotional skills.

Scientific research on how the brain works indicates that the formation of emotional skills is much easier in the 'formative' years from birth to the late teens. Looking at existing structures, school is the major activity in that age group. Since children are facilitated to sign up in schools, thanks to the initiatives of SSA, it offers a place to reach children with basic lessons for living that they may never get otherwisc.

HISTORICAL PERSPECTIVES OF EMOTIONAL INTELLIGENCE

The roots of Emotional Intelligence can be traced back to over 2000 years ago, when Plato wrote: 'All learning has an emotional base'. But the famous psychologist, E.L. Thorndike through his concept of social intelligence laid a solid foundation of the essence of emotional intelligence in 1920. Thorndike (1920) defined social intelligence as "the ability to understand and manage men and women, boys and girls – to act wisely in human relations", It can be described as a model of personality and individual behaviour in which people are presumed to be knowledgeable about themselves and the social world in which they live. Individuals actively use this knowledge to manage their emotions and direct their behaviour toward desired outcomes. Since then, scientists, educators and philosophers have worked to prove or disprovc the importance of feelings.

Gardner (1983) advanced Thorndike's ideas of social intelligence by proposing Multiple Intelligence Theory including inter-and intra – personal intelligences. He presented seven types of intelligence, namely: Verbal, musical, logical, spatial, kinesthetic, interpersonal, and intra personal in 1983. Afterwards, he added naturalist and existential dimensions. He described interpersonal intelligence as the ability to understand other people, what motivates them, how they work, and how to work cooperatively. Intrapersonal intelligence is the ability to develop an accurate model of the self and use it effectively to operate throughout life. Moreover, he described these skills as necessary for social interaction and the understanding of one's own emotions and behavioiurs.

Later on Sternberg (1988) also carried out the concept of social intelligence in the name of contextual intelligence through his Triarchic Theory of Intelligence. This component of one's intelligence (other components being componential and experiential) relates with one's capacity of making adjustment to various contexts with a proper selection of contexts so that one can improve one's environment in a proper way. As a follow up study, it was later on discovered that without having a high IQ (Intelligence Quotient) one can have high contextual intelligence i.e. the ability to lead one's life successfully (Zimbardo and Germing, 1996). The importance of "emotional factors" was also recognized by David Wechsler (1940) who urged that the 'non-intellective aspects of general intelligence' be included in any IQ measurement.

In 1948 another American researcher R.W. Leeper promoted the idea of 'emotional thought' which he believed contributed to logical thought. Historically speaking, the term 'emotional intelligence' was first coined by Salovey and Mayer (1990). The reconceptualised inter-

and intra- personal intelligences (Gardner, 1983) under a broader label of Emotional intelligence and proposed a more comprehensive framework on Emotional Intelligence in 1990. However, in 1995, Emotional Intelligence went through a phase of popularization by Goleman's (1995) work on 'Emotional Intelligence". He made a provocative claim that if IQ contributed up to 20% to life's success, the remaining was fulfilled through one's emotional intelligence and as a result predicted. "E.I. would contribute to the success at home, at school, and at work". He emphatically said, "E I help in knowing one's emotions, managing emotions, motivating one 's self, recognizing emotions in other and handling relationships".

Later Bar-On (1997) broadened the conceptual frame work of EI by incorporating various personality characteristics such as empathy, motivation, persistence, social skills, and warmth. Actually, he contributed the phrase Emotional Quotient (EQ).

EMOTION AND INTELLIGENCE – THEIR RELATIONSHIP

Conceptions of Emotions

Emotions are recognized as one of three or four fundamental classes of mental operations. These classes include motivation, emotion, cognition and (less frequently) consciousness (Mayer, Salovey and Caruso, 2000). Among the triad of motivation, emotion and cognition, basic motivations arise in response to internal bodily states and include drives such as hunger, thirst, need for social contact and sexual desires. Motivations are responsible for directing the organism to carry out simple acts to satisfy survival and reproductive needs. In their basic form, motivations follow a relatively determined time course and are typically satisfied in a specific fashion.

Emotions form the second class of this triad. Emotions appear to have evolved across mammalian species so as to signal and respond to changes in relationships between the individual and the environment. For example, anger arises in response to danger. Emotions follow no rigid time course but instead respond to external changes in relationships (or internal perceptions of them). Moreover, each emotions organize several behavioural responses to the relationship; for example, fear organizes fighting or fleeing. Emotions are therefore more flexible than motivations, though not quite so flexible as cognition.

Cognition, the third member of the triad, allows the organism to learn from the environment and to solve problems in novel situations. This is often in service to satisfying motives or keeping emotions positive. Cognition includes learning, memory and problem solving. It is ongoing and flexible intentional information processing based on learning and memory.

A good deal of research addresses how motivations interact with emotions and how emotions interact with cognition. For example, motives interact with emotions when frustrated needs lead to increased anger and aggression. Emotions interact with cognition when good moods lead a person to think positively. One would except that the interaction of emotion and cognition would also give rise to emotional intelligence.

Conceptions of Intelligence

Generally, the concept of intelligence encompasses a broad spectrum of abilities, including, in the words of Neisser (1979), "verbal fluency, logical ability, and wide general knowledge but common sense, with, creativity, lack of bias, sensitivity to one's own limitations, intellectual independence, openness to experience and the like". With the advent of intelligence testing, the original purpose of which was to predict success in school, the concept of intelligence has become restricted to the capacity for abstract reasoning.

Although intelligence is a potent predictor, it is far from a perfect one, leaving the vast amount of variance unexplained. As Wechsler (1940) put it, "individuals with identical IQs may differ very markedly in regard to their effective ability to cope with the environment". One way of dealing with IQs limited predictive ability is to redefine intelligence itself as a combination of mental ability and non-intellective personality traits (Mayer, Salovey and Caruso, 2000), Wechsler (1943) wondered, "whether non-intellective, that is, affective and co native(motivational) abilities are admissible factors in general intelligence. In this next sentence, he concluded they were. A few sentences thereafter, however, he qualifies the notion: they predict intelligent behaviour (as opposed to being a part of intelligence). Further, he defined intelligence as involving"....The aggregate or global capacity of the individual to act purposefully, to think rationally and to deal effectively with his environment (Wechsler, 1958).

Intelligence and Emotion

While analyzing the relationship between intelligence and emotion, Averill (2000) discusses two possibilities: intelligent use of emotions and emotions as a form of intelligence. The first leaves intact the traditional view of emotions as primitive, relatively automatic responses. For example, a wild animal may be domesticated and put to intelligent use by its trainer, without thereby making the animal any more intelligent. The second concept (emotions as a form of intelligence) is more radical. It presumes that emotions are determined by some of the same process that helps account for others forms of intelligent behaviour.

Interaction between intelligence and emotion manifests in meaningful pattern of responses. The human brain is an exceedingly complex organ that has evolved over millions of the years. Past adaptations are seldom discarded but rather, are maintained and incorporated into newer systems; thus, different types of cognitive processes undoubtedly exist. Some of these process (such as concept formation) may be more relevant to intelligent behaviour, whereas other (such as sensitivity to interpersonal cues) may be more relevant to emotion).

Humans are both the most intelligent and the most emotional of animal species; no infrahuman animal has the ranger or subtlety of emotions that human beings have. The most parsimonious explanation for this fact is that many of the same processes that mediate intelligence on one occasion may mediate emotion on another occasion. However, in this context, it is quite relevant to quote the observations by Zajonc (1998): At the basic level we share emotions with lower animals. Except for trivial features, cognitions are probably uniquely human. There are 'cognitive virtuosos' mathematical prodigies, mnemonics, geniuses – but there are no 'emotional prodigies'. We can speak of an 'intellectual giant' but an 'emotional giant' is an absurdity". He mentions Gaus and Pascal as examples of cognitive virtuosos. Averill (2000) while picking up this argument further, proposes that Dante and Meister Eckhart might be mentioned as their equals in the emotional domain. But Dante and Meister Eckhart were also highly intelligent. So it is not unreasonable to assume that the more intelligent a person, the greater the range and subtlety of his or her emotions. Emotions, after all, presume an ability to discriminate among complex and often conflicting situational cues: knowledge of social norms and standards regarding the appropriate occasions for, and expressions of, emotions; and the foresight to anticipate the consequences of one's behaviour.

DEFINITIONS OF EMOTIONAL INTELLIGENCE

Emotional intelligence is the set of abilities for how the people's emotional reports vary in their accuracy and how the more accurate understanding of emotion leads to better problem solving in individuals emotional life. More formally, it is defined as the ability to perceive and express emotions, assimilate emotions in thought, understand and reason with emotion and regulate emotion in the self and others (Mayer and Salovey, 1997). After publishing numerous articles, Mayer and Salovey have evolved the following definition of emotional intelligence: 'It is the ability to perceive emotions and emotional knowledge and to reflectively regulate emotions so as to promote emotional and intellectual growth'.

According to Goleman (1998). "Emotional Intelligence refers A to the capacity for recognizing our own feelings and those of others, for motivating ourselves, and for managing emotions well in us and in our relationships". He redefines it by adding some more attributes like self-awareness, impulse control and delaying gratification, and handling stress and anxiety. He further elaborates the concept by saying that 'there is an old fashioned word for the body of skills that emotional intelligence represents: 'character'.

Bar – on (1997) characterized emotional intelligence as "an array of non-cognitive capabilities, competencies and skills that influence one's ability to succeed in coping with environmental demands and pressures". The ability definition of emotional intelligence, as proposed by Mayer and Salovey, has its own set of competing constructs and concepts. One of the most closely related concepts, emotional competence, as defined by Saami (2000) is emotional competence is the demonstration of self efficacy in emotion – eliciting social transactions.

To conclude, the various definitions, discussed above, on emotional intelligence have led to the development of different models of emotional intelligence.

MODELS OF EMOTIONAL INTELLIGENCE

Currently several comprehensive models of Emotional Intelligence provide alternative theoretical frameworks for conceptualizing the construct. These models do not contradict one another but they do take somewhat different perspectives on the nature of emotional intelligence. These models are broadly classified as ability models and Mixed Models. Models that propose a pure ability definition of emotional intelligence are considered as Ability Models. Models that incorporate aspects of both the original definitions of emotional intelligence and attributes of personality are classified as Mixed Models of Emotional Intelligence.

ABILITY MODELS OF EMOTIONAL INTELLIGENCE

Earlier work of Salovey and Mayer (1990) defines emotional intelligence as "the ability to monitor one's own and others' feelings and emotions, to discriminate among them and to use this information to guide one's thinking and action". They initially postulated that emotional intelligence consists of the three categories of adaptive abilities: appraisal and expression of emotions, regulation of emotions and utilization of emotions in solving problems. The first category consists of the components of appraisal and expression of emotion in the self and the appraisal of emotions in others. The component of appraisal and expression of emotion in the self is further divided into the sub components of non-verbal perception and empathy. The second category of emotional intelligence, regulations, has the components of regulation of emotions in the self and regulation of emotions in others. The third category, utilization of emotion, includes the components of flexible planning, creative thinking, redirected attention and motivation. Even though emotions are at the core of this model, it also encompasses social and cognitive functions related to the expressions, regulation and utilization of emotions. This model talks only about perceiving and regulating emotion and omit thinking about feelings.

Mayer and Salovey (1997) revised the model of emotional intelligence to address these problems. The revised model gives more emphasis to the cognitive components of emotional intelligence and conceptualizes emotional intelligence in terms of potential for intellectual and emotional growth. It consists of four branches of emotional intelligence as follows:

1. Perception, Appraisal and Expression of Emotion

This branch concerns the accuracy with which individuals can identify emotions and emotional content.

2. Emotional Facilitation of Thinking

This branch concerns emotion acting on intelligences; it describes emotional events that assist intellectual processing.

3. Understanding and Analysing Emotions; Employing knowledge

This branch concerns the ability to understand emotions and to use emotional knowledge.

4. Reflective Regulation of Emotions to Promote Emotional and Intellectual Growth

This branch concerns the conscious regulation of emotions to enhance emotional and intellectual growth.

The perceptions, appraisal and expression of emotions are viewed as the most basic processes, while the reflective regulation of emotion requires the most complex processing. Further, each branch has associated with its stages or levels of abilities, which individuals master in sequential order.

MIXED MODELS OF EMOTIONAL INTELLIGENCE

Mixed models of Emotional Intelligence are substantially different from the mental ability models. These models blend emotional intelligence with other skills and characteristics such as well being, motivation and capacities to engage in relationships.

Goleman's Model of Emotional Intelligence

Goleman's (1995) treatment of emotional intelligence expanded the construct to include a number of specific social and communication skills influenced by the understanding and expression of emotions.

1. Knowing one's emotions
   - Recognizing a feeling as it happens
   - Monitoring feeling from moment to moment
2. Management of Emotions
   - Handling feelings so that they are appropriate
3. Motivating oneself
   - Marshalling emotions in the service of goal.
4. Recognising emotions in others
   - Empathic awareness
   - Attunement to what others need.

5. Handling relationships
    - Skills in managing emotions in others
    - Interacting smoothly with others

Bar - On's Model of Emotional Intelligence

Bar – On (1997) reviewed the psychological literature for personality characteristics that appeared related to life success and identified the following five areas with specific skills functioning relevant to success:

Intra Personal Skills

- Emotional Self Awareness
- Assertiveness
- Self-regard
- Self-Actualisation
- Independence

Inter - Personal Skills

- Interpersonal relationships
- Social responsibility
- Empathy

Adaptability Skills

- Problem Solving
- Reality Testing
- Flexibility

Stress Management Skills

- Stress tolerance
- Impulse control

General Mood

- Happiness
- Optimism

Bar-On's theoretical work combines what may qualify as mental activates e.g. Emotional Self Awareness with other characteristics that are considered separable from mental ability, such as personal independence, self-regard, and mood; this makes it a mixed model. Despite the breadth of his model, Bar-On is relatively cautious in his claims for his model of emotional intelligence. Although his model predicts success, this success is "the end – product of that which one strives to achieve and accomplish".

Moreover, his Emotional Quotient Inventory (EQ-i) relates to the potential to succeed rather success itself'. At a broader level, he believes that Emotional Quotient (EQ)., along with intelligence Quotient (IQ), can provide a more balanced picture of person's general intelligence (Mayer, Salovey, Caruso, 2000).

Critics of Emotional Intelligence Claim that it is a type of personality miscast as intelligence. Still others would argue that EI, if it were to be taken as a form of intelligence, would be subsumed by general intelligence (Graves, 2000), However, as it can easily be seen, the concept of EQ is a broad umbrella term that refers to inter and intra personal skills, being aware of emotions and using emotional and social activities. Most of the authors on this topic note that in order to function fully as a member of society, one has to possess both IQ and EQ (Gardnes, 1983; Goleman, 1995; Salovey and Mayer, 1990). Moreover it is EQ that might be as important as IQ for people to succeed in life. However, the models of EI appear to contain a mixture of different types of emotional Intelligence. Although each taxonomy differs in compositions, emotional and social skills and empathy seem to be the skills that appear in most models. With these issues kept in mind, the problem of assessing the emotional intelligence of elementary school teachers is addressed in the study.

Emotional Intelligence and Schooling of Children

Research shows that unlike IQ which is concerned relatively to be stable and unchangeable, Emotional Intelligence(EI) is acquired and developed through learning and repeated experience at any stage (Ashforth, 2001; Cherniss and Goleman, 1995; Cooper, 1997; Goleman, 1998). In this context EI skills are becoming more important as society creates new challenges for youth (Ross 2000). Emotional Quotient can be shaped by one's learning to be not only well-developed in intellectual abilities, but also in social and emotional skills as well (Pfeiffer, 2001). As Hamacheck (2000) writes that intellectual ability is essential for being successfully educated and being a contributing member of society. Emotional Intelligence is also equally essential, which can help people study toward their potentials and develop healthy interpersonal relationships. According to Byron (2001), understanding one's own emotional process can have far-reaching effect for social functioning and the quality of life. However, Richardson (2000) indicates that young people who lack social and emotional competence might end up becoming self centered and unable to empathize and relate to others.

Researchers found that pupils with high emotional intelligence tend to be better learners, more confident, optimistic, creative as well as being flexible, happier, successful at solving problems, being able to handle emotions much better (Abraham, 1999; cooper, 1997; Heins, 1996). There are many advantages of using EI at school both for teachers and for students. Using EI helps students learn emotional vocabulary and feel cared rather than controlled. On the one hand, it helps teachers identify the feelings and fears of students recognize their feelings and see to their unmet emotional needs (Abraham, 1999 Heins, 2001). Furthermore, EI might have significant relevance in the dynamic preparation and training of both the notice teachers and constituents (Byron, 2001). Teachers thereby may improve their potential to reach students with the socio-emotional learning activates during growth and development, and can also provide the necessary support to enhance learning activities and educational experience.

Many teachers have a habit of believing that the most important thing is the lesson plan in classroom process. The lesson plan and learning are more important than any feelings in general. The usual attitude is that the lesson plan should be followed, no matter at what emotional cost. Furthermore, learners with unmet emotional needs are usually seen as disruptions to the class and to the attainment of the lesson plan. While keeping strict adherence to the lesson plan, emotional needs of the children tend to be ignored (Heins, 2000). If on the contrary, the feelings of children were to be consistently addressed and validated and their emotional needs met, they may tend to be much more cooperative and respectful in the class. This is more important since the children need both emotional and intellectual development.

Similarly, a positive relationship between the teacher and learner is crucial if students are to be successful. When students perceive their teacher's motivation as a sincere interest in helping them to succeed, the motivational and emotional impact of the feedback tends to be more positive (Trucker, 2000) As Heins (1996) indicates that Emotional quotient (EQ) level of teachers and students are an important variable in creating a classroom in which EQ skills can be developed healthily. Another important variable in teacher's EQ is how they handle their own emotions, especially the negative ones. Effective and successful teachers are mainly those who can handle negative feelings in a healthy way. To assist students in developing skills, educators need to incorporate EQ skills along with academic skills into the curriculum. NCFSE (2000) also strongly emphasizes that 'emotional literacy" programmes directly alter the level of success, self esteem and well being of a person. They help reverse a tide of educational decline and thus strengthen schools.

QUALITIES OF AN EMOTIONALLY INTELLIGENT TEACHER

A Child in its early years needs a role model to emulate in shaping his / her own personality. An emotionally intelligent teacher can be a good role model for a child. One who is well aware of his / her own emotions and manages them successfully in a class room will be able to perform his / her role as a good teacher. She is able to carry out her class room transaction without any emotional blackout. She is capable of understanding her own feelings and their causes and recognizing the difference between feelings and action. Generally the children at primary and upper primary level are bundle of emotions. They have a tendency to emotionally react to any situation which at times leads to aggressive and self destructive behaviour. In this context, the teacher has to deal with them sympathetically and tactfully. Unless she knows how to control her own impulses towards such behaviours of children, She cannot handle them properly. In fact, there is no psychological skill more fundamental than resisting impulse. It is the root of all emotional self-control, since all emotions, by their nature, lead to one or another impulse to act.

An emotionally competent teacher has a good self-regard which is an ability to be aware of her and accurately appraise her. There is a link between teacher's self –regard and pupil's self-esteem. If a teacher has a high self-regard, the pupils will be likely to have high self-esteem also (Hums, 1982) If she treats students with respect, avoids ridicule and other belittling remarks, deals with everyone fairly and justly, and projecting a strong, benevolent conviction about every student's potential, then the teacher is supporting both self-esteem and the process of learning and mastering challenges. It is also important for him / her to control a child's misbehavior in a way which does not lower the self esteem of the child who is being disciplined, by using techniques which are non-confrontational and focused on his behaviour, not on his self. A teacher who is intelligent in emotions is assertive and has the ability to express herself. This trait of self expression does not imply that she should be aggressive in his / her behaviour. Positively his / her assertiveness would help children express their own feelings freely.

Since universalisation of Elementary Education (UEE) emphasizes not only education for all children but also education for every child, class rooms are becoming inclusive settings nowadays. They comprise a heterogeneous group including first generation learners, slow learners, differently able children, newly mainstreamed out-of-school children and of course, gifted children. They have a wide spectrum of attitudes, interests and abilities. Each of them has different needs to be addressed. Teacher should be able to solve their problems and help them accept and appreciate their individual differences. She needs to adopt a 'persistent, preserving, an disciplined approach in dealing with problematic situations' (Bar – On 2000).

Some extraordinary situations like free, flood and tsunami demand teacher's resourcefulness, sympathy and empathy and efficient leadership quality. Since children are emotionally affected easily in such critical situations, the emotionally competent teacher is empathic towards them and shares their feelings. He takes an active interest in their emotional well being and offers them psycho-care. A competent teacher is good at building inter-personal relationships in school. He is socially well-adjusted individual, adopt at inducing desirable responses in fellow teachers. This trait helps him build a good rapport with children. Maintaining interpersonal relationship is an asset to any institutions like school where co operation and belongingness promote better school climate for children to develop their personality.

In school settings, particularly at elementary level, anxiety provoking situations are often created by innocent children. The teacher is in a position to effectively cope with the situation and manage stress, Moreover, the expectations of head teacher, higher educational authorities and communities are varied and the teacher has to deal with them effectively and address them tactfully. So She / he should have stress tolerance if she wants to be a committed and dedicated teacher.

Some teachers are insensitive to children's individuality. They are demanding a mindless conformity to the rules and routines which would emotionally disturb them. An emotionally literate teacher is flexible and adjustable in catering to the different emotional and cognitive needs of the children.

Unless teacher's perception, feeling and thinking are strongly grounded in reality, she / he may not be able to approach the children's problems realistically. She / he should have respect for reality. All children are not equal in their mental ability. They differ in their academic performance naturally. She/ he should appreciate their accomplishments instead of accepting too much perfection from them.

Thus an emotionally intelligent teacher is able to

- Have good self regard and imbibe high self-esteem among children.
- Be aware of his / her emotions and make children understand their emotions.
- Be assertive in expressing her feelings and help children understand their feelings and express them appropriately.
- Be empathic, considerate and concerned about children and their feelings.
- Maintain good interpersonal relationship with fellow teachers and community and have a good rapport with children.
- Control his .her own impulses.
- Be flexible and realistic in solving children's problems.

NEED FOR THE STUDY

Learning does not take place in isolation from children's feelings. Being emotionally literate is as important as instruction in reading, writing and arithmetic. But emotions rarely have a place in schools today. The current educational paradigm does not insist upon the emotional development of children. It rather stresses the inculcation of market – logic and reinforces the concomitant drive to increased individualism by attributing quantitative values to qualitative phenomena through the all pervasive marks system which rapidly becomes the dominant goal of pupils. Encouraging individuals competition rather than group collaboration and solidarity is the order of the day. This paradigm strongly emphasizes rationality and logic while neglecting emotions and relationships. Reviewing the sorry state of affairs in schools. The National Curriculum Framework (2005) makes a critical remark, "schools across the country are obsessed with academic goals, but neglect character goals. Many children can't cherish themselves or love others......Almost all efforts are concentrated on cognitive skills. This exclusive focus on the cognitive to the total neglect of the affective in the learning process has long been recognized as a pedagogic aberration". The NCF (2005) elaborates further on the ills of lop sided focus on cognitive skills: "It needs to be asked if we are not spreading alienation albeit unwittingly, through education by undermining the affective, relational and experimental aspects of learning. Education of this kind turns children into cerebral machines that master facts and are mastered by them. But it leaves them deficient in emotional and relational skills. As a result, the more achievement oriented a person is, the less able he tends to be in relating to people, even dear ones, sensitively, reciprocally, and responsibly.

Laudable efforts are being made in Tamil Nadu to raise academic standards through various teaching methodologies such as joyful learning and activity based learning. These strategies have started paying dividends in improving children's cognitive skills. But emotional climate is far from satisfactory, Corporal punishment, teachers mis-behaviour, sexual abuse, and children's suicide rates are on the rise not only in private schools but also in government schools. Recently revised Tamil Nadu Educational Rules do not formally permit corporal punishment in schools but it is widely practiced in schools, In fact, research shows that nearly 10% of primary school children dropout from schools due to corporal punishment (Alavandar, 2000). Some of the case studies show that some teachers are inhuman, lacking empathy and interpersonal relationships.

Ram Abhinav took the extreme step of committing suicide following harassment at a city school. One Caroline Daffodil, a student of government higher secondary school, Ponneri, was hit with a bound register. She swooned and remained unconscious for nearly two hours without medical attention.

About 15 children in a Government Adi Dravidar school in Kancheepuram werc madc to crawl on their knees in the hot sun for 'talking in the class' (The Hindu, June 2003).

An 11 years old in popular school, terrified at canning, pulled in his hand instinctively, thrice; the infuriated teacher hit him on the face, leading to loss of an eye. At another, punishment was for children to walk on their bare knees in scorching sun some of them getting boils with infection.

Children of class VI in a school were admonished that those who could not recite an English poem the next day would be paraded naked in the assembly (Reminiscent of the Iraq prison), A student who was unsure of his performance set himself on fire that very night.

In a private school, a six year old was locked up in a one-fool shelf in a wooden cupboard for stealing a pen. Worse is the case of a four year old girl in LKG who was beaten black and blue because she had misspelled a word. The girl is now mentally disturbed and terrified of going to school. (The Hindu, Sep.2004).

Recently 13 students studying fifth and sixth standards were forced to hold cubes of dry ice in their palm without dropping. The carbon dioxide in the ice burnt the tender flesh of the boy's hands. The mistake they committed: playing with some sacks of match boxes stored in a house on their way to school (Deccan Chronicle, August 2005).

Instances of molestation and sexual assault on children in schools, and other forms of human rights violations are also reported from time to time, said the Chairperson of State Commission for Women (The Hindu, July2003) A physical education teacher of a private school in Chennai raped a nine-year old student and he had been repeatedly abusing other girls studying standard III

A strong case of teacher's mis-behaviour in the classroom has been brought into focus recently. Two teachers who were allegedly drunk during class hours at a panchayat Union School have been placed under suspension (Deccan Chronicle, October 2005).

These practices in schools show that some teachers and schools in poor light. They are inhuman, arrogant, and emotionally illiterate. The lack emotional and social competencies in handling children. They are not quite aware of their own emotions and don't know how to control their impulses. The lack empathy and love for children. Their interpersonal relationship with their fellow teachers and community are unbecoming of an emotionally intelligent teacher. For students, teachers are role models. "Teachers play a role unwittingly in propagating violence and terror in the classroom. A teacher who imposes 'discipline' in the classroom only by intimidating children with blows and slaps role-models as the problem solving strategy" (NCF 2005). Unless teachers are emotionally intelligent, they can't develop emotional and social competencies of children. Hence it becomes important to study the emotional intelligence of elementary school teachers.

REVIEW OF RELATED LITERATURE

CHAPTER NO.	TITLE
2	REVIEW OF RELATED LITERATURE
	2.1 Introduction
	2.2 Related Studies
	2.3 Conclusion

2

Review of Related Literature

INTRODUCTION

The most striking aspect of the emotional Intelligence literate is the breath, variety, and differences among authors regarding which abilities Emotional Intelligence is thought to entail (Goleman, 1995; Mayer and Salovey, 1995). Studies have been undertaken on various fields namely industrial and commercial organization and different work places like hospitals and educational institutions.

RELATED STUDIES

Culver et al. (1999) investigated the optimum academic performance and its relationship with emotional intelligence. Their study reviews the elemental of flow and describes educational activities and programmes which promote flow. The suggest how these can be tied to self directed learning strategies to prepare professionals for life – long learning. Work by Barret et al (2000) on sex differences in emotional awareness pointed out that woman consistently displayed more complexity and differentiation in their articulations of emotional experiences than did men, even when the effect of verbal intelligence was controlled. Abisamara's (2000) correlation study between emotional intelligence and academic achievement indicates a positive relationship when emotional intelligence is compared with the high achievers.

Another gender study on emotional intelligence by Petridis and Fumham (2000) noted that females scored higher than males on the social skills' factor of measured trait emotional intelligence, correlations between measured and self estimated scores were generally high among males than females and a regression analysis indicates that gender was significant predictor of self estimated emotional intelligence.

Madonna and Kathy (2001) conducted a study on Emotional Intelligence and Empathy: their relation to multicultural counseling, knowledge and awareness. Their results revealed no statically significantly sex differences, school counselors' multicultural education, emotional intelligence scores, and personal distress empathy scores accounted for significant variance in their self – perceived multicultural counseling knowledge. However, prior multicultural education, emotional intelligence and empathy were not significantly predictive of school counselors' self reported multicultural counseling awareness.

Mishra and Dhar (2001) investigated the relationship between thinking orientation and emotional intelligence among future managers and reported that students with whole brain thinking orientation possess significantly higher emotional intelligence in comparison to the ones with right and left brain thinking orientation. Students with right thinking orientation did not differ from students with left brain thinking orientation, irrespective of right brain or left brain thinking orientation.

Bruno *et al (2002)* studied the effectiveness of implementing a social and emotional learning programme for elementarily school students. A year long programme consisting of five units (listening, feeling, anger management, decision making and perspective taking) was designed to enhance their emotional and social intelligence. The programme was found effective by pre-test and post test analysis.

Roberts and Mathews (2002) conducted a study on "Can emotional intelligence be schooled? And pointed out that several issues that need to be addressed prior to developing and implementing emotional intelligence programmes and provide specific guidelines for the development, implementation and evaluation of future emotional programmes.

Hartley (2003) investigated the instrumentalization of the expressive in education. There is a resurgence of matters emotional in education. The concept of emotional intelligence is an example. The effective school seems set to become the affective school. He has made a strong emphasis on both the emotions and creativity in schools.

Liau et al ***(2003)*** studied the case for emotional literacy: the influence of emotional intelligence on problem behaviour in school students. Their findings indicated that emotional literacy, measured in terms of emotional intelligence, was linked to internalizing and externalizing problems behaviours. Emotional literacy also served as a moderating, factor between parental monitoring and externalizing problem behaviour.

Zeidner *et al.* *(2003)* in their study on development of emotional intelligence towards a multi level investment model, proposed a tentative investment model for emotional competencies in children that accommodates the multifaceted nature of emotional intelligence. Lower level competencies may provide a platform for developing more sophisticated emotion-regulation skills, with competencies becoming increasingly differentiated over time.

Pery *et al, (2004)* developed a new measure for assessing emotional intelligence of teachers in teaching situation and reported gender differences where female teachers reported greater likelihood of demonstrating emotional intelligence compared to male teachers. There was partial support for the four branch model of emotional intelligence in their findings.

Marc *et al (2004)* studied the emotional intelligence and its relation to everyday behaviour. Women scored significantly higher in emotional intelligence than men. Emotional intelligence, however, was more predictive of the life space criteria for men than of women. Low emotional intelligence was significantly associated with maladjustment and negative behaviour's for college aged males. But not for females.

Parker et al (2004) in an influential study observed that the academic success was strongly associated with several dimensions of emotional intelligence particularly in the context of emotional and social competencies during the transition from high school to university.

Mohanasundaram et al (2004) investigated the emotional intelligence of 269 teacher trainees studying at DIETs and TTIs, selected through stratified random sampling technique and reported that men and women trainees did not differ significantly in their emotional intelligence. When trainee' emotional intelligence was correlated with their academic achievement, low but significant correlation (0.24) existed between the two, but there was no correlation between the emotional intelligence of trainees and their performance in language and social science subjects.

Amirtha (2004) conducted a study on the personality of teachers in relation to their emotional intelligence using Bar-On's emotional Quotient Inventory and found that there is no significant gender difference in overall emotional intelligence, although women teachers have better impulse control and problems solving skills than men teachers. Age also does not influence the emotional intelligence of teachers, but elder teachers are found to have more empathy than the youngsters. In general, educational qualifications do not have a say over the overall emotional intelligence of teachers, albeit significant difference in problem solving, emotional self-awareness and stress tolerance skills where post graduate teachers are better than graduate teachers. No significant difference is found between arts and science teachers in their study. Experience and type of school do not influence the emotional intelligence of teachers. An important finding of the study is that the personality of teachers has significant impact on their emotional intelligence.

Shenwal (2004) studied the emotional intelligence of 200 children of fourth and fifth standards from two urban and two rural schools using an adopted version of the Multifactor Emotional Intelligence Scale (MEIS) and found that rural girls are much better on emotional intelligence than their urban and gender counterparts.

Annaraja and Jose (2005) in their study on the emotional intelligence of 300 B.Ed teachers trainees in Kerala State, observed that eighteen percent of the trainees have low level, 66% of them moderate level and 16% of them high level of emotional intelligence. No significant difference exists between rural and urban trainees in their self awareness, self-control, social skills and emotional intelligence except in two dimensions namely motivation and sympathy where the difference is found to be significant. Trainees with different optional of study such as English, Physical Science, Social Science, Natural Science and Mathematics show significant difference in their emotional intelligence in general but such difference does not exist in selected two dimensions namely self-awareness and self control.

The study of **Suresh and Rajalakshmi (2005)** on the emotional intelligence of school teachers reveals no significant gender difference and also no rural urban divide. But teachers from government schools have significantly higher emotional intelligence than those of private schools. Similarly language teachers exhibits higher performance in their Emotional Intelligence score than other subjects teachers

Latha *et al (2005)* studied the effect of Emotional Intelligence on teaching effectiveness in private school teachers and found that emotional intelligence in general, does not differentiate teaching effectiveness of school teachers. Its impact is very minimal except in two specific dimensions like teachers' sense of humour and mastery in the subject. Another study on the relationship between teacher effectiveness and Emotional Intelligence was conducted by Dash and Behera (2004) on a sample of 100 junior college teachers. They found that there is a significant positive relationship between teacher effectiveness and Emotional Intelligence. Dimension wise analysis reveals that many dimensions of teacher effectiveness namely information source, motivation, advisor and guide relationship with pupils, fellow teachers, principals and parents, teaching skills, professional knowledge and classroom management have significant positive relationship with emotional intelligence. Whereas the relationship in dimensions of teacher effectiveness such as disciplinarian, general appearances and habits in relation to classroom, co-curricular activities, and personal characteristics with emotional intelligence is insignificant. The study also reveals that the high Emotional Intelligence teachers have higher teacher effectiveness as compared to low emotional intelligence teachers.

CONCLUSION

Studies conducted so far suggest that positive relationship exists between Emotional Intelligence and academic achievement. Investigations carried out in India have mostly focused on the population of children, teacher trainees at B.Ed., and D.T.Ed levels and high and higher secondary school teachers. No study has been conducted, as far as investigator knows, on elementary school teachers. hence the present project has been undertaken.

3

Methodology

INTRODUCTION

This chapter describes the methodology of the study including the statement of the objectives, research design and procedure. The research design details the selection and validation of the tool, the sample and conduct of the field work.

OBJECTIVES OF THE STUDY

The objectives of the study are as follows:

1. To study the level of Emotional Intelligence of teachers working in elementary schools.
2. To find out if there is any difference in the Emotional Intelligence of teachers with respect to their gender, age, educational qualification and experience.
3. To find out if there is any difference in the Emotional Intelligence of teachers working at different levels of schools namcly primary, middle, high and higher secondary schools.
4. To find out if there is any difference in the Emotional Intelligence of teachers working in Government and Private aided schools

5. To find out if there is any relationship among the ten components of Emotional Intelligence of the elementary school teachers.
6. To determine the relative importance of each of the ten components in the prediction of the emotional intelligence of elementary school teachers.
7. To suggest, if necessary, suitable teacher development programmes for developing the Emotional Intelligence of teachers at elementary level.

OPERATIONAL DEFINITIONS

(i) Emotional Intelligence is defined as, in the words of Bar-On, "an array of non-cognitive capabilities, competencies, and skills that influence one's ability to succeed in coping with environmental demands and pressures".

(ii) By elementary school Teachers, it is meant that the teachers work in primary and middle schools and also those teaching in elementary sections i.e. 6, 7, 8 standards of high and higher secondary schools.

METHOD OF STUDY

This research is classified as descriptive research and incorporates the use of a survey.

DEVELOPMENT OF TOOL

Development of tool involves the review of existing instruments development and standardized for measuring the Emotional Intelligence of elementary school teachers and the selection of a suitable tool and its validation for the present research.

Measures of Emotional Intelligence

The development of theoretical models of Emotional Intelligence has resulted in the development of various tools to measure the concept. With so many tests available it would be useful to have an overview of the existing scales of measurement for selecting an appropriate tool for the present study. The content of emotional intelligence tests varies due to the fact that there is different interpretation of the term 'emotional intelligence'. There are three major prevailing approaches in assessing it namely ability, competence and skill approaches.

Ability Scales

Mayer and Salovey (1997), the researchers who first developed a scientifically testable proposition on emotional intelligence view it as an array of abilities that can be measured by one's ability to 'read' emotions in faces, or in group interactions. They first constructed an ability scale namely Multifactor Emotional Intelligence Scale (MEIS). This scale measures emotional intelligence assuming that Emotional Intelligence is an intelligence *per se,* in that it relates to processing information. It had four components. The first, emotional perception, involves such abilities as identifying emotional in faces, music, and stories. The second, emotional facilitation of thought, involves abilities such as relating emotions to other mental sensations such as colour and taste and problem solving. The third area, emotional understanding, involves emotional problems such as knowing which emotions are similar or opposites and what relations they convey. The fourth area, emotional management, involves understanding the implications of social acts on emotions and the regulation of emotion in the self and others.

Later they (Mayer and Salovey), along with Caruso (1999) developed a more comprehensive test named Mayerr, Salovey and Caruso Emotional Intelligence Test (MSCEIT). It is also an ability test designed to yield overall Emotional Intelligence score as well as subscale scores for perception, facilitation, understanding and management. Each branch has several subtests. The testee's score depends on answering each question with the best answer. Both MIES and MSCEIT scale were found to be highly reliable. The four MEIS branch scores had coefficient alphas raining from 0.81 to 0.96 with a full scale internal consistency of 0.96. The research version of MSCEIT had branch score alphas ranging from 0.59 to 0.87. Validity of these measures is established by relating them to other tests. For example, when MSCIET scores were compared with those of Bar-On, EQ-I, the overall 'r' was 0.36 MIES correlated significantly with empathy (r=0.33).

EMOTIONAL COMPETENCE INVENTORY

Goleman views emotional intelligence as a set of competencies that can be measures by his Emotional Competency Inventory (ECI). The Emotional Competency Inventory is a 360 feedback tool. It includes 25 competencies arranged in five clusters namely self-awareness, self regulation, motivation, empathy and social skills. One's score is a reflection of feedback from their boss, their peers and those who report to them at work. This instrument is designed for use only as a development tool, not for hiring or compensation decisions for use only as a development tool, not for hiring or compensation decision. The Emotional Competency Inventory model has changed from their boss, their peers and those who report to them at work. This instruments is designed for use only as a development tool, not for hiring of compensation decisions. The Emotional Competency Inventory model has changed from the original model published in Daniel goleman's (1998) book 'Working with Emotional Intelligence'. The following changes were made:

- Five clusters reduced to four clusters.
- Self – regulation and Motivation were combined to form Self management and 25 competencies were reduced to 20.
- Managing Diversity was removed as it was highly correlated with empathy.
- Commitment was removed as it was highly correlated with the leadership competency.
- Optimism was removed. It clustered with achievement orientation and Initiative. It was felt that there were better instruments in the field dedicated to measuring this factor.
- Team capabilities were removed. It clustered with heavily with collaboration.
- Innovation was removed as it was highly correlated with achievement orientation.

This tool has been developed by Richard Boyatziz and Daniel Goleman which is designed to assess competencies from four quadrants. It is an observer rating scale where people who know the individual rate him or her.

Emotional Quotient Inventory

Bar-on (1997) developed a self – report instrument called 'Emotional Quotient Inventory (EQ-i) based on 19 years of his research on emotional intelligence. The tool, designed to measure a number of constructs related to emotional intelligence, was tested on over 48000 individuals worldwide. The Bar-on Emotional Quotient Inventory (EQ-i) consists of 133 items and employs a five point Lickert scale ranging from, "Very Seldom or not true of me to very often true of me or true foe me.

The EQ-I renders a total EQ score and the following five EQ composite scale scores:

1. Intrapersonal EQ
2. Interpersonal EQ
3. Stress Management EQ
4. Adaptability EQ
5. Gender Mood EQ

The inventory comprises fifteen subscale scores, those components of which were discussed in the models of Emotional Intelligence.

The internal consistency of the EQ-i Scales ranges from a low of 0.69 to a high of 0.86 with overall internal consistency co-efficicient of 0.76. The stability reliability was found to be 0.73. The Emotional Quotient Inventory was again revised by Bar-On (2000) and he published an abbreviated version of Emotional Intelligence which includes 66 items.

Emotional Quotient Map

Another self report scale is Emotional Quotient Map (cooprr 1996/ 1997) which divides Emotional Intelligence into five attributes namely the current environment, emotional literacy, emotional quotient, competencies, emotional quotient values and attitudes and emotional quotient outcomes

SELECTION AND VALIDATION OF TOOL FOR THE PRESENT STUDY

After reviewing the different scales available on Emotional Intelligence Bar – On's Emotional Quotient Inventory (shorter version) was found to be most suitable tool for measuring the Emotional Intelligence of elementary school teachers for the following reasons:

- It is suitable to Indian setting because India was one of the seven countries sampled by Bar-On for its standardization.
- It has different components of Emotional Intelligence so that specific interventions may be given on required area in future.
- It is methodologically sound and scientifically validated.
- It has already been used on teacher population in India.

BAR – ON'S EMOTIONAL QUOTIENT INVENTORY

Description of the Tool

The Emotional Quotient Inventory was developed by Reuven Bar On to measure Emotional (or non – cognitive) Intelligence. This tool is the first scientifically developed and validated measure of Emotional Intelligence. It measures one's ability to deal with daily environmental pressures and demand. The Bar-On Emotional Quotient Inventory assessment highlights the emotional and social strengths and weaknesses that affect how an individual performs and interacts with an institution.

This tool is a self-report questionnaire consisting of 66 items which measure ten different components of Emotional Intelligence namely self regard, interpersonal relationships, impulse Control, Problem Solving, Emotional Self-Awareness, Flexibility, Reality Testing, Stress Tolerance, Assertiveness, Empathy. There are five response categories ranging from "not true", "seldom true", "sometimes true", "often true" and "true". The number of items in each dimensions of the Emotional Quotient Inventory is given Table 1.

Table 1

Components of Emotional Intelligence and their Items

Sl. No.	Components	Item Numbers
1.	Self Regard (SR)	6, 12*,.,21,27*, 36*, 43, 51,56,64
2.	Interpersonal Relationship (IR)	15, 20, 31,35*, 50, 55,63*
3.	Impulse Control (IC)	7*,38*,44*,58*,65*
4.	Problem Solving (PS)	1,9,14,23,29,46
5.	Emotional Self-Awareness (ES)	3,5,11*,17*,25*,57*
6.	Flexibility (FC)	8*,13*,22*,28,38,45*,-52*,66*
7.	Reality Testing (RT)	4,19*, 26*, 34*, 42, 48*
8.	Stress Tolerance (ST)	2,10,16,24*,32*,40,53,60*
9.	Assertiveness (AS)	18,33*,41*,47*,54*,62*
10.	Empathy (EM)	30,37,49,59,61

* Negative items

The total score of all the 66 items yield the total emotional quotient score of person

Administration

Instruction for Administration given is as follows: "This inventory consists of series of statements which follow five response categories.

Read each item carefully and decide how it describes you in the given point scale and indicate your choice by circling the corresponding number in the (separate) answer sheet. There is no right or wrong answers and there is no time limit. Work rapidly and give your immediate response to each item.

SCORING PROCEDURE

The responses should be scored as per the scoring key given in Table 2.

Table 2

Scoring Key for E Q Inventory

Response		Score for	
		Positive Item	Negative Item
Not True	1	0	4
Seldom True	2	1	3
Some Times True	3	2	2
Often True	4	3	1
True	5	4	0

RELIABILITY

The Emotional Quotient Inventory was found to have high degree of reliability (Bar-On, 1997), Based on seven population samples, the internal consistency coefficients for the Emotional Quotient Inventory subscales were analyzed. The average Cranach Alpha Coefficients were high for all of the subscales, ranging from 0.69 to 0.86 with an overall average internal consistency co-efficient of 0.76. Further test-test reliability studies indicated that there was consistency coefficient of 0.76. Further test-retest reliability studies indicated that there was consistency in the findings from one administration to the next. One month and four month test retest reliability studies indicated that there was consistency in the findings from 0.78 to 0.92 and 0.55 to 0.82. These findings reveal that the Emotional Quotient Inventory is highly reliable.

Validity

Bar-On established the validity of this tool by conducting studies in six different countries (India is one the six different countries), This tool possess content validity and face validity. Further, the convergent validity of the tool was found to be 0.57. The divergent validity of the tool was 0.12 with an intelligence scale. Moreover, the criterion group validity was established as 0.819. These values indicate that the tool is highly valid.

VALIDATION OF THE TOOL

Bar – One's Emotional Quotient Inventory was translated into Tamil so that the teachers at elementary level could easily understand it. The translated version was received by three experts and their suggestion incorporated. As many as 100 teachers were randomly selected from schools (both primary and middle) belonging to cluster resource centers in Cuddalore block for the pilot study. It was personally administrated on the teachers. All the responses were quantified and computer analyzed. The Cronbach Alpha Reliability was found to be 0.9102. By spilit – half method the reliability was high as 0.8892. Using the Spearman – Brown Prophecy formula the reliability for the whole test was calculated to be 0.889. Since the Emotional Quotient Inventory was found to be reliable on the elementary school teacher population in the pilot study, it has been selected for the final study without any modifications.

SAMPLING

Proportionate Stratified Random Technique has been used for the selection of sample, Cuddalore District was the catchment area where the project was undertaken. The District was stratified into different blocks and they are fourteen in number. Schools were stratified according to their levels namely primary, middle, high and higher secondary schools. Stratification was also done in type of schools namely Government school and Private Aided School. Schools were randomly selected from each block but number of schools selected was decided in proportion to the actual number of schools located in each block. Due consideration was also given to municipal primary and middle schools in sample selection. There are 1601 schools in Cuddalore District. Among them 1094 are primary schools, 322 middle schools, 95 high schools and 90 higher secondary schools. In high and higher secondary schools, teachers handling elementary sections (classes VI to VIII) were also involved in the study (see Table 3.3). The sample design is given in Table 3.

Table 3

Sample Design of Places

Sl. No.	Name of the Block	No. of CRCS	No.of School Attached with the block				
			P	UP	HS	HSS	TOTAL
1.	ANNAGRAMAM	15	73	15	7	6	101
2.	BHUVANAGARI	9	62	15	6	5	87
3.	CUDDALORE	20	91	38	5	15	150
4.	KAMMAPURAM	13	89	18	15	4	120
5.	KATTUMANNARKOIL	14	90	24	4	5	129
6.	KEERAPALAYAM	9	65	33	5	4	107
7.	KUMARATCHI	13	87	29	4	12	132
8.	KURUNJIPADI	17	103	26	11	4	144
9.	MANGALORE	10	80	26	7	7	120
10.	NALLUR	11	80	26	8	6	120
11.	PANRUTI	14	79	19	10	9	117
12.	PARANGIPETTAI	10	101	21	6	4	132
13.	VIRUDHACHALAM	12	85	21	4	6	116
14.	VEYVELI		9	11	3	3	26
	TOTAL	222	1094	322	95	90	1601

Table 4

Sample Design of Study

S. No.	Block	Primary			Middle			HS / HSS		Total
		PU	MU	Aided	PU	MU	Aided	Govt	Aided	
1.	CUDDALORE	3	1	1	1	1	-	1*	0	8
2.	ANNAGRAMAM	3	1	1	1	-	-	—	1*	7
3.	PANRUTI	3	1	1	-	-	1	1#		7
4.	NEYVELI	-	-	1	-	1	-	1*		3
5.	KURUNJIPADI	5	-	1	-	-	1	—	1#	8
6.	VIRUDHACHALAM	3	1	1	-	-	1	1#		7
7.	NALLUR	3	1	1	1	-	-	1*		7
8.	MANGALORE	4	-	1	1	-	-	1#		7
9.	KAMMAPURAM	4	-	1	1	-	-	1*		7
10.	PARANGIPETTAI	4	-	1	1	-	-	1*		7
11.	BHUVANAGARI	3	-	1	1	-	-	1#		6
12.	KEERAPALAYAM	3	-	1	1	-	1	-	1*	7
13.	KUMARATCHI	3	-	2	1	-	—	-	1*	7
14.	KATTUMANNARKOIL	3	-	2	1	-	—	1#	-	7
	Total									95

Note: *HSS # HS

Number of Schools selected ranges from 3 to 8 from all the fourteen blocks. Cuddalore and Kurinchipadi blocks have the largest number of schools, 150 and 144 respectively where as Neyveli Block has only 26 schools in its fold. Altogether 95 schools were selected for the final study (Table 3.4). From each school, only three or four teachers were randomly selected depending upon the number of teachers on position in the school concerned,. Number of teachers involved in the study frame each block ranges frame 3 to 23. Altogether, three hundred teachers were selected for the final study.

TABLE 5

Distribution of Sample with respect of variables

VARIABLE	CHARACTERISTICS	NO.OF TEACHERS	PERCENTAGE %
GENDER	WOMEN	173	57.67
	MEN	127	42.33
AGE	Group 1 (21-30)	31	10.33
	Group 2 (31-40)	148	49.34
	Group 3 (41-50)	64	
	Group 4 Above 50	57	
QUALIFICATION	Group 1 D.T.Ed	102	34.00
	Group 2 Degree with DT Ed	76	25.33
	Group 3 Degree with B.Ed.	50	16.67
	Group 4 Post Graduate	72	24.00
EXPERIENCE	Group 1 / 1 -5 years	51	70.00
	Group 2 / 6-10 years	80	26.67
	Group 3 / 11-15 years	50	16.67
	Group 4 / 16-20 years	57	17.00
	Group 5 above 20 years	68	22.66
LEVEL OF SCHOOL	Primary	168	56.00
	Middle	86	28.67
	High and Higher secondary	46	15.33
TYPE OF SCHOOL	Government	191	63.77
	Private / Aided	109	36.33

FIELD WORK

Field work comprised the training of investigators on the method of data collection for the present investigation.

Training

Fieldwork for the study involved the training of DIET faculty members as field investigators in the data collection. A one-day workshop was conducted at DIET Vadalur for 14 faculty members including Senior lecturers and lecturers. The workshop agenda included orientation on the proposed survey and its major details regarding the tool for data collection and sample design.

DATA COLLECTION

Each of the fourteen DIET faculty was assigned to one of the 14 blocks in Cuddalore District. The data collection phase lasted for a period of seven days. The batching and scrutiny of data was done after the completion of data collection to facilitate individual scrutiny of the filled in instruments. The data were classified with respect to variables. Table 3.5 describes the number of samples and their percentage with reference to the variables studied.

DATA ANALYSIS

The collected and scrutinized data were tabulated and analyzed using SPSS

4

Analysis of the Data

INTRODUCTION

The main objective of the project, as already mentioned, is concerned with studying the Emotional Intelligence of teachers. By administering Bar On 'EQ scale, the data were collected and analyzed. The mean and standard deviation of Emotional Intelligence (EI) the teachers have been found to be 190.02 and 27.62, respectively (Table 1). The maximum Emotional Intelligence score that could be obtained is 264. The maximum score teachers obtained in the present study has been 255 and the minimum 108. The mean score (190.02) is far above 50% of the maximum score. So, it may be concluded that Emotional Intelligence of elementary school teachers is rather high. The SD 27.62 indicates that there is no wide dispersion of scores.

Component Wise analysis of the Emotional Intelligence also shows that their performance is relatively high in all the ten components (Table 1>> regarding the component's 'self – regard'(SR) the mean and SD have been found to be 28.28 and 5.14 respectively. They are also good at interpersonal relationship (IR) with the mean score of 22.15 and SD, 4.26. While their 'impulse control' (IC) mean score is 14.09, their 'problem solving' (PS) skills have got the mean of 19.84. In 'emotional self awareness' (ES) which is a vital component of the Emotional

Intelligence, their mean is 15.48 and SD 3.26. Their 'flexibility' (FL) means score is found to be 21.76 with the SD 01'4.71. While their performance in 'reality testing' (RT) is rather high with the mean score of 16.94, their 'stress tolerance' (ST) is equally on the higher side. Their 'assertiveness' (AS) mean score (13.76) while comparing with the other components is relatively low even though it is above 50%, their mean score on the components 'empathy' (EM) is 15.81 which is high above the 50% of the maximum score. So, it may be concluded that elementary school teachers generally have high Emotional Intelligence. Component wise analyses also support the general conclusion except in a single component namely 'assertiveness' implies that teachers are not assertive enough to express their feelings and opinions freely without fear.

Table 1

Mean and Standard Deviation of Emotional Intelligence score Elementary School Teachers

Component	N	Minimum	Maximum	Mean	SD	Mean%
SR	300	15.00	36.00	28.28	5.14	78.56
IR	300	4.00	28.00	22.15	4.26	79.00
IC	300	1.00	20.00	14.09	4.02	70.45
PS	300	7.00	24.00	19.84	3.84	82.67
ES	300	6.00	24.00	15.48	3.26	64.50
FL	300	6.00	32.00	21.76	4.71	68.00
RT	300	5.00	24.00	16.94	3.26	70.58
ST	300	11.00	32.00	22.11	4.92	69.09
AS	300	3.00	22.00	13.76	3.44	57.33
EM	300	6.00	20.00	15.81	3.06	79.05
EI	300	108.00	255.00	190.22	27.62	72.05

Comparison of Different Groups in respect of their Emotional Intelligence

Gender and Emotional Intelligence

A research question often posed is: Are men and women equal in their Emotional Intelligence? The present research demonstrates that they are. Men and Women teachers do not differ significantly in their Emotional Intelligence score (Table 4.2). The mean score of women teachers is 191.41 with the SD of 25.49 which is slightly above the Grand Mean of 190.02.

Men teachers' mean score is 188.66 with the SD, 30.30 which is below the Grand Mean 190.02, These minor variations are due to chance, as is evidenced from the quite insignificant 'I' value of 0.039.

Similar findings are reported by Bar-On (2000), Mohanasundaram et al. (2004), Amirtha (2004) and Suresh and Rajalakshmi (2005).

However, there are certain components of Emotional Intelligence namely impulse control, emotional self awareness and reality testing which differentiate women from men involved in teaching at elementary level.

Table 2

't' Tcst Gender wise comparison of the Emotional Intelligence of Teachers

Component of EI	Male (N = 127)		Female (N = 173)		t	Significant Level
	M	SD	M	SD		
SR	28.09	5.46	28.41	4.90	0.525	NS
IR	21.92	4.46	22.32	4.12	0.808	NS
IC	13.13	4.24	14.80	3.70	3.631	0.01
PS	19.84	4.10	19.83	3.63	0.023	NS
ES	16.02	3.64	15.08	2.89	2.478	0.05
FL	21.36	4.95	22.06	4.51	1.266	NS
RT	16.49	3.40	17.27	3.12	2.066	0.05
ST	22.38	4.80	21.92	5.01	0.798	NS
AS	13.80	3.39	13.72	3.47	0.200	NS
EM	15.57	3.27	15.99	2.88	0.038	NS
EI	188.66	30.30	191.41	25.49	0.039	NS

While women are better able to 'control their impulse' with the mean score of 14.80, their men counterparts with the mean score, 13.13 are not able to achieve the Grand Mean of 14.09, not to speak of equalizing their score. They differ significantly at 0.01 level with the '1' value, 3.631 (Table 2) Amirtha's study (2004) on high school teachers also reports that women teachers are better in controlling their impulses that men teachers. But men teachers have higher 'emotional self awareness' with the mean score of 16.02 than women teachers (15.08). They do differ significantly with the 't' value of 2.48 but at 0.05 level. However the women are strongly grounded in 'reality is testing' with the mean score of 17.27 when compared to men whose mean score is 16.49. Their difference is real and not due to chance as it is evident from the '1' value (2.06) which is significant at 0.05 level. In general, however, there are more similarities than differences in the Emotional Intelligence of men and Women teachers. So it may generally be concluded that men and women teachers are equally Emotionally Intelligent, albeit minor differences in a few components like impulse control, emotional self awareness and reality testing. Women teachers appear to be stronger in controlling their impulses and understanding ground reality than their men counterparts but the latter have a better emotional self awareness.

Age and Emotional Intelligence

Unlike I.Q. Emotional Intelligence can improve throughout life (Goleman, 1998). Life offers chance after chance to hone one's emotional competence. In normal course of a life time, Emotional Intelligence tends to increase as people learn to handle distressing emotions better and to listen and to empathies. In short, the people become more matured when they progress in age. They become more intelligent in their emotions. An evaluation by Bar-On of Emotional Intelligence in more than 3000 men and women ranging from teenagers to people in their fifties found small but steady and significant increases as people go from age group to age group, with a peak occurring in the forties (Bar – On 1997). The present research also evidently proves that age differentiates teachers in their Emotional Intelligence. In the present study teachers have been divided into four groups according to the age. Group I comes under the bracket of 21 – 30. Group II has the range between 31 and 40, whereas Group III comprises teachers belonging to 40's (41-50). The group V belongs to 'greying' population of above 50. 'F' test has been applied to find out if there is any significant difference among the four groups of teachers in the Emotional Intelligence score and the 'F' value 2.94 is found to be significant at 0.05 level (Table 3).

Further component wise analysis shows these groups differ significantly (0.05 level) in self regard, emotional self awareness and assertiveness and 'F' values are 3.506, 3.745 and 2.832 respectively.

Since 'F' values are significant for these groups, 't' test has been applied to find out the difference among the sub-groups in their Emotional Intelligence in general and component wise in particular. Looking at Table (4) Group I and Group II differ significantly with the latter putting up higher performance (Mean = 192.90) than the former (Mean = 180.03). The 't' value is 2.538 which are significant at 0.05 level. Another two groups of teachers who differ in their Emotional Intelligence in general are the youngest (Group I) and the oldest (Group IV) among the four. Teachers with the above 50 years of age have obtained the higher mean score 194.14 which is not only higher than the youngest group of 21-30 but also the grand mean of 190.02. Bar-

On (2000) also suggests that Emotional Intelligence increases with the age, at least up until the fifth decade of live. Similar findings have been reported by other (Denny and Palmer, 1991 and Goleman 1998).

Table 3

ANOVA Teacher's Age and Emotional Intelligence

Components	Sources	Sum of Squares	Df	Mean Square	F	Sig
	Between Groups	271 107	3	90.369	3.506	0.05
SR	Within Groups	7628.930	296	25.773		
	Total	7900.037	299			
	Between Groups	64.955	3	21.652	1.196	NS
IR	Within Groups	5359.992	296	18.108		
	Total	5424.947	299			
	Between Groups	122.892	3	40.964	2.576	NS
IC	Within Groups	4707.678	296	15.904		
	Total	4830.570	299			
	Between Groups	112.914	3	37.638	2.605	NS
PS	Within Groups	4276.083	296	14.446		
	Total	4388.997	299			
	Between Groups	115.887	3	38.629	3.745	0.05
ES	Within Groups	3052.950	296	10.314		
	Total	3168.837	299			
	Between Groups	80.254	3	26.751	1.211	NS
FL	Within Groups	6539.942	296	22.094		
	Total	6620.197	299			
	Between Groups	60.853	3	20.284	1.923	NS
RT	Within Groups	3122.067	296	10.548		
	Total	3182.920	299			
	Between Groups	140.834	3	46.945	1.960	NS
ST	Within Groups	7091.313	296	23.957		
	Total	7232.147	299			
	Between Groups	98.457	3	32.819	2.832	0.05
AS	Within Groups	3430.779	296	11.590		
	Total	3529.237	299			
	Between Groups	24.957	3	8.199	0.877	NS
EM	Within Groups	2766.950	296	9.348		
	Total	2791.547	299			
	Between Groups	6600.218	3	2200.073	2.940	0.05
EI	Within Groups	221467.3	296	748.200		
	Total	228067.5	299			

Component wise analysis shows that Group I and Group II alone differ significantly in self regard with the mean scores 25.94 and 29.01 respectively. The 't' value 3.174 is significant at 0.05 level (Table 4) one of the core competencies of Emotional Intelligence identified by all researchers is emotional self awareness. Teachers of above 50 (Group IV) have obtained the higher mean score 16.68 than the teachers of twenties (Group I) whose mean score is 15.16 and the difference with 't' value (2.064) is significant at 0.05 level. Again Group IV outperforms Group II whose mean value is 15.03 which is surprisingly lower than that of youngest (Group 1) also.

The difference between the teachers of 50s and 30s is more significant with the 't' value of 3.514 at 0.01 level.

Regarding assertiveness, Group IV and Group II with the higher mean scores of 14.09 and 14.16 respectively differ significantly from Group I, its mean score being 12.61. Teachers become more assertive when they become older. But one surprisingly contradictory finding is the difference between Group II and Group III. Teachers of 30s are more assertive than those of 40s and they differ significantly too. The older the teachers become, the higher the self regard and stronger their assertiveness are. To conclude, teachers become more emotionally intelligent when they are getting older and older up to period of a time.

Educational Qualification and Emotional Intelligence

Minimum educational Qualification prescribed for elementary school teachers is a Diploma in Teacher Education (D.T.Ed) Now B.T. teachers (graduation with B.Ed.) are being gradually appointed at upper primary level. As part of professional development a large number of teachers have acquired higher educational qualifications. In fact there are 102 teachers with only D.T.Ed., qualification in the sample, categorized as group I in the sample. As many as 76 teachers have acquired a bachelor degree along with D.T.Ed., (Group II). The Group III consists of 50 teachers who are graduates with bachelor degree in education (B.Ed.). It is interesting to note that as many as 72 teachers (about one fourth of the total sample) have acquired post graduate qualification like M.A or M.Sc or M.Com. They are classified as Group IV. F test has been applied to find out whether the teachers of different educational qualifications differ in their Emotional Intelligence scores., In general, no significant difference is found among the four groups of teachers (Table 5) in their total Emotional Intelligence score., However, component wise analysis shows that there exists significant difference among teachers of various qualifications with special reference to emotional self awareness and stress tolerance when 't' test is applied (Table 6). Teachers with post graduate qualifications (Group IV) significantly differ from the other three groups with the higher mean score of 16.43 in emotional self awareness.

Table 4

t-Test Age wise Comparison of the Emotional Intelligence of Teachers

Dimension	Group	N	M	SD	t	df	Sig
	21-30	31	25.94	5.29	3.174	1.77	0.01
	31-40	148	29.01	4.81			
	21-30	31	25.94	5.29	1.530	93	NS
	41-50	64	27.69	5.20			
	21-30	31	25.94	5.29	1.972	86	NS
SR	>50	57	28.32	5.47			
	31-40	148	29.01	4.81	1.787	210	NS
	41-50	64	27.69	5.20			
	31-40	148	29.01	4.81	0.886	203	NS
	>50	57	28.32	5.47			
	41-50	64	27.63	5.20	0.647	119	NS
	>50	57	28.32	5.47			
	21-30	31	15.16	3.62	0.209	1.77	0.01
	31-40	148	15.03	2.97			
	21-30	31	15.16	3.62	0.528	93	NS
ES	41-50	64	15.58	3.60			
	21-30	31	15.16	3.62	2.064	86	0.05
	>50	57	16.68	3.13			
	31-40	148	15.03	2.97	1.147	210	NS
	41-50	64	15.58	3.60			
	31-40	148	15.03	2.97	3.514	203	0.01
	>50	57	16.68	3.13			
	41-50	64	15.58	3.60	1.193	119	NS
	>50	57	16.68	3.13			
	21-30	31	12.61	3.38	2.171	1.77	0.05
	31-40	148	14.16	3.64			
	21-30	31	12.61	3.38	0.715	93	NS
	41-50	64	13.09	3.29			
	21-30	31	12.61	3.64	1.991	86	0.05
AS	>50	57	14.09	2.92			
	31-40	148	14.16	3.64	2.064	210	0.05
	41-50	64	13.09	2.92			
	31-40	148	14.16	3.64	0.122	203	NS
	>50	57	14.09	3.29			
	41-50	64	13.09	2.92	1.763	119	NS
	>50	57	14.09	3.26			
	21 30	31	180.03	26.93	2.538	1.77	0.05
	31-40	148	192.92	25.40			
	21-30	31	180.03	26.93	0.863	93	NS
	41-50	64	185.47	29.64			
	21-30	31	180.03	26.93	2.196	86	0.05
EI	>50	57	194.14	29.73			
	31-40	148	192.90	25.40	1.857	210	NS
	41-50	64	185.47	29.64			
	31-40	148	192.90	25.40	0.299	203	NS
	>50	57	194.14	29.73			
	41-50	64	185.47	29.64	1.604	119	NS
	>50	57	194.14	29.76			

Table 5

ANOVA Educational Qualification and Emotional Intelligence of Teachers

Components	Sources	Sum of Squares	Df	Mean Square	F	Sig
	Between Groups	119.10	3	39.703	1.150	NS
SR	Within Groups	7780.927	296	26.287		
	Total	7900.037	299			
	Between Groups	82.153	3	27.834	1.517	NS
IR	Within Groups	5342.794	296	18.050		
	Total	5424.947	299			
	Between Groups	26.172	3	8.724	0.537	NS
IC	Within Groups	4804.398	296	16.231		
	Total	4830.570	299			
	Between Groups	76.966	3	25.655	1.761	NS
PS	Within Groups	4312.030	296	14.568		
	Total	4388.997	299			
	Between Groups	89.982	3	29.994	2.884	0.05
ES	Within Groups	3078.855	296	10.402		
	Total	3168.837	299			
	Between Groups	57.027	3	19.009	0.857	NS
FL	Within Groups	6563.170	296	22.173		
	Total	6620.197	299			
	Between Groups	30.873	3	10.291	0.966	NS
RT	Within Groups	3152.047	296	10.649		
	Total	3182.920	299			
	Between Groups	227.860	3	75.953	3.210	0.05
ST	Within Groups	7004.287	296	23.663		
	Total	7232.147	299			
	Between Groups	65.608	3	21.869	1.869	NS
AS	Within Groups	3463.629	296	11.701		
	Total	3529.237	299			
	Between Groups	22.746	3	7.582	0.811	NS
EM	Within Groups	2768.801	296	9.354		
	Total	2791.547	299			
	Between Groups	4351.629	3	1450.543	1.919	NS
EI	Within Groups	223715.9	296	755.797		
	Total	228067.5	299			

Teachers with higher educational qualification especially post graduates (Group IV) have obtained higher mean score of 23.56 than diploma holders (21.44) and degree holder with diploma (25.53) in stress tolerance and they differ significantly from other (Table 6). These findings support the logical conclusion that highly educationally qualified teachers are more aware of their emotions. They appear to cope with the stressful situation in the classroom better than relatively less qualified teachers.

Table 6

t-Test Educational Qualification and Emotional Intelligence of Teachers

Dimension	Group	N	M	SD	t	df	Sig
	1	102	15.29	3.42	0.277	176	NS
	2	76	15.16	2.99			
	1	102	15.29	3.42	0.596	150	NS
	3	50	14.96	2.85			
	1	102	15.29	3.42	2.160	172	0.05
ES	4	72	16.43	3.41			
	2	76	15.16	2.99	0.370	124	NS
	3	50	14.96	2.85			
	2	76	15.16	2.99	2.416	146	0.05
	4	72	16.43	3.41			
	3	50	14.96	2.85	2.498	120	0.05
	4	72	16.43	3.41			
	1	102	21.44	4.74	0.100	176	NS
	2	76	21.51	4.81			
	1	102	21.44	4.74	1.005	150	NS
	3	50	22.30	5.36			
	1	102	21.44	4.74	2.919	172	0.01
ES	4	72	23.56	4.74			
	2	76	21.51	4.81	0.858	124	NS
	3	50	22.30	5.36			
	2	76	21.51	4.81	2.618	146	0.01
	4	72	23.56	4.74			
	3	50	22.30	5.36	1.379	120	NS
	4	72	23.56	4.74			

Experience and Emotional Intelligence

Teaching experience at elementary level of education would provide teachers with lot of learning experience. Are experienced teachers more intelligent in their emotions? Do they stand apart from novice? These questions are addressed in the study. Teachers have been classified into five groups with five years of experience as one block.

Group I has put in 1-5 years of experience, Group II has worked for 6 to 10 years. Group III and IV are categorized with 11-15 years and 16-20 years, respectively. Teachers with more than 20 years of experience belong to Group V. 'F' test has been applied to find out the difference among them in Emotional Intelligence (Table 7). Results indicate that they do not differ significantly not only in total emotional intelligence but also in specific components. So it may be concluded that groups are homogenous and experience does not differentiate teachers in acquiring Emotional Intelligence competencies.

Table 7

ANOVA Teaching Experience and Emotional Intelligence of Teachers

Components	Sources	Sum of Squares	Df	Mean Square	F	Sig
SR	Between Groups	81.687	4	20.422	0.771	NS
	Within Groups	7818.350	295	26.503		
	Total	7900.037	299			
IR	Between Groups	43.638	4	10.910	0.598	NS
	Within Groups	5381.308	295	18.242		
	Total	5424.947	299			
IC	Between Groups	103.726	4	25.932	1.618	NS
	Within Groups	4726.844	295	16.023		
	Total	4830.570	299			
PS	Between Groups	87.369	4	21.842	1.498	NS
	Within Groups	4301.628	295	14.582		
	Total	4388.997	299			
ES	Between Groups	85.249	4	21.312	2.039	NS
	Within Groups	3083.587	295	10.453		
	Total	3168.837	299			
FL	Between Groups	14.740	4	3.685	0.165	NS
	Within Groups	6605.456	295	22.391		
	Total	6620.197	299			
RT	Between Groups	83.734	4	20.934	1.993	NS
	Within Groups	3099.186	295	10.506		
	Total	3182.920	299			
ST	Between Groups	151.609	4	37.902	1.579	NS
	Within Groups	7080.538	295	24.002		
	Total	7232.147	299			
AS	Between Groups	12.940	4	3.235	0.271	NS
	Within Groups	3516.297	295	11.920		
	Total	3529.237	299			
EM	Between Groups	29.863	4	7.341	0.784	NS
	Within Groups	2762.184	295	9.363		
	Total	2791.547	299			
EI	Between Groups	2666.426	4	666.607	0.872	NS
	Within Groups	225401.1	295	764.071		
	Total	228067.5	299			

Level of School and Emotional Intelligence of Teachers

Elementary teachers work at four levels of schools namely primary, middle high and higher secondary. Whether these levels of schools do have any say over the Emotional Intelligence is a valid research question because each level of school has its own infrastructure, faculty and students as well as problems. For example, higher secondary schools have better library facilities than other schools. Teachers working at four levels of schools are classified into four groups and 'F' test has been applied (Table 8). It is found that there is no significant difference among them in their Emotional Intelligence. So it may be concluded that teachers' Emotional Intelligence is not influenced by the level of school they work.

Table 8

ANOVA Level of School and Emotional Intelligence of Teachers

Components	Sources	Sum of Squares	Df	Mean Square	F	Sig
SR	Between Groups	24.048	3	8.016	0.301	NS
	Within Groups	7875.989	296	26.608		
	Total	7900.037	299			
IR	Between Groups	39.131	3	13.044	0.717	NS
	Within Groups	5385.816	296	18.195		
	Total	5424.947	299			
IC	Between Groups	15.978	3	5.326	0.327	NS
	Within Groups	4814.592	296	16.266		
	Total	4830.570	299			
PS	Between Groups	9.355	3	3.118	0.211	NS
	Within Groups	4379.641	296	14.796		
	Total	4388.997	299			
ES	Between Groups	25.658	3	8.553	0.805	NS
	Within Groups	3143.178	296	10.619		
	Total	3168.837	299			
FL	Between Groups	5.821	3	1.940	0.087	NS
	Within Groups	6614.375	296	22.346		
	Total	6620.197	299			
RT	Between Groups	17.408	3	5.803	0.543	NS
	Within Groups	3165.512	296	10.694		
	Total	3182.920	299			
ST	Between Groups	109.613	3	36.538	1.518	NS
	Within Groups	7122.534	296	24.063		
	Total	7232.147	299			
AS	Between Groups	39.506	3	13.169	1.117	NS
	Within Groups	3489.731	296	11.790		
	Total	3529.237	299			
EM	Between Groups	20.494	3	50.721	0.730	NS
	Within Groups	2771.052	296	9.361		
	Total	2791.547	299			
EI	Between Groups	684.138	3	228.046	0.297	NS
	Within Groups	227383.3	296	768.187		
	Total	228067.5	299			

Type of School and Emotional Intelligence

Teachers work in schools run by the Government as well as managed by the private body aided by the Government so the latter is called private aided school and the former Government School. Do the teachers working in these types of schools differ in their Emotional Intelligence? To address this issue, 't' test has been applied and the finding clearly shows that there is no significant difference between them in general Emotional Intelligence as well as in component wise analysis (Table 9)

Table 9

't' Test Type of Management and Emotional Intelligence

Component of EI	Govt (N = 191)		Private Aided (N=109)		t	Significant Level
	M	SD	M	SD		
SR	28.70	4.82	27.54	5.61	1.880	NS
IR	22.21	4.16	22.06	4.45	0.301	NS
IC	14.26	4.09	13.80	3.90	0.950	NS
PS	19.93	3.89	19.68	3.74	0.538	NS
ES	15.44	3.35	15.54	3.09	0.259	NS
FL	21.94	4.68	21.45	4.76	0.872	NS
RT	16.95	3.33	16.92	3.16	0.090	NS
ST	22.09	4.84	22.15	5.08	0.089	NS
AS	13.83	3.49	13.63	3.35	0.470	NS
EM	16.00	3.06	15.49	3.03	1.403	NS
EI	191.31	27.17	188.25	28.40	0.934	NS

Findings of comparison of different groups in respect of their Emotional Intelligence suggest that gender, educational qualification, experience, type and level of schools do not influence the Emotional Intelligence of teachers. Age alone appears to differentiate their Emotional Intelligence.

CORRELATIONAL ANALYSIS

The inter –correlations among ten components namely self regard (SR), interpersonal relationship (IR), impulse control (IC), Problem Solving (PS), emotional self awareness (ES), flexibility (FL), reality testing (RT), stress tolerance (ST), assertiveness (AS), and empathy (EM) are positive and significant (Table 4.10), The only exception is between empathy and emotional self-awareness where the relationship is low and insignificant even though positive. The high degree of relationship is found between self-regard and interpersonal relationships (0.62) and self regard and stress tolerance (0.59). This may mean that ability to be aware of one and accurately appraise one's self facilities the ability to create and maintain relationships. Teachers who have a high self-regard would be able to sustain cordial relationship with fellow teachers as well as maintain good rapport with students. Moreover, those who understand themselves properly would be able to manage stress and anxiety provoking conditions.

Relatively high correlation between inter-personal relationship and stress tolerance (0.58) demonstrates maintaining good relationship with fellow teachers and children involves the tolerance of stress which is necessary in school settings. The fairly high correlation obtained between inter-personal relationship and flexibility (0.55) shows that creating and sustaining relationship and flexibility (0.55) shows that creating and sustaining relationships demand flexibility in teachers thinking and behaviour. The fairly close relationship between the inter-personal relationship and problem solving (0.54) implies that both of them require a persistent, preserving and disciplined approach' in sustaining relationships and solving problems.

Impulse control, highly correlated with stress tolerance (0.58) implies that the ability to be composed facilitates effective management of stressful classroom situations. Its relationship with problem solving (0.54) and flexibility (0.55) is rather high. Controlling one's impulses enables a teacher to focus on the problem in question and solve it quickly. There is also moderately high correlation between impulse control and reality testing (0.47) which implies that the ability to accurately and realistically assess the immediate situation is facilitated by the control of hostile and aggressive impulses. Problem solving correlates significantly well with stress tolerance (0.48) and empathy (0.48) and empathy (0.47). In fact decision making and problem solving help people coping with stressful situations as is evidenced from the findings of Bar-On (1997).

Table 10

Inter Correlations among ten components of Emotional Intelligence

	SR	IR	IC	PS	ES	FL	RT	ST	AS	EM
SR		0.62**	0.44**	0.53**	0.41**	0.48**	0.43**	0.59**	0.52**	0.38**
IR			0.45**	0.54**	0.44**	0.55**	0.35**	0.58**	0.45**	0.42**
IC				0.31**	0.33**	0.54**	0.47**	0.51**	0.29**	0.14*
PS					0.29**	0.329**	0.29**	0.48**	0.25**	0.47**
ES						0.44**	0.35**	0.38**	0.40**	0.08
FL							0.40**	0.51**	0.47**	0.20**
RT								0.37**	0.36**	0.20**
ST									0.40**	0.30**
AS										0.20**
EM										

** Significant at 0.01 level
* Significant at 0.05 level

Emotional Self awareness, the vital component of Emotional Intelligence, correlates moderately well with flexibility (0.44) and significantly with assertiveness (0.40) emotional self awareness, an on-going attention to one's internal states, is facilitated by flexibility in mind, "Then only it is possible to be aware of both our mood and our thoughts about that mood" (Goleman, 1955). its relationship with assertiveness suggests that awareness of one's emotions is a pre-requisite for expressing one's self and his emotions firmly and clearly.

Flexibility has moderately high correlation with stress tolerance (0.51) and assertiveness (0.47). it is logical to assume that ability to adjust to different school environments when teachers are on transfer helps them effectively manage anxious situations. It is also equally important that flexible mind-set without emotional rigidly enables the expression of feelings openly and adequately. The significant correlation between flexibility and reality testing (0.40) suggests that emotional flexibility plays no less important role in assessing real situations more accurately. In fact reality testing correlates significantly with stress tolerance (0.37) and assertiveness (0.36) These relationship suggests that unless teacher's perception, feeling and thinking are strongly grounded in reality, She / he may not able to cope with stress and asset herself boldly in tough situations. Only a realistic approach helps the teachers nurture the individuals talents of children and appreciate their accomplishments without exacting too much from them in the name of perfections, at the emotional cost of children. The significant correlation between assertiveness and stress tolerance (0.40) implies that only assertive people can manage the stressful situations effectively.

Table 11

Correlation between components and Emotional Intelligence

Component	r value	Significant level
SR	0.81	0.01
IR	0.80	0.01
IC	0.67	0.01
PS	0.66	0.01
ES	0.59	0.01
FL	0.74	0.01
RT	0.60	0.01
ST	0.78	0.01
AS	0.64	0.01
EM	0.48	0.01

The correlations between each of the ten components and Emotional Intelligence range from 0.48 to 0.81 (Table 11). They are positively and significantly correlated. The highest degree of relationship between Emotional Intelligence and self regard (0.81) and inter-personal relationship (0.80) has been obtained. That very strong connection exists between Emotional Intelligence and stress tolerance (0.78) and with flexibility (0.74) is evident from the present research. It is also interesting to note that Emotional Intelligence has a fairly high correlation with impulse control (0.67), with problem solving (0.66), with assertiveness (0.64), with reality testing (0.60) and with emotional self-awareness (0.59) but empathy is only moderately highly correlated with Emotional Intelligence (0.48).

A stepwise regression analysis was done to arrive at the fit model by introducing step by step each component (Table 12). All components except empathy have been found to be accountable for Emotional Intelligence. Empathy was left out due to co linearity. The R2 value 0.991 given in Table 12 shows that the proportion of the dependent variable (Emotional Intelligence) variance can be attributed to, or explained by variance in the independent variables (the components). Hence it may be concluded that 99 percent of the observed variable in the Emotional Intelligence of teachers can be explained by the variance in their self-regard, flexibility, stress tolerance, interpersonal relationship, reality testing problem solving, assertiveness, impulse control and emotional self-awareness. The Durbin – Watson value of 1.936 also emphatically supports the assumption that independent error is tenable in the model evolved.

Table 12

Regression Analysis Model Summary

MODEL	R	R SQUARE	ADJUSTED R SQUARE	STANDARD ERROR OF THE ESTIMATE	DURBIN WATSON
9	0.996	0.991	0.991	2.59875	1.936

Predicators: (Constant), SR, FL, ST, IR, RT, PS, AC, IC AND ES

Dependent Variable : EI

The multiple regression equation was set up as follows:

Emotional Intelligence EI =

6.923 + 1.081 SR + 0.0991 FL + 1.012 ST+ 1.063 RT + 1.251 PS + 1.014 AS + 0.911 IC + 0.831 ES

The beta – coefficients of the components namely self-regard (0.201), flexibility (0.183), Stress tolerance (0.180) inter personal relationship

(0.183) reality testing (0.126), Problem Solving (0.174) assertiveness (0.126), impulse control (0.133) and emotional Self awareness (0.098) are given table 13. The influence of self regard on Emotional Intelligence is twice that of emotional self-awareness. Both stress tolerance and inter personal relationship are almost equal in sharing the domain of Emotional Intelligence, next only to self-regard. They are followed by problem solving a vital component with more cognitive dimension. Flexibility shares more than three fourth of the variance of self regard. Impulse control has more than moderate influence on Emotional Intelligence. Reality testing and assertiveness are equal in exerting their moderate influence on Emotional Intelligence.

Table 13

Beta Coefficients

Model	Dimensions	Un-standardized coefficient		Standardized Co-Efficient	t	Sig
		B	STD Error			
9	(Constant)	6.923	1.087		6.370	0.000
	SR	1.081	0.044	0.201	24.448	0.000
	FL	0.991	0.044	0.169	23.394	0.000
	ST	1.012	0.043	0.180	23.566	0.000
	IR	1.187	0.053	0.183	22.589	0.000
	RT	1.063	0.056	0.126	19.048	0.000
	PS	1.251	0.050	0.174	25.048	0.000
	AS	1.014	0.056	0.126	18.232	0.000
	IC	0.911	0.049	0.133	18.463	0.000
	ES	0.831	0.055	0.098	15.117	0.000

Dependent Variable EI

Components of Emotional Intelligence and Elementary School Teachers

Teachers' self regard plays a critical role in determining their Emotional Intelligence. Their emotional competence also depends crucially on their interpersonal relationships they maintain with teachers, students and community as well their stress tolerance with which they cope with anxiety provoking situations on the school campus. Their problem solving skills do contribute to their emotional competence capabilities. Emotional flexibility certainly facilitates their improvement of Emotional Intelligence skills. To what extent they are capable of controlling their impulses determine their Emotional Intelligence capacity. Realistic assessment of children's strengths and limitations not only in cognitive but also in affective domain helps them to be emotionally competent in addressing the children's needs. They need to be assertive also in certain situations where their feelings need proper expression. But surprisingly the missing component of elementary school teachers' Emotional Intelligence is empathy which is a basic requirement of an emotionally competent teacher. It may be one of the causes for their lack of emotional bonding with children resulting in corporal punishment and other mis-behaviours in schools.

5

Findings and Implications

INTRODUCTION

The project was undertaken with a view to studying the Emotional Intelligence of teachers working at elementary stage of education and integrating of teachers working at elementary stage of education and integrating it within the discourse of classroom process. It aimed at finding out the difference between men and women teachers in respect of their Emotional Intelligence. It also attempted to study whether teachers' age, educational qualification, teaching experience and level and type of school where they work influence their Emotional Intelligence skills. Finally, it tried to investigate the relationship between ten components, namely self-regard, interpersonal relationship, impulse control, problem solving, emotional self awareness, flexibility, reality testing stress tolerance, assertiveness and empathy, and their relationships with emotional intelligence in total.

The translated and validated version of Bar-On's Emotional Quotient Inventory was canvassed on 300 teachers working in primary and middle schools and elementary sections of high and higher secondary schools of both types-government and private aided drawn from 14 blocks in Cuddalore District through proportionate Stratified Random Sampling Procedure. The data collected were analyzed and the results discussed.

The main findings are first presented and their implications are discussed later in this chapter.

FINDINGS

The findings are as follows

1. The Emotional Intelligence of elementary school teachers is rather high. Component wise analysis shows that their performance is relatively low in 'assertiveness' and 'emotional self- awareness dimensions"
2. Men and Women teachers, in general, do not differ significantly in their Emotional Intelligence. While women teachers are stronger in 'impulse control' and reality testing' than men teachers, the latter are more aware of their emotions (emotional self awareness).
3. Age differentiates elementary school teachers in their Emotional Intelligence. Increases with age until the fifth decade of life. the older teachers are stronger in assertiveness, higher in self regard and better in their awareness of emotions.
4. Educational qualification does not significantly influence the emotional intelligence of teachers. However teachers with higher qualifications at post graduate level have more emotional self awareness and handle stress better than the teachers with less qualifications.
5. Elementary teachers do not differ significantly in their Emotional Intelligence in respect of their teaching experience.
6. Irrespective of the level of schools they work namely primary, middle, high and higher secondary teachers exhibit similar performance in Emotional Intelligence.
7. Type of Management of schools per se does not differentiate teachers in their Emotional Intelligence.
8. There is a positive and significant correlation between the ten components of Emotional Intelligence. The correlation between each of the ten components and Emotional Intelligence range from moderately high (0.48) to very high (0.81). The highest degree of relationship exists between self-regard and emotional intelligence (0.81) and the lowest but moderately high correlation is found between empathy and emotional intelligence (0.48).

9. Ninety –nine percent variance in the Emotional Intelligence of teachers can be explained by the variance in their self –regard, flexibility stress tolerance, interpersonal relationship reality testing, problem solving, assertiveness, impulse control and emotional self– awareness. The only component left out due to co-linearity is empathy.
10. The beta – coefficients of the components show that the influence of self-regard (0.201) on Emotional Intelligence is twice that of emotional self awareness (0.098), which is the least influencing one. Both stress tolerance (0.180) and inter-personal relationship are almost equal in sharing the domain of Emotional Intelligence, next only to self regard. They are followed by problem solving (0.174), Flexibility (0.169) shares more than three-fourth of the variance of self regard. Impulse control (0.133) has more moderate influence on Emotional Intelligence. Reality testing (0.123) and assertiveness (0.126) are equal in exerting their moderate influence on Emotional Intelligence

IMPLICATIONS

The present research shows that the teachers working at elementary stage exhibit higher level of performance in their Emotional Intelligence. However, the components that have been tested are rather general. They are only potential Emotional Intelligence skills. The teachers might have already known the skills. But practicing them in classroom setting demands different emotional and social competencies from the teachers.

Specific interventions targeted on elementary school teachers should be made by organizing teacher – development programmes such as in service training, workshop and action research projects.

The in-service training programmes will help the teachers become emotionally competent in developing the wholesome personality of children. Researches indicate that the teachers gain considerable benefit from in-service training programmes focusing emotional skills. A qualitative study (Fer, 2004) on the evaluation of Emotional Intelligence in-service programme for school teachers found that the training provided opportunists for teachers to synthesis information and skills derived from Emotional Intelligence activities. it helped them to adopt ways of using Emotional Intelligence activates in the classroom. Through the training programme, teachers will be made more aware of their feelings and emotion. Emotional awareness is the most important one since it serves as a good basis for other skills. They will be trained to retain their impulses. Which will by any large reduce the evils of corporal punishment and other undesirable teacher behaviour on the school campus. They will be persuaded to rethink their methods of punishing children.

Since there are far more similarities than differences between men and women teachers with respect to their emotional intelligences, a uniform training programme may be designed for both of them.

As older teachers are more "matured" and emotionally competent than the younger age groups, the relatively young teachers may be given wide exposure to the application of Emotional Intelligence skills in the classroom. Byron (2001) study also found that Emotional Intelligence workshop has significantly increased the EQ of novice teachers. It is effective in enhancing their emotional knowledge and skills. Hargreave's (2000) study, which interviewed the teachers in order to investigate emotions of teaching and educational change, indicated that elementary teaching was characterized by creating greater emotional intensity.

Since educational qualification, teaching experience and level and type of schools do not differentiate teachers in respect of their Emotional Intelligence a common programme for developing emotional competence of the teachers may be organized.

Findings of correlation and regression clearly reveal that empathy does not contribute even marginally to the Emotional Intelligence of the teachers. It may imply that teachers are not empathic towards children in classroom makes communication healthier. So, teachers may be specially trained on empathy related skills.

Action research project may be undertaken to improve the Emotional Intelligence of teachers as well as students by designing an integrated emotional intelligence curriculum within the existing school curriculum frame work. Action researches (E.g. Fattinger *et al 2000)* support that EQ curriculum improves social and personal skills of students.

CONCLUSION

Education for promoting emotion should be recognized as an essential element of the educational process in the classroom since it facilitates the attainment of educational goals. In fact, for the teacher, emotion can become a valuable tool for the development all round personality of children. But emotional incompetence of teachers affects the emotional ecology of schools negatively. The findings of this research, in general, indicate that Emotional Intelligence of teachers is rather high but the potential skills are not translated into emotional and social competencies in classroom. The most important component that does not contribute to the Emotional Intelligence of elementary school teachers in this study is empathy that appears in most models of Emotional Intelligence.

The lack of empathy among teachers leads to the increasing indicidence of corporal punishment, teacher misbehavior, children's suicide rates in schools. Unless teachers love children and understand their feelings, children don't develop empathy for other people and other cultures. It is high time teachers improved their emotional competencies so that they can play good role models for children to become emotionally literate citizens in future.

BIBLIOGRAPHY

1. **Abisamara, Nada (2000)** *Relation between Emotional Intelligence and academic achievement of eleven graders,* unpublished dissertation Auburn University at Montgomery.
2. **Abraham, R. (1999)** *Emotional Intelligenece in Organisations,* A conceptualization, Genetic, Social and general psychology monographs 125 (2), 209 -225.
3. **Alavandar, R (2000).** *A study not the dropouts from Primary Schools in Kalraya Hills.* A DPEP project Report, Chennai,.
4. **Amirtha, M. (2004)** *A study on the personality of teachers in relation to their Emotional Intelligence,* Unpublished M.Phil Dissertation Annamalai University, Annamalai Nagar.
5. **Annaraja, P., and Jose, S. (2005)** *Emotional Intelligence of B.Ed., Trainees,* Research and Reflections, Vol. 3 No.2
6. **Ashforth, E. (2001)** *The handbook of Emotional Intelligence (Book Review).* Personnel Psychology, 54 (3), 721-725.'
7. **Averill, J.R. (2000)** *Intelligence, emotion, and creativity: From tracheotomy to trinity.* In R. Bar – On and J.D.A. Barker (eds). The handbook of Emotional Intelligence (PP 3-31) San Francisco: Jossey- Bass

8. **Bar – On, R. (1997).** *The Emotional Quotient Inventory* (EQ-i): A test of Emotional Intelligence, Toronto, Canada: Multi – Health Systems.

9. **Bar – On R (2000).** *Emotional and social Intelligence: Insights from the Emotional Quotient Inventory.* In R. Bar – On and J.D.A. Parker (Eds) The handbook of Emotional Intelligence. San Francisco: Jossey- Bass).

10. **Barren, L.F., Richard, D.L., Sechrest. L.E. and Gray, E.S. (2000)** *Sex differences in emotional awareness.* Psychological and Social Psychological Bulletin. 1027-1035.

11. **Boyatzis, R.E., Goleman, D., and Hay / Mc.Ber. (1999):** Emotional Competence Inventory. Boston: Hay Group.

12. **Bruno, K., England, E. and Chembliss. C. (2000)** *The et Tectiveness of implementing a social and emotional learning programme for elementary students.* Academic. uofs.edu/ organization/psycon/abstracts.

13. **Byron, C.M. (2001)** *The effects of emotional knowledge education in the training of novice teachers.* Digital Disserrtation, 62 (5), 1797 A (Publication No. ATT 30 I 4883).

14. **Chemiss, C, and Goleman, D (1998).** *Bringing Emotional Intelligence to workplace* Retrieved December 17, 2001 from http://www.eiconsortium .org/research/technical report.

15. **Cooper, R.K. (1997).** *Applying Emotional Intelligence in the workplace. Training & Development,* 51 (120- 31-38) Retrieved November 19, 2001 from Proudest Database.

16. **Culver, R., Binghamton, N.Y and Yokomoto, C (1999).** *Optimum academic performance and its relation to Emotional Intelligence.* Frontiers in Education Conference. Nov. 10-13, San Juan, Puerto Rico, 9fie Enging Pitt. Edn / fie / 99 / papers / 1585.pdf.

17. **Dash D.N., and Bchera, N.P. (2004).** *Teacher effectiveness in relation to their Emotional Intelligence,* Journal of Indian Education, Vol XXX No.3

18. **Denny, N.W., and Palmer, A.M (1981).** *Adult age differences on Traditional and Practical Problem solving measures.* Journal of Gerontology., 36, 323-328.

19. **Fer, S. (2004)** Qualitative evaluation of Emotional Intelligence in – service program for secondary school teachers. The Qualitative Report Vol. 9 Nov.4 pp 562-588, http://www.Nova.Edue / sss/QRJ qr9/fer.pdf.

20. **Finley, D., Pettinger, A., Rutherford, T., and Timmes, V (2000)** *Developing Emotional Intelligence in a multiage classroom.* (Report No. PSO 28662) Chicago: Saint Xavier University and Skylight Professional Development Field – based Masters Programme (ERIC Document Reproduction Service No. ED 44442571).

21. **Gardner, H (1983).** *Frames of mind: The theory of multiple intelligences.* New York: Basic Books.

22. **Goleman, D., (1995)** *Emotional Intelligence New York: Bantam*

23. **Goleman, D (1998)** *Working with Emotional Intelligence* **New York; Bantam.**

24. **Graves, M.L.M. (2000)** *Emotional Intelligence, general intelligence, and personality: Assessing the construct validity of Emotional Intelligence test using structural equation modeling.* Digital Dissertation, 61 (04) 2255B (Publication No. AAT 9968121)

25. **Hamachek, D. (2000)** *Dynamics of self understanding and self-knowledge: Acquisition, advantages and relation to Emotional Intelligence* Journal of Humanistic Counseling Education & Development, 38 (4),. 230-243, Emotional Intelligence interactions with students. Teaching and Teacher Education 16(8) – 811.

26. **Hartley, D. (2003).** *The instrumentalisation of the expressive in education.* British Journal of Education Studies, 51 (1), 6-19.

27. **Henis, S. (1996)** *Emotional Intelligence for everybody: A practical guide to Emotional Intelligence.* Clearwater, Florida; Aristotle Press. Retrieved December. 17, 2001 from http:eqi.org./eqe96-1.htm.

28. **Heins S. (2001a).** The importance of developing Emotional *Intelligence.* Retrieved December 17, 2001 from http:eqi.org./eqe96-1.htm.

29. **Heins S. (2001b).** *Tips for teachers.* Retrieved December 17, 2001 from http:eqi.org./eqe96-1.htm.

30. **Latha A., Ramasamy, S., and Ananthasayanan, R. (2005).** *Study of Emotional Intelligence and its effect on teachers' effectiveness among school teachers.* Journal of Educational Research and Extension Vol. 42 (3). PP 20-29.

31. **Liau, A.K. Liau, A.W., Teoh, G.B.S., and Liau, M.T.L. (2003).** *The case for emotional literacy: the influence of Emotional Intelligence on problem behaviour's in Malaysian Secondary School Students.* Journal of Moral Education 32(1). 51-66.

32. **Madonna, G.C., and Kathy, A.G. (2001).** *Emotional empathy and their relation to multicultural counseling knowledge and awareness.* MC 81@ Columbia. edn.

33. **Mare, A.B., Mayer, J.D., and Rebecca, M.W (2004)** *Emotional Intelligence and its relation to everybody behaviour.* Personality and individual differences, 36, 1387 – 1402.

34. **Mayer, J.D., and Salovey, P. (1995).** *Emotional Intelligence and the construction and regulation of feeling.* Applied and Preventive Psychology, 4, 197-208.

35. **Mayer, J.D., and Salovey, P. (J 1997).** *What is Emotional Intelligence?* In P. Salovey and D. Sluyter (Eds.) *Emotional development and Emotional Intelligence: Implications for educators* (pp 3-31) NewYork: Basic Books).

36. **Mayer J.D., Salovey, P., and Caruso, D.R. (1999).** Working manual for the MSCEIT Research Version 1.1. cited in R – Bar – On and J.D., Parker (Eds) (2001) *The handbook of Emotional Intelligence,* San Francisco: Jossey Bass.

37. **Mayer J.D., Salovey, P., and Caruso, D.R. (2000).** Models of *Emotional Intelligence.* In **R.J. Sternberg (ED)** *Handbook of intelligence* (2nd ed., pp 396-421) New York: Cambridge University Press.

38. **Mishra, P., and Dhar, V. (2001)** *Emotional Intelligence as a correlate of thinking orientation among future managers.* Indian Journal of Industrial Relations, 36 (3) 323-338. Emotional Intelligence and achievement of teacher trainees at Primary level. *The Educational Review.* Vol. 47, No. 8 pp 13-16.

39. National Council of Educational Research and Training (2000). *National Curriculum Frame Work for School Education (NCFSE).* New Delhi: NCERT.

40. National Council of Educational Research and Training (2005). *National Curriculum Frame Work (NCF).* New Delhi: NCERT.

41. **Neisser. U. (1979).** The concept of intelligence. In R.J. Sternberg and D.K. Detterman (Eds) *Human Intelligence; Perspectives on its theory and measurement* Norwood, N.J: Ablex.

42. **Parker. J.D. A., Summerfeldt, L.J.. Hogan, M.J., and Majeski., S.A. (2004)** *Emotional Intelligenceand academic success:* Examining the transition from high school to university. Personality and individual differences, 36, 163-172.

43. **Pfeiffer, S.I. (2001).** *Emotional Intelligence: Popular but elusive construct.* Roeper Review, 23 (3), 138-143. Retrieved September 9, 2001, from proquest database.

44. **Richardson, R.C. (2000)** *Teaching Social and emotional competence.* Children Schools, 22(4), 246-252. Retrieved September 9, 2001 from Proquest database.

45. **Roberts, R.D., and Mathew, G. (2002).** *Can Emotional Intelligence be schooled: A Critical Review.* Educational Psychologist 37 (4), 215 – 231.

46. **Ross, M.R. (2000).** An assessment of the professional development needs of middle school principals around social and emotional learning issues in schools. Digital Dissertation, 6 (01) 85A (Publication No. AA 19958665).

47. **Saarni, C. (2000).** Emotional competence: A Developmental perspective. In R. Bar-On & J.D.A. Parker (Eds). *The handbook of Emotional Intelligence:* San Francisco: Jossey Bass.

48. **Salovey P., and Mayer, J.D. (1990)** *Emotional Intelligence. imagination,* Cognition, Personality 9, 185-211.

49. **Shenwal V.K. (2004).** *Emotional Intelligence: The Indian Science Reviewed in Indian.* Educational Review. V 01 . 40, No.2

50. **Sternberrg, R.J. (1988).** The triarchic mind: *A new theory of human intelligence.* New York: Penguin.

51. **Strenborg, R.J. (1999).** (Review of Goleman's Book *"Working with Emotional Intelligence")* Personnel Psychology, 52, 780-783.

52. **Suresh, I., and Rajalakshmi (2005).** *Emotional Intelligence among school teacher.* Meston Journal of Research in Education, PP 4-6.

53. **Thorndike, E.L. (1920).** *Intelligence and its uses.* Harper Magazine, 140, 227-235.

54. **Tucker, K. (2000).** *The development of empathy and role – taking skills in pupil from grades six to nine.* (Report NO PS028500) Finland:

55. University of Helsinki (*ERIC Document Reproduction Service No. ED 440-753).*

56. **Wechsler, D. (1940).** *Non intellective factors in General intelligence.* Psychological Bulletin, 37, 444-445.

57. **Wechsler. D. (1943).** *Non intellective factors in General intelligence.* Journal of Abnormal Psychological 38, 100 – 104.

58. **Wechsler. D. (1958).** *"The measurement and appraisal of adult intelligence".* Baltimore. M. 0: The Williams & Wilkins Company.

59. **Zajonc. R.B. (1998). Emotions.** In D.T. Gilbert. S.T. Fiske., and G.Lindzey (Eds) *Handbook of Social Psychology* (Vol. 1, pp, 591632). Boston, M.A: Mc Graw-Hill. Leidnerr, M. Mathews, G., Roberts. R.D. and Macgenn, C. (2003). *Development of Emotional Intelligence towards a multilevel investment model.* Human Development, 46 (2-3) 69-96.

60. **Zimbardo, P.G., and Germing, R.J. (1996).** *"Psychology and Life".* New York: Harper CoUins.

APPENDIX

Emotional Quotient Inventory

Read each statement and decide which one of the following five possible responses and best describes you. Mark your choices by encircling the number that corresponds to your answer.

1. Never	2. Rarely	3. Sometimes	4. Often	5. Always

1. My approach in overcoming difficulties is to move step by step	1	2	3	4	5
2. I know how to deal with upsetting problems	1	2	3	4	5
3. Its fairly easy for me to express feeling	1	2	3	4	5
4. I try to see thing as they really are, without fantasizing or day dreaming about them	1	2	3	4	5
5. I am in touch with my emotions	1	2	3	4	5
6. I feel sure of myself in most situations	1	2	3	4	5
7. It is a problem controlling my anger	1	2	3	4	5
8. Its difficult for me to begin new things	1	2	3	4	5
9. When faced with a difficult situation, I like to collect all the information about it that I can	1	2	3	4	5
10 I believe that I can stay on top of tough situations	1	2	3	4	5
11. Its hard for me to share my deep feelings with others	1	2	3	4	5
12. I lack self confidence	1	2	3	4	5
13. Its hard for me to make adjustments in general	1	2	3	4	5
14. I like to get an overview of a problem before trying to solve it	1	2	3	4	5
15. I am fairly a cheerful person	1	2	3	4	5

16. I can handle stress, without getting too nervous	1	2	3	4	5
17. Its hard for me to understand they way I feel	1	2	3	4	5
18. When I am angry with others, I can tell them about it	1	2	3	4	5
19. I have had strange experiences that cannot be explained	1	2	3	4	5
20 Its easy for me to make friends	1	2	3	4	5
21. I have good self respect	1	2	3	4	5
22. Its difficult for me to change my opinions about things	1	2	3	4	5
23. When facing a problem, the first I do is stop and think	1	2	3	4	5
24. I do not hold up well under stress	1	2	3	4	5
25. I don't get express my intimate feelings	1	2	3	4	5
26. People do not understand the way I think	1	2	3	4	5
27. I don't feel good about myself	1	2	3	4	5
28. Its easy for me to adjust to new conditions	1	2	3	4	5
29. When trying to solve a problem, I look at each possibility and then decide on the best way	1	2	3	4	5
30 I would stop and help a crying child find his or her parents, even if I had to be some where else at this time.	1	2	3	4	5
31. I am fun to be with	1	2	3	4	5
32. I feel that it is hard for me to control my anxiety	1	2	3	4	5
33. When I disagree with someone, I am unable to say so	1	2	3	4	5
34. I tend to fadeout and loose contact with that happens around	1	2	3	4	5
35. I don't get along well with others	1	2	3	4	5
36. Its hard for me to accept myself just the way I am	1	2	3	4	5
37. I care what happens to other people	1	2	3	4	5
38. I am impatient	1	2	3	4	5
39. I am able to change old habits	1	2	3	4	5
40 I know how to keep calm in difficult situations	1	2	3	4	5
41. Its hard for me to say 'No' when I want to	1	2	3	4	5
42. I get carried away with my imagination and fantasies	1	2	3	4	5
43. I am happy with the type of person I am	1	2	3	4	5
44. I have strong impulses that are hard to control	1	2	3	4	5
45. Its generally hard for me to make changes in my daily life	1	2	3	4	5
46. In handling situations that arise, I try to think of as many approaches as I can	1	2	3	4	5
47. Its fairly easy for me to tell people what I think	1	2	3	4	5
48. I tend to exaggerate	1	2	3	4	5
49. I am sensitive to the feeling of others	1	2	3	4	5
50 I have good relations with others	1	2	3	4	5
51. I feel comfortable with my body	1	2	3	4	5
52. Its hard for me to change my ways	1	2	3	4	5
53. I believe in my ability to handle most upsetting problems	1	2	3	4	5
54. Others think that I lack assertiveness	1	2	3	4	5
55. People think that I am sociable	1	2	3	4	5
56. I am happy with the way I look	1	2	3	4	5
57. Its hard for me to describe my feelings	1	2	3	4	5

58. I have got a bad temper	1	2	3	4	5
59. Its hard for me to see people suffer	1	2	3	4	5
60 I get anxious	1	2	3	4	5
61. I avoid hurting other people's feelings	1	2	3	4	5
62. Its difficult to stand up for my rights	1	2	3	4	5
63. I don't keep in touch with friends	1	2	3	4	5
64. Looking at both my good and bad points, I feel good about myself	1	2	3	4	5
65. I tend to explode with anger easily	1	2	3	4	5
66. It would be hard for me to adjust if I were forced to leave my home	1	2	3	4	5

3. Moral Anxiety of Higher Secondary Students

1

Problem and its Perspectives

INTRODUCTION

God has made different religions to suit different aspirants, times and countries. All doctrines have many paths; but a path is by no means God Himself. Indeed, one can reach God if one follows any one of the paths; with whole-hearted devotion. Suppose there are errors in the religion that one has accepted; if one is sincere and earnest, then God Himself will correct those errors.

According to Hinduism, no prophet is unique in the sense that he is the greatest of all. All receive their message from the one source and present it to men to suit their particular needs. In the teachings of Christ, Buddha, Mohammed and Krishna one may see apparent differences due to the peculiar requirements of the people whom these prophets taught. But in their communion with reality they all experienced the same goodness, beauty and truth. The common inner experiences of prophets are not noticed by their followers; the apparent external differences in their teachings account for much of religious quarrelling and controversy.

A religion which regards ultimate reality as impersonal truth and at the same time recognizes the validity of its concrete manifestations for the benefit of struggling aspirants cannot but admit the validity of all religious ideals and show them respect. The situation is quite different with those for whom the Personal God is the ultimate reality. To accept the doctrine of exclusive salvation and develop the concept of 'either-or' are natural for them. Hinduism has never developed the theory of a jealous God or exclusive salvation; the idea of a chosen people is alien to it. In the Hindu monotheism all other deities are either absorbed in the Supreme God or accepted as parts of Him. Whereas in the Semitic monotheism they are not tolerated. The Bhagavad-Gita says that people under the compulsion of desires, following their own natures, worship other deities with suitable rituals. The supreme God does not frown upon such worship; on the contrary, He deepens their faith in their respective ideals and enables them to obtain the object of their desires. The ultimate fulfillment of desires, however, comes from Him alone who is the real dispenser of the fruits of worship. To a disciple who criticized the questionable rituals of a certain Hindu sect, Sri Ramakrishna said that the members of that sect, too, if sincere, would enter God's mansion- it might be by the back door. Religion is normally imbibed through education.

Education should bring about a change in any individual for the betterment of the society. Individuals in the society are involved in various related activities linked to the individual, family and society. He is forced to voice his opinions and develop his own likes and dislikes. His experience in different situations provides him with a set of moral values and attitudes. The building up of a person's character is closely related to moral anxiety.

Generally in our society, the moral anxiety can be perceived in the people with various attitudes. Those who are inclined in the path of religion are found to be morally anxious most of the time. The subjective introspection may be continuously occurring in their religious path. Positive or negative responses of religious concepts are prevention of character, faith in God, prayer and worship and are some of the religious attitudes.

EMERGENCE OF THE PROBLEM

Religious beliefs and practices have been a universal feature of human society, "Men have probably thought about sacred things from the time they began to think at all, but thinking about why one thinks about sacred things is a relatively recent enterprise.

Religion may be defined as man's belief in supernatural forces outside himself, which forces, he is convinced, influence human events. As a concrete experience, religion is accompanied by emotions, especially of fear, awe, or reverence.

The objective or scientific study of the religious life had seemed too many a contradiction in terms, a mere act of violence on the part of scientist toward a sphere of life he does not understand.

Dr. Radhakrishnan (1948) "Religion is not the acceptance of academic abstractions or the celebrations of ceremonies but kind of life and experience. It is an insight into the nature of reality (Dharshana) or experience of reality (Anubhava)." In this book Religion and society' points out that "Religion is necessary to educated man and helps him to rise above his baseness and work upwards" (1952).

He also quoted "Religion is an attitude which gives meaning and unity to existence and it is not a set of dogmas to be universally accepted" in the book called 'Recovery of Faith' (1956).

The attitude towards religion is a positive or negative evaluations, emotional feelings, and action tendencies towards particular religions with respect to social objects. It is a favorable or unfavorable responses involving some kind of actions inherently or overtly towards God.

DIFFERENT RELIGIOUS CONCEPT

Different religions are differing forces in the economy of God; all working for the good of mankind. Different faiths are necessary to suit the diversity of human temperaments. Some men are emotional, some rational, some introspective, some active; again, there are those who wish to contemplate an abstract ideal, and those who wish to worship through concrete symbols. If there were only one religious discipline, there would be no hope for those who did not respond to it. Hence it is fortunate that there are many religions instead of only one, as many would prefer to have it. The greater the number of religions, the more chances people will have to satisfy their spiritual hunger.

The different religions emphasize different facets of the supreme reality. Islam, perhaps more than any other religion, stands for the brotherhood of men among its own devotees. With the Moslems there are no social distinctions. It is inspiring to read about the pilgrimage of the Moslems to Mecca. There hundreds of thousands of the faithful discard their differing dress, whether of prince, ordinary citizen, or beggar, put on the seamless white garment which makes the chieftain indistinguishable from the shepherd, and proceed to the holy shrine to declare their surrender to almighty Allah. Before God all Moslems are equal.

With the Christians the central idea is: 'Watch and pray, for the kingdom of heaven is at hand' – which means, purify your minds and be ready for the coming of the Lord. And one cannot but admire the love of God, which innumerable Christians show through love of men, to whose service they devote their time, energy, and material resources. The idea of 'sharing' is perhaps the most striking feature of Christianity in practice.

Judaism has clung to the idea of God's power and justice and the Jewish people with dauntless patience have faced the ordeals and sufferings through which they have passed for two thousand years without losing their faith in God's power and justice.

Buddhism teaches how to attain peace through renunciation and service. In these days of selfishness and competition, it is a joy to see Buddhist monk serving people with infinite love and infinite compassion, as taught by their prophet.

Hinduism makes the realization of God, who is both within and without, the central fact of life. Thousands of Hindus are willing, even today, to renounce everything- including the world itself- to experience the reality of God.

Human beings differ from one another in size, shape, and colour of skin, but an underlying humanity is common to all. One may not be able to lay one's finger on it, yet it exists all the same. Likewise the universal religion, in the form of God-consciousness, runs through all faiths, whether primitive, ethical, or highly mystical.

Thus the different religions are like different photographs of the same building from different angles; but all of them are genuine pictures. None can exhaust the infinite power, beauty, love, and goodness of God.

MEANING OF RELIGION

Religion is something personal, leading to a larger impersonality of significance which is implanted in the personality of individuals. It is an inward turning of the mind towards its source, gradually by stages, rather than an outward meandering in the social field of work and entertainment, so that the intensity of a religious achievement cannot be observed by outward activity or conduct.

Religion is nothing but a spirit which you adopt in your life and attitude in general so that, if that is absent, religion becomes a corpse, a skeleton, without flesh and blood in it. It may have all the appearances of a living organism, but it has no life in it. So we can have lifeless religions, yet they may look like religions - just as a dead body may look like a human being, but it is not a human being because it is has lost its value, which is the spirit of existence.

DEFINITION OF RELIGION

There are many definitions of religion, and most have struggled to avoid an overly sharp definition on the one hand, and meaningless generalities on the other. Some have tried to use formalistic, doctrinal definitions and others have tried to use experiential, emotive, intuitive, valuation and ethical factors.

Sociologists and anthropologists see religion as an abstract set of ideas, values, or experiences developed as part of a cultural matrix. Primitive religion was indistinguishable from the sociocultural acts where custom and ritual defined an emotional reality.

Other religious scholars have put forward a definition of religion that avoids the reductionism of the various sociological and psychological disciplines that relegate religion to its component factors. Religion may be defined as the presence of a belief in the sacred or the holy. For example Rudolf Otto's "The Idea of the Holy," formulated in 1917, defines the essence of religious awareness as awe, a unique blend of fear and fascination before the divine. Friedrich Schleiermacher in the late 18th century defined religion as a "feeling of absolute dependence."

The Concise Oxford Dictionary (1990) defines religion as "Human recognition of superhuman controlling power and especially of a personal God entitled to obedience." This definition would not consider some Buddhist sects as religions. Many Unitarian Universalists are excluded by this description. Strictly interpreted, it would also reject polytheistic religions, since it refers to "a personal God."

Merriam-Webster's Online Dictionary defines the religion as "A cause, principle, or system of beliefs held to with ardor and faith." This is a curious definition because it does not require elements often associated with religion, such as deity, morality, worldview, etc. Also it requires that a person pursue their religion with enthusiasm. Many people identify themselves with a specific religion, but are not intensely engaged with their faith.

Webster's New World Dictionary (Third College Edition): "Any specific system of belief and worship, often involving a code of ethics and a philosophy." This definition would exclude religions that do not engage in worship. It implies that there are two important components to religion:

This dual nature of religion is expressed clearly in the Christian Scriptures (New Testament) in Matthew 22:36-39: "Teacher, what is the great commandment in the law? Jesus said unto him, Thou shalt love the Lord thy God with all thy heart, and with all thy soul, and with thy entire mind. This is the first and great commandment. And the second is like unto it, Thou shalt love thy neighbor as thyself."

DEFINITION OF RELIGION BY ACADEMICIANS

Alfred North Whitehead defines religion as: "what the individual does with his own solitariness." Religion can be further defined as: "... a system of social coherence based on a common group of beliefs or attitudes concerning an object, person, unseen being, or system of thought considered to be supernatural, sacred, divine or highest truth, and the moral codes, practices, values, institutions, traditions, and rituals associated with such belief or system of thought."

Clifford G. defined religion as a cultural system meaning, "A religion is a system of symbols which acts to establish powerful, pervasive, and long-lasting moods and motivations in men by formulating conceptions of a general order of existence and clothing these conceptions with such an aura of factuality that the moods and motivations seem uniquely realistic."

Don Swenson defines religion in terms of the sacred as, "Religion is the individual and social experience of the sacred that is manifested in mythologies, ritual, ethos, and integrated into a collective or organization."

Paul Connelly also defines religion in terms of the sacred and the spiritual aspect meaning, "Religion originates in an attempt to represent and order beliefs, feelings, imaginings and actions that arise in response to direct experience of the sacred and the spiritual. As this attempt expands in its formulation and elaboration, it becomes a process that creates meaning for itself on a sustaining basis, in terms of both its originating experiences and its own continuing responses."

THE CONCEPT OF RELIGIOUS ATTITUDE

Religious attitude is a positive or a negative response or tendency towards various aspects or religion like faith in God, the knowledge that the soul is different from the body, preservation of character, formal religion, priest, future life, spirits and spirit world.

An important attitude is response or reaction to the value. It is a favorable or an unfavorable response involving some kind of action inherently or overtly towards God. The existence of an attitude towards something is quite impossible without having the knowledge about the thing.

VARIOUS ASPECTS OF RELIGION

Nature of God

Every religion has its own adoption of God. The ways and means, the rites and sacrifices may vary, but the supremacy of God was always unquestionable and indisputable. God is the creator ruler, and supreme authority of all the times. The most essential aspect of God is his cosmic nature. God has been conceived by people of various religions as both as personal and impersonal and also immanent and transcendent. He reveals himself through incarnations to the world. He is the creator and destroyer. He is the Supreme Being. He is full of perfection. He is the cause of all cosmic change yet he remains unchanged. God is omnipresent, Omniscient and Omni potential. He is the redeemer of souls.

Prayer and worship

Prayer and worship are important religious activities practiced in every religion. The human soul cries to a power that can help him when he is in need.

Prayer is a humble request to God. It is a religious observance, public or private. Veneration to supernatural is displayed through appropriate acts, rites or ceremonies. A form of adoration to pay respect is divine worship.

Priests

In almost all religions, religious activities are performed by priests of some type. The priests exercise great influence upon the people. They dominate all religious function, both inside and outside the temples, churches and mosques on all sacred occasions.

Future Life

The ultimate aim in leading a spiritual life is attainment of Moksha, Nirvana or a life after death. All religions speak about the present life with future orientation. Hindus speak about the transformation of human consciousness into divine consciousness which is possible only by breaking the cycle of birth and rebirth. For Christians life in this world ends with death but it is the beginning of life with Christ. Church is a group of pilgrims marching towards the heavenly Jerusalem.

Formal Religion

All religions have got a formal aspect related to it. It is mainly concerned with the structure of the religion. The scripture, place of worship, festivals, patterns of rites etc. constitute the structure of whatever religion one practices.

Spirits and Spirit World

The general meaning of spirit is that which gives life to the physical organism in contrast to its purely material element, the breadth of life. Hinduism has faith in the existence of spirits which can visit the world and can have contact with people. The notion of spirit is worldwide and discussed in every religion. Spirits are invisible and can bring good or evil to man.

RELIGIOUS BELIEF

Religious belief usually relates to the existence, nature and worship of a deity or deities and divine involvement in the universe and human life. Alternately, it may also relate to values and practices transmitted by a spiritual leader. Unlike other belief systems, which may be passed on orally, religious belief tends to be codified in literate societies, religion in non-literate societies is still largely passed on orally. Religious beliefs are found in virtually every society throughout human history.

SPIRITUALITY

Members of an organized religion may not see any significant difference between religion and spirituality. Or they may see a distinction between the mundane, earthly aspects of their religion and its spiritual dimension. Some individuals draw a strong distinction between religion and spirituality. They may see spirituality as a belief in ideas of religious significance such as God, the Soul, or Heaven, but not feel bound to the bureaucratic structure and creeds of a particular organized religion. They choose the term spirituality rather than religion to describe their form of belief, perhaps reflecting a disillusionment with organized religion and a movement towards a more modern more tolerant, and more intuitive form of religion.

MYTH

The word *myth* has several meanings. A traditional story of ostensibly historical events that serves to unfold part of the world view of a people or explain a practice, belief, or natural phenomenon; can be termed as a myth. A person or thing having only an imaginary or unverifiable existence is usually referred to as a myth. A metaphor for the spiritual potentiality in the human being is said to be a myth in the minds of educators.

RELIGIONS AS ABSOLUTELY TRUE

Religions can be viewed as absolutely and unchangingly true. Jewish and Christian and religions model which hold that God relates to humanity through covenants that he established a covenant with all humanity at the time of Noah called the Noahide Laws, and that he established a covenant with Israel through the Ten Commandments, and also Jesus Christ did establish a covenant with his people through the New Testament. Exclusivists hold that one particular set of religious doctrines is the "One True Religion," and all others are false to the extent that they conflict with the true one, so that the development of the True Religion is tied inexorably to one prophet or holy book. All other religions are seen as either distortions of the original truth or original fabrications resulting from either human ignorance or imagination, or a more devious influence, such as false prophets or the influence of another rival supernatural entity such as Satan. Many kinds to be over ruled by this absolute both in religion.

Religions faith and positive attitude to words religion usually help people to develop a less anxious and more tolerant personality features. The deep faith one develops over the process of experience in this own religious beliefs can lay the foundation for a better conscious effort to over curve situations that could cause over anxiousness.

DEFINITIONS OF ANXIETY

Anxiety according to Mower, "is a learned response, occurring to signals which are unconditioned stimuli that are premonitory to situations of injury or pain. "Anxiety is an emotional and non-adjective response which a person is making to his conflicts. In dealing with anxiety status Mac Curdy (1925) writes, "The anxiety is directed against mental images of a dangerous nature which in psychosis comes in to full consciousness. The fear, as such, is rational, if the reality of the stimulus were only granted".

According to Freud, "anxiety is a consequence of the frustration of needs, particularly the frustration that occurs in conflict situations". Freudian theory also says that a person is largely unaware of the sources or causes of anxiety, but that psychoanalysis helps the patient uncover the sources of conflict in his or her previous history.

In motivational terms anxiety is anticipation of pain, psychological or physical. This definition has three components: First of all the definition classifies the nature of the state, namely, a state of apprehension or distress; then the nature of the stimulus is given, namely, a real or imagined threat, and finally the definition tells what is threatened, namely, the self.

Anxiety can be defined as an individual's fear laden overreaction, to an adjustment situation. The threatening implications of the situations are felt because the individual already sense that he cannot cope with the situation. It becomes a threat to his self esteem. 1925, defines anxiety as, "Mental distress with respect to some anticipated frustrations".

THE CONCEPT OF MORAL ANXIETY

Anxiety is an unpleasant, emotional state of high energy that involves a complex combination of emotions that include fear, apprehension, and worry. It is often accompanied by physical sensations such as heart palpitations, nausea, chest pain, shortness of breath, or tension headache.

Anxiety is often described as having cognitive, somatic, emotional, and behavioral components (Seligman, Walker & Rosenhan, 2001). The cognitive component entails expectation of a diffuse and uncertain danger. Somatically the body prepares the organism to deal with threat (known as an emergency reaction): blood pressure and heart rate are increased, sweating is increased, blood flow to the major muscle groups is increased, and immune and digestive system functions are inhibited. Externally, somatic signs of anxiety may include pale skin, sweating, trembling, and papillary dilation.

Emotionally, anxiety causes a sense of dread or panic and physically causes nausea, and chills. Behaviorally, both voluntary and involuntary behaviors may arise directed at escaping or avoiding the source of anxiety. These behaviors are frequent and often maladaptive, being most extreme in anxiety disorders. However, anxiety is not always pathological or maladaptive: it is a common emotion along with fear, anger, sadness, and happiness, and it has a very important function in relation to survival. Anxiety can be somewhat of a mental illness.

DEVELOPMENT OF MORALITY

While some philosophers, psychologists and evolutionary biologists hold that morality is a thin crust hiding egoism, amorality, and anti-social tendencies, others see morality as equally a product of evolutionary forces and as evidence for continuity with other group-living organisms. One approach argues that moral codes are founded on emotional instincts and intuitions that were naturally selected in the past because they aided survival and reproduction (inclusive fitness), and that they still generally prescribe behavior that enhances individual fitness and/or group well-being. Selected psychological and behavioral tendencies, and their abstraction in to moral codes or religions, are seen to be common to most or all human cultures.

MORAL CODES

Moral codes are often complex definitions of right and wrong that are based upon well-defined value systems. They dictate proper personal conduct. Although some people might think that a moral code is simple, rarely is there anything simple about one's values, ethics, etc. or, for that matter, the judgment of those of others. The difficulty lies in the fact that morals are often part of a religion and more often than not about culture codes. Sometimes, moral codes give way to legal codes, which couple penalties or corrective actions with particular practices. Note that while many legal codes are merely built on a foundation of religious and/or cultural moral codes, overtimes they are one and the same.

Examples of moral codes include the Golden Rule; the Noble Eightfold Path of Buddhism; the ancient Egyptian code of Ma'at;the ten commandments of Judaism, Christianity, and Islam; the yamas and niyama of the Hindu scriptures; the ten Indian commandments; and the principle of the Dessek.

Another related concept is the moral core which is assumed to be innate in each individual, to those who accept that differences between individuals are more important than Creators or their rules. This, in some religious systems (e.g. Taoism and Gnosticism), is assumed to be the basis of all aesthetics and thus moral choice. Moral codes as such are therefore seen as coercive part of human politics.

MORALITY IN JUDICIAL SYSTEMS

The law is considered a living governing system constructed by present and historical debate and moral consensus among juries, and more generally, all citizens under the system. This system is used to maintain order, righteousness, and justice in everyday life. Individual actions or events can be summoned to court for review, investigation, and prosecution if it is believed that there has been a breach of morality (meaning, a violation of the law) or if a law's moral implication is questioned. A verdict is a lawful determination of guilt, and a guilty party is one that has committed an immoral act.

In most systems, the lack of morality of the individual can also be a sufficient cause for punishment, or can be an element for the grading of the punishment. Especially in the systems where modesty (i.e., with reference to sexual crimes) is legally protected or otherwise regulated, the definition of morality as a legal element and in order to determine the cases of infringement, is usually left to the vision and appreciation of the single judge and hardly ever precisely specified. In such cases, it is common to verify an application of the prevalent common morality of the interested community that consequently becomes enforced by the law for further reference.

The government of South Africa is attempting to create a Moral Regeneration movement. Part of this is a proposed Bill of Morals, which will bring a biblical-based "moral code" into the realm of law. This move by a nominally secular democracy has attracted relatively little criticism.

ANXIETY AND EGO-DEFENSE MECHANISMS

In Freud's view, the human is driven towards tension reduction, in order to reduce feelings of anxiety. Anxiety an aversive inner state that people seek to avoid or escape. Humans seek to reduce anxiety through defense mechanisms. Defense Mechanisms can be psychologically healthy or maladaptive, but tension reduction is the overall goal in both cases. A comprehensive list of Defense Mechanisms was developed by Anna Freud, Sigmund's daughter.

Anna remained with her Father throughout his life, never marrying. In Freudian terms, she remained trapped in her Oedipus complex, never giving up her longing to possess her father sexually. However, because of a strong ego and super ego, this id based desires were sublimated into psychological creativity which advanced Freudian theory, her father's greatest love.

FREUD SPECIFIED THREE MAJOR TYPES OF ANXIETY

Reality Anxiety: the most basic form, rooted in reality. Fear of a dog bite, fear arising from an impending accident. (Ego Based Anxiety) Most Common Tension Reduction Method: Removing oneself from the harmful situation.

Neurotic Anxiety: Anxiety which arises from an unconscious fear that the libidinal impulses of the id will take control at an in opportune time. This type of anxiety is driven by a fear of punishment that will result from expressing the id's desires without proper sublimation.

Moral Anxiety: Anxiety which results from fear of violating moral or societal codes, moral anxiety appears as guilt or shames this conception of Anxiety; can be seen as a reason why Freud concentrated on strengthening the Ego through psychoanalysis.

Defense Mechanisms

When some type of anxiety occurs, the mind responds in two ways:

First, problem solving efforts are increased, and secondly, defense mechanisms are triggered. These are tactics which the Ego develops to help deal with the id and the Super Ego. All Defense Mechanisms share two common properties:

They can operate unconsciously

They can distort, transform, or falsify reality is some way.

The changing of perceived reality allows for a lessening of anxiety, reducing the psychological tension felt by an individual.

NEED FOR THE STUDY

According to Gandhiji, for the all-round development of the child, education should provide the right understanding about attitude and morality among the students. Particularly during the adolescent age, the maturity level usually develops and awareness about morality and religious values also begins to emerge. It is also evident that during this stage, lot of anxiety and stress is revealed. This could be due to the lack of understanding about morality. For the purpose of getting more insight into this concept, there is a need to study the moral anxiety and religious attitude of students at the secondary school level.

If clarity of the various aspects related to the moral anxiety and religious attitude is unearthed, students at the secondary level can be helped to develop the right level of moral anxiety and also a positive religious attitude.

STATEMENT OF THE PROBLEM

Religious Attitude and Moral Anxiety Among the Higher Secondary School Students".

OPERATIONAL DEFINITIONS

Religious attitude

The investigator defines religious attitude as attitude towards religion and its concepts in students. Religious attitude in this study refers to the scores obtained by using the Religious Attitude scale designed by Rajamanickam (1966).

Moral anxiety

This study refers to the 'anxiety towards morality' in students. By this, the investigator means the scores obtained by administering the scale of Moral Anxiety standardized by Lawrence R.Good and Katherine C.Good.

Higher Secondary School Students

Higher Secondary school students in this study refer to the students studying in XI and XII classes.

OBJECTIVES OF THE STUDY

1. To find out the level of Religious attitude of higher secondary school students.
2. To find out the level of moral anxiety of higher secondary school students.
3. To find out the significant difference between boys and girls of higher secondary school in their religious attitude.
4. To find out the significant difference between students studying in standard XIth and XIIth in their religious attitude.
5. To find out the significant difference between students studying in English and Tamil medium of the higher secondary schools in their religious attitude.
6. To find out the significant difference between students studying in Government and Private higher secondary schools in their religious attitude.
7. To find out the significant difference between boys and girls of higher secondary schools in their moral anxiety.
8. To find out the significant difference between students studying in standard XIth and XIIth in their moral anxiety.
9. To find out the significant difference between student studying in English and Tamil medium of the higher secondary schools in their moral anxiety.
10. To find out the significant difference between students studying in Government and Private higher secondary school in their moral anxiety.
11. To find out the relationship between religious attitude and moral anxiety of higher secondary school students.

LIMITATIONS OF THE STUDY

Due to lack of time and resources available the study has been limited to the following.

1. The present investigation is confined to the students studying in Higher Secondary school level XIth & XIIth.

2. The study has been restricted only to the students studying in government schools and private schools.
3. The study has been limited to Dharmapuri District, (Tamil Nadu) only.
4. The study has been limited to English and Tamil Medium only.
5. It includes a sample size of 300 higher secondary school students only.

CONCLUSION

The first chapter is chiefly concerned with the conceptual frame work of the problem chosen for the study. This chapter gives an overview of the problem, its statement, and its significance. It also includes the objectives, and limitations of the study. It also gives an elaborate explanation of the meaning of the terms, religious attitude and moral anxiety.

2

Review of Related Literature

INTRODUCTION

In this chapter, the related literature, enfolds studies related to the variables used in the present investigation. After going through the related studies regarding the religious attitude and moral anxiety among the Higher Secondary School students the researcher can conceptualize the research problem clearly and precisely.

According to Best (1963), the familiarity with the literature in any problem area helps the students to discover, the known facts, the attempted methods and the manner in which the problems are solved. The investigator feels that the study of related literature helps in acquiring information about the studies done in the field, avoid duplication and further guides in carrying out the investigation successfully. In the following chapter, a review is made on the studies conducted in India and abroad related to the present study.

STUDIES RELATD TO RELIGIOUS ATTITUDE

Studies Done Abroad

Horne and William Stender.H (1945) administered a questionnaire containing observation of daily prayer, Holy communion, church going and practice of baptism to denominational and non-denominational college students. It was found out that denominational students tend towards religious orthodoxy that non-denominational students.

The study by Telford (1950) on ten thousands students at the university of Utah tried to correlate religious background of the student the degree of antagonism toward church. It was found out that females were more favourable to church and that church attitude was found positively related to church affiliation and attendance.

Weima, J. (1965) of Catholic University of Nijmegen. Netherlands examined authoritarianism, religious conservatism and socio centric attitudes in Roman Catholic groups. A Dutch version of F. scale and Anti-Semitic Scale, an anti-protestant scale and a religious conservatism scale were used to evaluate attitudes in catholic students. Measures of authoritarianism were found to correlate positively with measures of Anti-Semitism, anti-communism and religious conservatism. Difference is examined in the light of official catholic attitudes to jews and protestants. It is positive in both cases. A study by Robert Young, K., David Dustin, S. Holtzman and Wayne H. (1996) of the University of Texas investigated change in attitude towards religion in a Southern University. This describes study changes in attitude towards organised religion as measured in three surveys taken over a periods of nine year. The attitude of the respondents who in each survey were under graduate students at the University / of Texas became less favourable towards organised religion during that period. Several variables were found to be related to attitude towards organised religion. These include sex, grade point average major academic field, religious preference, and frequency of church attendance.

John Kottman, E. (1966) University of Lowa conducted a semantic study of religious attitude. During 1965, one hundred and forty one male and twenty six female students at the University of Lowa participated in testing the hypothesis that a positive correlation exists between intension and religious attitude. In general sematic terminology "one who relies largely on words and disregards observations is said to have an intentional orientation". Five kinds of intentional manifestations were measured by one scale; also administered were excerpts from three test designed to measure attitudes towards God, the Bible, and Church. In order to avoid bias religious affiliations were not asked for. These data supports hypothesis that persons who are most intentional tend to have the strongest religious attitude. Although the correlations; not high, they point to the existence of the hypothesized connection.

Pang, Henry (1968) of Middle Bury College examined religious attitudinal dimensions of altruism, conformity, devotion, fundamentalism, mysticism, superstition, and total religiosity in 10 students denominational groups of eighty students.. It was generalized that the Ss would reflect attitudes of their respective denominations. The groups differed in mysticism (P<0.05) and the other dimensions (P>0.01).

Maranell, Gary, M. (1968) of the University Kansas made a factor analytic study of some selected dimensions of religious attitude. eight conceptually distinct / dimension of religious attitude were translated into attitude scales. The religious attitude of urban clergy men of eleven denominations in four regions of the country was surveyed. Resulting scale scores were correlated for the total population and the resulting correlation matrix was factor analyzed. The factors were orthogonally rotated. The two factor were (1) a conservative fundamentalist attitude cluster and (2) a more liberal socially concerned religious attitude factor.

John Roscoe (1968) investigated religious beliefs of American College Students. This study is part of a research study of student values. One thousand five students from seventeen colleges and universities returned the polyphonic values inventory (PVI). The schools included major universities, teachers colleges and liberal art colleges. Two of the twenty multiple-choice questions of PVI sampled students religious beliefs. 52 percent of the students were protestant, 25 percent Catholic, 12 percent with no religious affiliation and 5 percent were Jewish. 73 percent of the students expressed belief in personnel God. Of the 73 percent 28 percent subscribed to the traditional Judeo-Christian concept of the God of Bible. 88 percent of the catholic and 83 percent of the protestants expressed belief in a personnel God. Jewish students were more liberal in their beliefs than Christian Students. 24 percent of students considered the Bible as the inspired religious book, not all of which is completely realizable but which directs men's thought towards God.

Thomas Thai, V. (1969) made an investigation of religious attitudes, ideals, and personality traits of the four groups of catholic college students. The religious attitude scale, the test in ideals, the Guilford-Zimmerman Temperament survey and information questionnaires were used to test the students with regard to their religious attitudes, ideals, personality traits and backgrounds. The subjects were eight hundred and eighty four catholic men and women, fresh men and women, fresh men and seminars, students enrolled at twenty two catholic and non catholic college and universities of New York. Men students were, however found to score significantly higher in the ideal of altruistic interest, on self interest and on social approval. Significant difference between the mean religion attitudes, religious values, altruistic interest, emotional stability and personal relations were found in favour of women students. Women students excelled the n on students in their religious practices of the students participated in the study about 83 percent of the men and 90 percent of the women, stated that religion had influenced their individual lives either "very strongly" or "strongly". Pearson product moment co-efficient of correlation were found to be significant at the 0.01 level between religious attitude and religious values, between religious values and some personality traits namely, restraint, emotional stability, friendliness, and personal relations.

In a study by Prezyna, Wlady Slaw (1969), investigated the relationship between the religious attitude and personality characteristics. The religious attitude scale applied in the study was constructed by the author. Personality was investigated with sixteen PF in its polish version standardized on polish – population. The sample consisted on sixty women and forty men. Results reveal the high positive religious intensity group to possess on the average more emotional maturity, more super ego control greater, self control, higher sensitivity and contact with the environment. The lower group was characterized by the opposite features.

Hcpburn and Lawrence R. (1971), found that systematic information concerning adolescent views towards religions is very limited though at least one study reported as early as one thousand and nine hundred perceptively related the general nature of adolescence to an undefined sense of incompleteness. Religious interest ranks high among adolescent students but it is not nearly so marked among non student peers. Conflict between liberal religious teachings and scientific views of the world appears to be implicated in adolescent students concern over religion. Since commitment has many dimensions, it poses measurement difficulties. Some investigators define dimensions of religion as belief, practice, experience knowledge, and consequence or effect in everyday life. Development of valid approaches to the academic study and religion can provide expanded educational opportunities since religion elicit attitudinal responses from people whether or not they are religious.

Lewis, et.al., investigated religiosity among Indo-Chinese students for about 400 in Utah. Findings showed that the major students adopted western Christian Religions in which most of them affiliated with ethnic congregation. Religion rate was important in their life and reported high amount of religious participation.

Ponton, et.al, (1988) administrated the religious oriented inventor, the quest scales (Baston C.D. 1976) and a culturally adapted social distance scale to a Venezuelan sample of two hundred and seventy five University Students. The results indicated the extrinsic religiosity correlated positively. With prejudice, intrinsic religiosity correlated negatively.

Boisvert, Donald Luc undertook a sociological study of religion and nationalism in Quebec society. He argues that religion was a stage for the expression and unification of three sets of polarities found within Quebec society. Nationalism versus religion, the elite versus the masses and popular religiosity versus clerical authority. The review of the relationship between the Catholic Church and Quebac society was dealt with and the basic foundation for the subsequent analysis were made by religion.

Deonandan, Kalovvatie (1990) conducted a study on Religion and the struggle for Hegemony in Nicaragua in the university of Queen in Kingston. The thesis established the Church's counter-revolutionary offensive had undermined the position of the liberation theology advocates a id weakened the church bused communities. The revolutionary religions to promote progressive changes in Nicaraguan

Loewenthal, et. al., (1993) made their study on Family size, religiosity and contextually assessed stress were examined in relation to eleven symptoms of depression in fifty six orthodox Jewish women. The major findings were the religiosity and family size were highly confounded, but the effects did differ. Religiosity related to the absence of several symptoms, There is association between family size, religiosity and depressive symptoms.

Krause, Neal (1993) made his study regarding measuring religiosity, which consists of organizational religiosity, subjective religiosity and religious beliefs. His sample size was 936 individuals. The findings examined the impact of religiosity on feelings of life satisfaction among adults.

Francis, Leaslie J. (1993) made his studies on personality and Religion among college students in United Kingdom. The samples of one hundred and twenty six undergraduates were tested using the scale of attitude to Christianity. According to him, the findings had an inverse relationship between psychotism and religiosity, while neither neurotism nor extraversion is positively or negatively related to religiosity.

Gaston and Brown L.B. (1993) studied on heterogeneous groups of Australian one hundred and five female ninety five male including high school and University students Catholic and Anglican church goers and senior citizens using free response and rating of gender based traits show that religion and non-religious prototype are gender typed since Ss assigned to feminine traits to religious target person and masculine traits to non religious target persons. The prototype may make it easier for women to be religious that it two men.

Charies (1993) investigated the dimensionality of religion in the prediction of self reported religious behaviour through the differentiation of religiousness into measure of belief and motivation. one hundred and sixty one students at Christian Protestant colleges participated. Religious belief was measured through eleven primary god concept factors. Both motivation and god concept factors significantly added predictive variance over each other with respect to self reported religious belief.

Medoff, and et.al., (1993) investigated the relationship between deviant social behaviour and membership in fundamentalist Christian denominations at the state level. Four dependent variables arc used to measure deviant social behaviour (1) Murder rate (2) Suicide rate (3) Divorce rate (4) Abortion rate. The rate of deviant social behaviour is hypothesized to be a function of the states socio economic characteristics and an index of religious fundamentalist attitudes. The results show that fundamentalism has a significant effect on sexual morality, abortion, birth rates and marriage.

Brinkley Ellen. H. (1995), made a study on, "Faith in the world: examining religious right attitudes about texts". It described theological views about written texts, related attitudes exhibited by current protestors, and attitudes created for English language arts teachers. The study suggested that an awareness of the religious perspective might help to lead to more constructive outcomes to the conflicts among teachers, individual students and parents.

Indian Studies

Adinarayan S.P. and Rajamanickam M. (1962) conducted a study on Attitude towards religion, and spiritual and the supernatural belief of the students. The sample of 300 students from Annamalai University was tested by attitude towards religious scale by the investigator. The major findings were: students belonging to higher socio economic level expressed religious attitude more than the students of lower. Rural and urban backgrounds influenced the religious socio-economic level. Rural and urban backgrounds influenced the religious attitude of the students.

A study by Dutt, N.K. (1965) Punjab University, Chandigarh, investigated attitudes of the University students towards religion. A 30 item Likert scale was prepared for eighty two items after item analysis. Results of the final scale on two hundred students showed that girls were significantly more religious than boys. No difference was found due to academic discipline.

Rajamanickam, M.(1966) made his study of religious and related attitudes of the students and professional groups in south India for his Ph.D. in Annamalai University. The sample of 1400 students from Andhra, Kerala, Madras, and Mysore were collected by using the tool Religious Attitude scale constructed by the investigator. The major findings were religious attitude was correlated with conservatism in both the groups, and it was highest for the arts students. Students were more religious than professionals. Men students went to places of worship more than the women students.

Tandom, B.K. (1967) conducted his study on the attitude towards religion of higher secondary school students in Uttar Pradesh towns. A sample of 3917 students, both boys and girls from twenty one towns of Uttar Pradesh were selected for the study. The tools used were the Attitude scale of fifty items by the investigator and Saxena's supplementary questionnaire to the Attitude scale of Religion and Adjustment inventory. The major findings were: Students in general had a favorable attitude towards religion. The communities having favorable religious attitude in the descending order were Hindu, Muslim, Sikh and Christian.

Kapil, H.K. and Aggarwal, Sushma (1967) studied changing pattern of values amongst women in modern Hindu society. A study of ninety six women revealed a definite trend of decline in traditional values to the peripheral area. More than ninety three percent of the respondents expressed absolute faith in transmigration of souls and religious scriptures and ninety five percent supported religious observances. Conversely, except for a lukewarm traditional support for disapproval of divorce, there was a definite decline in the time honoured value of joint family system or disapproval of nuclear family non acceptance of women as the bread earner or giving her equal right of education with man.

The study by Misra, S.L. (1970) made a comparative study of religion-caste differences in concept formation ability of Young adults. Hypothesized that Hindu and Muslim students would different their concept formation ability and difference would be found between Hindu Caste and Muslim sects. Two hundred and eighty eight, 14-19 years old students were selected. Twenty four students represented each of the Hindu caste and students seventy students represented each of the two Muslim sects. Lovell's concept formation test and Trist Hargreave's tests were administered. On both tests Muslim students scored Higher than Hindu students No significant difference is found within the groups, although the Hindu castes differed from the scheduled castes on both the tests wish the scheduled castes scoring lower.

This study by Telode, R.D. and R.V. Dable (1980) was conducted on religiosity as a function of sex and type of education. This study was conducted / on under graduate students of which 30 were science students and thirty were arts students. Sample was also selected to include fifteen boys and fifteen girls among arts and science students. Bushans (1971) religiosity scale was used. The study revealed that

1. Arts students were more religious than science students.
2. Girls are more religious than boys.

Gupta A., (1980) conducted a study on relationship between religious attitude and mental health of the Tibetian adolescents. His major objectives of the study were to establish. The tools employed were the Religiosity questionnaire locally constructed by the investigator. The major findings were found to be religious, mentally healthy and possessing positive personality character ties in being warm hearted, self sufficient, controlled and tense.

Hassan M.K. and Khalique (1981) conducted a study on religiosity and its correlates among college students. The samples of four hundred and eighty college students from Ranchi University were tested by using scale of Religiosity. Some of the major findings were: Muslims tend to have higher degree of religiosity than Hindus. The sex did not influence religious attitude of both Hindus and Muslims. Positive correlation between religiosity and anxiety was reported.

Rizvi, S.A.H (1986) conducted thesis for his Ph.D. in Alligarh Muslim University. His study was on attitudes towards religious education in relation to certain value orientations. The sample was 200 postgraduate students of the Hindu and Muslim communities in the Alligarh Muslim University. They were tested by using the tools Rajamanickam's religious attitude scale. It was found that the majority of students had moderate attitude towards religious education. Irrespective of the difference in their gender, socio-economic status and religion students had similar view.

Roquiya Zainuddin (1994) attempted to know the level of religiosity and spiritually in relation to certain personality needs. The major aspect of this study is concerned with the relationship between the spiritual orientation and personality needs based on Murrya's classification of psychogenic need on one hand, and religiosity and needs on the other hand. The sample consisted of two hundred and twenty teachers of various faculties. The tools used were (1) Meenakshi Personality Inventory (2). Religiosity scale and (3) Spiritual Orientation Inventory. Multiple regression analysis was sued to treat the data. The results revealed that aggression was found to be a significant factor of spirituality. The N-achievement was a significant negative predictor of religiosity and the need-exhibition was a significant positive contributor to religiosity.

Sayed Flroj and S. Karunanidhi (1995) Madras University attempted to find out the of foot of religious (y on values. The sample was selected from the students of various colleges Madras University. The data were collected by using Rajamanicak's Religious Attitude Scale (1989) and the value scale developed by Malla Reddy (1992). Results of the study show that those who are high on religiosity were found to traditional in their values. Whereas low A religiosity people are modern in their in their values.

STUDIES RELATED TO MORAL ANXIETY

Studies Done Abroad

Sigmund Freud (1995) describes how the ego is a range of mechanisms to handle the conflict between the Id, the ego and the super ego, which is why they are often called 'Ego-Defense Mechanisms'. He has discussed elaborately on anxiety and tension.

1. Moral anxiety
2. Neurotic anxiety
3. Objective anxiety

Kierkegaard (1959) relates anxiety decision, commitment, choice, and awareness. Wherever there is a decision or an opportunity to actualize a possibility, there is anxiety. In order for self-development to advance, anxiety must be experienced. Anxiety is referred to as a "school" and as "one of the best teachers", since through facing anxiety, awareness is increased. The normal person faces anxiety and moves ahead. The neurotic is viewed as a "shut-up" person, who constricts his awareness and individuality in order to avoid anxiety, and thereby becomes automation.

Feldhusen, Denny and Condon (1965) investigated the difference between high and low anxious children in convergent and divergent thinking and found that the difference on divergent thinking was no significant among the children.

Justice Maclene Carol (1989) made a study on "The Effect of Literature instruction with an emphasis on Kohlberg's moral development stages on secondary students' moral reasoning, and abilities'. Major purpose of the investigation was to determine whether there were significant differences in moral reasoning between groups of students who received literature instruction emphasizing on Lawrence Kohlberg's moral stages of development (experimental) and a group of students who received instruction by conventional teaching (control). An additional purpose of the investigation was to determine whether this teaching strategy depends on students' intelligence, writing skills etc. In the findings of the investigation, literature course which contained moral reasoning of students was below the mean intelligence scores on the test of moral development.

Wilhelm et al (1989) studied about fear and anxiety in low vision and totally blind children and education for the visually handicapped. They selected one hundred and thirty nine visually impaired children of age group 6-16 years. They were administered on a fear survey and a Manifest Anxiety scale. Students were classified into totally blind and low vision groups. Fear and anxiety scores were similar to those classifications. The general level of anxiety for the total sample when compared with general population showed that fear of students tends to reflect concern for injury to the body.

Jainvely (1991) examined the subjective construction of morality in the prevailing social atmosphere and argued that attribution of responsibility was involved in moral judgment. Responsibility was understood in direct ways and the social perspective also influenced further attribution. Data, supporting the social aspects of moral judgment were also presented in this study, in which sixty four Indian college teachers responded to a modified version of Lawrence Kohlberg's Heniz Dilemma. Traditional Indian (Hindu) thought or morality was also discussed along with the implications for the moral development.

Cart, Wright, Robert, H. and Stephen (1992) investigated on 'social control in alternative religions-A familiar perspective'. In the study the family models were pervasive in both the theological self conceptions of alternative religious organizations and the sociological scholarship on them. It around that the models provided useful directions for studying alternative religions. Since both the institutions frequently enmesh their members in contrasting social environments, it facilitated the occurrence of sustained systematic abuse.

Wilson, Kenneth and Deborah, K. (1992) studied on the 'Moral judgment development for the effect of education and occupation', presenting various conceptualization of moral judgment development which was synthesized into a single longitudinal study. As hypothesized, adolescent moral judgment development and educational attainment exerted significant direct effects on adult moral judgment development. Moral judgment development occupational attainment exerted significant direct effect indirectly through career satisfaction and work related variables. There were also equal to or greater than educational attainments in the predirective power.

Taylor et al (1992) made a study on 'Theoretical and therapeutic considerations for the anxiety disorders', which reviewed the theoretical, and therapeutic considerations for four types of anxiety disorders: Panic disorder, generalized anxiety, social phobia and obsessive-compulsive disorder. Emphasis was placed on the physiological commitments and neuropsychological bases of these illnesses. Furthermore, pharmacological treatment was related to the underlying substrate of the disorder, which was never possible.

Indian Studies

Pandit K.W. (1964) studied the role of anxiety in academic learning and achievement of school boys. The sample consisted of 145 boys from an elementary school in Delhi. The important findings were: 1. anxiety had a negative relationship with learning and academic achievement; subjects having less anxiety were found to be superior in learning and achievement irrespective of the task difficulty to those having more anxiety. 2. High learners and achievement in the retest, while the highest anxiety group showed poor performance in the retest. 4. Subjects with low intelligence and high anxiety did not improve in achievement up to the expectation as a result of induced anxiety. 5. Better achievement did not act as reinforcement in improving achievement of high anxious low achievers. Anxiety interfered with the retention of learning.

Patel A.D. (1977) collected a total sample of876 student teachers, both male and female, from thirteen colleges of education. Stratified random sampling technique was followed. It was found that the relationship of anxiety and achievement between student teachers was negative but not significant. The mean performance of the high and the low anxiety group was 47.6percent and 50.2percent respectively.

Annamma A.K.(1980) studied on the value, aspirations and adjustment of college students in Kerala. The major findings were: 1. A majority of the college students were conformists with a stable system of values and without rebellious tendencies. 2. The younger college students were more oriented to spiritualism as compared to the older group, which were more materialism oriented. 3. The academic achievement, residential background and father's education and occupational status had no relationship to value orientation of college students.

Ramachandran (1989) investigation the influence of anxiety and adjustment on performance. The main objective of the study was to find out the relationship between academic performance and anxiety.

The major finding of the study was that there was low negative correlation between academic performance and anxiety.

Gupta, Rajan 1989) (investigated on the values and moral judgement of adolescents of two representative centers of western and eastern states of Uttar Pradesh. The sample of the study covered eighty boys and eighty girls. The tool used was Moral Judgement Test developed by the researcher. The major findings were: Regional differences influenced the different personal values of adolescents; regional differences influenced different personal values of adolescents; regional differences influenced different moral judgement areas of adolescents.

Namrata (1992) conducted a study on two hundred and one boys and two hundred and eight girls, to find out the relationship between personality traits, stress, anxiety and achievement. The major findings was that the students who had a lower level of anxiety tended to score high in school examinations.

Geethanathan P.S. (1998) studied student's moral judgment in relation in relation to certain personal and demographic variables such as locality, sex and class in which studying, and certain psychological variables such as socio-economic status, intellectual ability and attitude towards religion. The sample comprised of thousand four hundred students equally distributed between the two localities. The tools were used to collect the data were Moral Judgment Questionnaire and Raven's Progressive Matrices Test. The major findings were: students of different classes in schools and of different age groups differed significantly in their moral judgment; urban students exhibited higher moral judgment than their rural counterparts; boys and girls did not differ significantly; students of different intellectual abilities differed significantly; and students of different socio-economic strata differed significantly with respect to their moral judgment. Students belonging to different subgroups differed significantly in attitude towards religion in their moral judgment

CONCLUSION

The study of related literature has helped the investigator to have a clear perspective of the problem chosen for the present investigation. The researcher has formulated the hypotheses for the present study. Designing of the method of research / description of the variables, sample selection, selection of suitable tools, administration and scoring methods are being discussed in the succeeding chapter.

3

Research Design and Methodology

INTRODUCTION

"Research design is a catalogue of the various phases and facts relating to the formulation of a research effort. It is an arrangement of the essential conditions for collection and analysis of data in a form that aims to combine relevance to research purpose with economy in the procedure.

Every human being is endowed with inner drives. They influence his thoughts, his attitudes, his emotions and his behavior. Religion which is at the same time anubhava (an experience of reality) and darsana (a vision in to reality influences man's behavior much more than any other reality. The sense of 'beyond' which man feels in himself compels him to go in search of it. The metaphysical in our day to day existence.

After gaining adequate theoretical perspective about religious attitude and moral anxiety of Higher secondary school students suitable hypotheses were proposed and appropriate design has been devcloped to collect the required data to prove the hypotheses statistically.

HYPOTHESES

1. The level of Religious attitude of higher secondary school students is neutral.

2. The level of moral anxiety of higher secondary school students is average in Nature.
3. There is no significant difference between boys and girls of higher secondary schools in their religious attitude.
4. There is no significant difference between students studying in standard XI and XII in their religious attitude.
5. There is no significant difference between students studying in English and Tamil medium of the higher secondary schools in their religious attitude.
6. There is no significant difference between students studying in Government and Private higher secondary schools in their religious attitude.
7. There is no significant difference between boys and girls in the higher secondary schools in the moral anxiety.
8. There is no significant difference between students studying in Standard XI and XII in their moral anxiety.
9. There is no significant difference between students studying in English and Tamil medium of the higher secondary schools in their moral anxiety.
10. There is no significant difference between students studying in Government and Private higher secondary schools in their moral anxiety.
11. There is no significant difference between the religious attitude and moral anxiety among the higher secondary schools students.

RESEARCH TOOLS SELECTED FOR THE PRESENT STUDY

As the present study investigates the religious attitude and moral anxiety Higher secondary school students, the tools taken by the investigator are as follows.

1. Religious attitude scale by Rajamanickam.M.
2. Moral Anxiety scale by Lawrence R.Good and Katherine.C

RELIGIOUS ATTITUDE SCALE

Description

In order to measure attitude towards religion, Rajamanickam's religious attitude scale was used. Religious attitude scale consists of

60 statements pertaining to various aspects of religion. 30 statements are positive and 30 are negative statements. The scorer has to check whether the statement is positive or negative. If positive 1 mark may be entered on the scoring sheet if strongly agree response is underlined. If agree is underlined 2 may be entered, 3 for unable to decide, 4 for disagree and 5 for strongly agree.

If the statement is negative strongly agree response will receive 5, agree 4, unable to decide 3, disagree 2, and strongly disagree 1.

Thus for the whole scale the lowest possible score is 60 which is excrement pro-religious attitude and highest possible score is 300 which in extreme anti-religious attitude.

The individuals score may be sub-divided into six components on the basis of value areas like.

1. Nature of God
2. Prayer and Worship
3. Formal Religion
4. Priests
5. Future life
6. Spirits and Spirit world

Administration of Test

The investigator established rapport with the students and explained the purpose of the investigation. The investigator made the students to sit properly in the class. Their responses would be kept confidential in the strict sense. The religious attitude scale was distributed to the students and asked to record their responses by putting a tick mark in the five point scale which is shown below.

They were asked to answer all 60 statements without omission and encouraged to clarify doubts regarding items.

Scoring

If the statement is positive, then the following marks were allotted which is given below.

Strongly Agree	**Agree decide**	**Unable to**	**Disagree**	**Strongly disagree**
1	2	3	4	5

If the statement is negative then the following marks were allotted as given below.

Strongly Agree	Agree decide	Unable to	Disagree	Strongly disagree
5	4	3	2	1

SCORNING KEY FOR RELIGIOUS ATTITUDE SCALE

Description	Item Number	Strongly Agree	Agree	Unable to decide	Disagree	Strongly disagree
Positive item	1,2,4,5,6,7,8,9,10, 11,15,17,19,20,27, 28,29,31,32,33,34, 36,37,42,46,47,48, 5054,57.	1	2	3	4	5
Negative item	3,12,13,14, 16,18, 21,22,23,24,25,26, 30,35,38,39,40,41, 43,44,45,49,51,52, 53,55,56,58,59,60	5	4	3	2	1

TABLE SHOWING RANGE OF SCORES AND LEVELS OF ATTITUDE

RANGE OF SCORES	LEVEL OF ATTITUDE
60-90	Extremely pro-religious
91-150	Moderately pro-religious
151-210	Neutral
211-270	Moderately Anti-religious
271-300	Extremely Anti-religious

If the scores fall in between 60 and 90 they are referred to extremely pro-religious attitude, the scores in between 91 and 150 moderately pro-religious, the scores in between 151 and 210 – neutral, the scores in between 211 and 270 moderately anti-religious and the scores in between 271 and 300 extremely anti – religious.

MORAL ANXIETY SCALE

Description

In order to measure the anxiety the anxiety towards morality, Lawrence R.Good and Katherin C.Good scale was used. It consists of 34 statements and each statement can be answered as true or false.

Administration

The investigator established rapport with the students and explained the purpose of the investigation. The investigator made the students to sit properly in the class and informed them to read the statements carefully to decide whether the statements are true or false. The moral anxiety questionnaire was distributed to the students and they were informed to mark in the appropriate space for each statement.

They were asked to answer all the 34 statements without omission and encouraged to clarify it necessary.

Scoring

The score for moral anxiety questionnaire is the total number of statements which has been answered 'true'. The score on this questionnaire can range from'0' to '34'.

Interpretation of the score

As Sigmund Freud stated, some worry about doing what is morally right is necessary in social situations. Such worry helps one to be considered and concerned about others in the society.

Thus a very low level of moral anxiety (a score of 8 or less) may suggest an indifference to the needs of others, a kind of egoism and independence from concern fellow human beings.

At the other end of the continuum, however, a very high level of moral anxiety (scores of 22 or greater) may relate to an inability to relax and enjoy life.

Some one that worried about violating moral principles may adopt a rigid, self-effecting approach life. Worry may take so much energy that there may be little left for actual socially concerned behaviour.

Scores ranging from 9 to 21, the average, suggest a reasonable balance of independent motivation and socially responsible behavior.

MORAL ANXIETY SCORE

Low	Average	Very high level
8 and less suggest to concern about fellow human beings	9 to 21 Balance of socially Balance of socially responsible behavior	22 and greater inability to relax and enjoy life.

PILOT STUDY

A Pilot study was conducted among 50 higher secondary school students to establish the reliability and validity of the different tools used in the present study.

ESTABLISHING RELIABILITY AND VALIDITY

The reliability of a test may be defined s the degree of consistency with which, the test measures, what it does measure. The reliability of the tool was calculated using odd even method.

Religious attitude scale

Reliability and Validity

In order to establish the reliability of the religious attitude scale, odd even mean method was used. The reliability of religious attitude scale, was found to be 0.64.

The index of validity which is the square root of reliability was found to be 0.80. The Questionnaire was valid.

Moral anxiety scale

In order to establish the reliability of the moral anxiety scale, odd even method was used. The reliability of moral anxiety sale was found to be 0.66.

The index of validity which is the square root of reliability was found to be .81. The Questionnaire was highly valid.

MAIN STUDY

The tools used for this study are given below:

1. Religious Attitude scale by Rajamanickam.
2. Moral Anxiety sale by Lawrence R.Good and Katherine C.Good.

The above two tools were used for collection of data for the main study with the following procedures followed. After administering the test, the responses were scored using the scoring keys and each students assigned various scores.

SAMPLE FOR THE MAIN STUDY

The investigator in the present study used the stratified random sampling technique. The samples selected for the study were higher secondary school students from Dharmapuri District in Tamil Nadu.

The sample was stratified on the basis of (Gender male and female) the classes (XIth and XIIth standard) The type of school management (Government and Private) and the medium of instruction (English and Tamil medium schools). The size of sample was 300 students, taken from six schools in Dharmapuri District of Tamil Nadu State.

TABLE 1

DISTRIBUTION OF THE SAMPLE SELECTED FOR THE STUDY

Serial No.	Name of School	Gender		Class		Medium		Type of Management		Total
		Male	Female	XI	XII	English	Tamil	Govt.	Private	
1.	Govt.Higher. Secondary School, Lakkiampatti	25	25	25	25	0	50	50	0	50
2.	Senthil Matric Higher Secondary School, Gandhi Nagar	25	25	25	25	50	0	0	50	50
3.	Government Higher Secondary School, Hale Dharmapuri	25	25	25	25	0	50	50	0	50
4.	Vijay Vidhalaya Matric Higher Secondary School, Dharmapuri	0	50	50	0	50	0	0	50	50
5.	Don Bosco Matric Higher Secondary School, Gundalpatty	50	0	50	0	50	0	0	50	50
6.	Government Higher Secondary School, Adhiyamankottai	25	25	25	25	0	50	50	0	50
	Total	**150**	**150**	**200**	**100**	**150**	**150**	**150**	**150**	**300**

STATISTICAL TECHNIQUES USED IN THE MAIN STUDY

Suitable descriptive and inferential statistical techniques were used in the interpretation of the data to draw out a meaningful picture of results from the collected data. In the present study, following statistical techniques were used.

1. Mean
2. Standard Deviation
3. Correlation
4. 't' test
5. Quartile Deviation

CONCLUSION

This chapter outlines the design of the present study, the procedure followed and the nature of the sample. It describes the hypothesis to be tested, the tools to be used and the methods of administration and scoring. The method of investigation designed was found to be quite appropriate and effective for the study. The various statistical techniques were implemented to analyse and systematize the data that were obtained through the test in finding out Religious attitude and moral anxiety among the higher secondary school students. Further, these results were discussed in the light of the hypotheses formulated.

4

Analysis and Interpretation of the Data

INTRODUCTION

This chapter highlights the analysis of data obtained to assess the religious attitude and moral anxiety among the higher secondary school students. Using appropriate statistical techniques hypothesis framed for the present study were verified and the findings interpreted and discussed in the light of previous research studies. Hence the present chapter, serves as guide to research, to show how all the major parts of the projects the objectives, the review of literature, hypotheses, and statistical techniques work together to address the Central research questions. At the outset, the following hypothesizes have been formulated keeping in mind the objectives of the present study.

HYPOTHESIS -I

The level of religious attitude of higher secondary school students in neutral in nature.

From the above table it is clear that the level of religious attitude among higher secondary school. Students are neutral in nature and the hypothesis is accepted.

Table 1

Showing the Level of Religious Attitude among the Higher Secondary School Students

Variables	Level	Number	Percentage
Religious Attitude	Moderately pro- religious	60	20.00
	Neutral	216	72.00
	Moderately Anti – religious	24	8.00
	Total	300	100.00

HYPOTHESIS

The level of moral anxiety among the higher secondary school students is average in Nature.

Table 2

Showing the Level of Moral Anxiety Among the Higher Secondary School Students

Variables	Level	Number	Percentage
Moral Anxiety	Average	172	57.33
	High	128	42.67
	Moderately Anti – religious	24	8.00
	Total	300	100.00

From the above table it is clear that the level of moral anxiety among the higher secondary school students is average in nature, confirming the Hypothesis.

HYPOTHESIS - III

There is no significant difference between boys and girls of higher secondary school in their religious attitude.

Table 3

Significant difference between mean score of Religious Attitude of higher secondary school students based on gender

Variables	Gender	Number	Mean	S.D.	SEMD	C.R. value	L.S.
Religious attitude	Boys	150	175.60	29.28	2.391	1.92	N.S.
	Girls	150	169.75	23.08	1.885		

From the above table it is clear that there is no significant difference between boys and girls in their religious attitude. Thus the null hypothesis is accepted.

HYPOTHESIS - IV

There is no significant difference between students studying in standard XIth and XIIth in their religious attitude.

Table 4

Significant difference between mean score of Religious Attitude of Higher Secondary School Students based on the Standard XIth and XIIth Classes

Variables	Class	Number	Mean	S.D.	SEMD	C.R. value	L.S.
Religious attitude	XI	200	172.36	26.93	1.904	0.29	NS
	XII	100	173.30	25.69	2.569		

From the above table it is clear that there is no significant difference between students studying in XI and XII in their religious attitude. So the null hypothesis is accepted.

HYPOTHESIS - V

There is no significant difference between students studying in Tamil and English medium of higher secondary school in their religious attitude.

Table 5

Significant difference between mean score of Religious Attitude of Higher Secondary School Students based on Medium of Instruction

Variables	Medium of Instruction	Number	Mean	S.D.	SEMD	C.R. value	L.S.
Religious attitude	English	150	169.34	29.59	2.416	2.20	0.05
	Tamil	150	176.01	22.57	1.843		

From the above table it is clear that there is significant difference between English and Tamil medium higher secondary school students in their religious attitude at .05 level. Thus the null hypothesis is rejected.

HYPOTHESIS - VI

There is no significant difference between students studying in Government and private of higher secondary schools in their religious attitude.

Table 6

Significant difference between mean score of Religious Attitude of Higher Secondary School Students based on Type of Management

Variables	Type of Management	Number	Mean	S.D.	SEMD	C.R. value	L.S.
Religious attitude	Government	150	176.01	22.575	1.843	2.20	0.05
	Private	150	169.34	29.594	2.416		

From the above table it is clear that there is a significant difference between Government and private higher secondary school students in their religious attitude at .05 level. Thus the null hypothesis is rejected.

HYPOTHESIS - VII

There is no significant difference between boys and girls in the higher secondary schools in the moral anxiety.

Table 7

Significant difference between mean score of Moral Anxiety of Higher Secondary School Students based on Gender

Variables	Medium of Instruction	Number	Mean	S.D.	SEMD	C.R. value	L.S.
Moral	Boys	150	21.06	5.794	.473	0.76	N.S.
Anxiety	Girls	150	20.55	5.907	.482		

From the above table it is clear that there is a significant difference between boys and girls in their Moral anxiety. Therefore the null hypothesis is accepted.

HYPOTHESIS - VIII

There is no significant difference between students studying in standard XIth and XIIth in their moral anxiety.

Table 8

Significant difference between mean score of Moral Anxiety of Higher Secondary School Students based on the Standard XIth and XIIth Classes

Variables	Class	Number	Mean	S.D.	SEMD	C.R. value	L.S.
Moral	XI	200	21.58	5.618	.397	3.30	0.01
Anxiety	XII	100	19.26	6.013	.601		

From the above table it is clear that there is a significant difference between students studying std XIth and XIIth in their Moral anxiety at .01 level. The null hypothesis is rejected based on the level of significance.

HYPOTHESIS - IX

There is no significant difference between students studying in English and Tamil medium of the higher secondary schools in their moral anxiety.

Table 9

Significant difference between mean score of Moral Anxiety of Higher Secondary School Students based on Medium of Instruction

Variables	Medium of Instruction	Number	Mean	S.D.	SEMD	C.R. value	L.S.
Moral	English	150	22.46	5.230	.427	5.11	0.01
Anxiety	Tamil	150	19.15	5.976	.488		

From the above table it is clear that there is a significant difference between English and Tamil medium higher secondary school students in their moral anxiety at 0.01 level. Therefore the null hypothesis is rejected.

HYPOTHESIS - X

There is no significant difference between students studying in Government and Private Secondary schools in their moral anxiety.

Table 10

Significant difference between mean score of Moral Anxiety of Higher Secondary School Students based on Type of Management

Variables	Type of Management	Number	Mean	S.D.	SEMD	C.R. value	L.S.
Moral	Government	150	19.15	5.976	.488	5.11	0.01
Anxiety	Private	150	22.46	5.230	.427		

From the above table it is clear that there is a significant difference between Government and Private higher secondary school students in their Moral Anxiety at .01 level. Thus the null hypothesis is rejected.

HYPOTHESIS - XI

There is no significant relationship among Religious attitude and moral anxiety.

Table 11

Showing the correlation among Religion Attitude and Moral Anxiety

Variables	Number of Students	Correlation	L.S.
Religious attitude Moral anxiety	300	0.04	N.S.

From the above table it is clear that there is no significant relationship among Religious attitude and moral anxiety. Therefore, the above hypothesis is rejected.

CONCLUSION

The analysis and interpretation of data reveals that there is no significant association between Religious attitude and moral anxiety among the higher secondary school students. The religious attitude of the higher secondary school students is found to be the neutral category. The majority of the high secondary school. Students fall in the average group with regard to moral anxiety. The next chapter deals with the major findings and summary of the study.

5

Summary and Findings

INTRODUCTION

The investigation was an attempt to study the religious attitude and moral anxiety of the higher secondary school students. Apart from this students attitude to various aspects of religion such as nature of God, Prayer and Worship, Formal Religion, Priests, Future Life, Spirit and Spirit world were also investigated on the basis of Sex, religious affiliation, gender type of management, classes and medium of instruction.

It is observed that there is no relationship between religious attitude and moral anxiety of the higher secondary school students. It is assumed that people's religious attitude may go with moral anxiety. The objectives and hypothesis the methodology and the major findings are presented.

In this study the sample of be 300 students from higher secondary schools in Dharmapuri District were tested using Religious attitude scale and moral anxiety. the information were collected, the data were statistically treated, analyzed, interpreted, discussed and concluded.

STATEMENT OF THE STUDY

The present investigation is titled as, "Religious attitude and Moral anxiety of higher secondary school students.

OBJECTIVES OF THE STUDY

1. To find out the level of Religious attitude of higher secondary school students.
2. To find out the level of Moral Anxiety of higher secondary school students.
3. To find out the significant difference between boys and girls of higher secondary school in their religious attitude.
4. To find out the significant difference between students studying in standard XIth and XIIth in their religious attitude.
5. To find out the significant difference between students studying in English and Tamil medium of the higher secondary schools in their religious attitude.
6. To find out the significant difference between students studying in Government and Private higher secondary schools in their religious attitude.
7. To find out the significant difference between boys and girls of higher secondary schools in their moral anxiety.
8. To find out the significant difference between students studying in standard XIth and XIIth in their moral anxiety.
9. To find out the significant difference between student studying in English and Tamil medium of the higher secondary schools in their moral anxiety.
10. To find out the significant difference between students studying in Government and Private higher secondary school in their moral anxiety.
11. To find out the relationship between religious attitude and moral anxiety of higher secondary school students.

HYPOTHESES OF THE STUDY

1. The level of Religious attitude of higher secondary school students is neutral.
2. The level of moral anxiety of higher secondary school students is average in Nature.
3. There is no significant difference between boys and girls of higher secondary schools in their religious attitude.

4. There is no significant difference between students studying in standard XIth and XIIth in their religious attitude.
5. There is no significant difference between students studying in English and Tamil medium of the higher secondary schools in their religious attitude.
6. There is no significant difference between students studying in Government and Private higher secondary schools in their religious attitude.
7. There is no significant difference between boys and girls in the higher secondary schools in the moral anxiety.
8. There is no significant difference between students studying in Standard XIth and XIIth in their moral anxiety.
9. There is no significant difference between students studying in English and Tamil medium of the higher secondary schools in their moral anxiety.
10. There is no significant difference between students studying in Government and Private higher secondary schools in their moral anxiety.
11. There is no significant relationship among the religious attitude and moral anxiety of students in the higher secondary schools.

SAMPLE OF THE STUDY

The sample population consisted of 300 higher secondary school students studying in Government and Private schools in Tamil Nadu. Six schools from the Dharmapuri District of Tamil Nadu have been chosen randomly for the study. Out of the sample of 300 students, 150 are male students and 150 are female students.

MAJOR FINDINGS OF THE STUDY

The major findings have been arrived at the present investigation are as follows:

1. It was found that the level of religious attitude among higher secondary school students is neutral in nature.
2. It was found that the level of moral anxiety among higher secondary school students is average in nature.
3. It was found that there is no significant difference between boys and girls in relation to their religious attitude.

4. It was found that there is no significant difference between students studying in standard XIth and XIIth in their religious attitude.
5. It was found that there is significant difference between English and Tamil medium higher secondary school students in their religious attitude
6. It was found that there is significant difference between Government and Private higher secondary school students in their religious attitude.
7. It was found that there is no significant difference between boys and girls in their moral anxiety.
8. It was found that there is a significant difference between students studying in standard XIth and XIIth in their moral anxiety.
9. It was found that there is a significant difference between English and Tamil medium higher secondary school students in their moral anxiety.
10. It was found that there is a significant difference between Government and Private higher secondary school students in their moral anxiety.
11. It was found that there is no significant relationship among Religious attitude and moral anxiety.

EDUCATION IMPLICATIONS

The aim of education is to develop abroad mindedness and universal outlook in the students with the right wisdom. This study would provide a chance for the students to be more religious and moral oriented some schools it appears that there is no systematic religious or moral instruction given to students. The religious practices were carried out at the homes of the students in most cases. It appears that such students are not having any strong view about the nature of god and religious principles.

The education system must impart values in students such as tolerance, patience, understanding, truthfulness, gratitude faith in God, self respect and also in the education at should raise it perspective the humanity and acquire the value of brotherhood, mercy, love etc.

The study also observes that the students do not have sufficient knowledge about any aspect of the religion they believe. When they grow old the same attitude to religion is carried by them, thus resulting in lack of building moral values and religious faith.

Morality is the beginning for into any religious group. At the same time by religious path one can enter in the goal of spiritual attainment. So, education should give clarity to the students about the need for moral values, and religious faith. Education should provide a proper understanding about every individual's life goal in relation to material and spiritual aspects.

Well-conducted classes on Religious or moral institutions could help students to become tolerant and respectful towards others. The school could organize sports events, cultural events and exhibitions encouraging students participation which would further improve development of values, provision and opportunities for students to work in collaboration with one another and to enhance religious tolerance.

Finally, education can only provide the right understanding in life to balance the religious and moral aspects concerning an individual.

SUGGESTIONS FOR FURTHER RESEARCH

Some suggestions with regard to possibilities of the research in the field of education are offered with a view to stimulate prospective research workers in this area.

1. The influence of institutions like home, school and political ideologies upon the religious attitude of the students.
2. Religious attitude in relation to personality traits such as introverts and extroverts.
3. The present study is limited to Government and private higher secondary school students and it could be extended to the University Level Students.
4. A similar study may be undertaken in other states of Tamil Nadu.

CONCLUSION

Good citizens contribute to the primary aims of education to bring about a change and get then to be realized and envisaged in the long run.

Moral anxiety is a progressive and positive level in the human life towards attaining spiritual development.

Education also provides opportunity to raise subjective moral questions regarding behaviour of their own self or others. Such type of introspective questions and moral anxiety in a behaviour is seen in students, especially at the adolescent period. Encouraged by the life of their teachers and the religious living atmosphere at home and the parents, they may be morally anxious and their gives rise to the concept of religious attitude which can be closely linked to the moral anxiety of individuals.

BIBLIOGRAPHY

1. **Adinarayan, S.P. and Rajamanickam M.** "A Study of Student Attitude towards Religion, the Spiritual and the Supernatural". Journal of Social Psychology, 1962, Vol.57 (1), pp.105-111.
2. **Boerce, C.G. (2001) Anxiety Hall C.S. (1954) "**A Primer of Freudian Psychology", Cleveland: World.
3. **Boisvert, Donad Luc (1990),** "Religion and Nationalism in Qubec the saint - Jean - Baptiste celebrations in sociological perspective", Dissertation Abstract International, Vol-52 (11), May 1992, P.3964.
4. **Deonandam, Kalowatie (1990),** "Religion and the struggle for hegemony in Nicaragua", Dissertation Abstract International, Vol.52 (11) May 1992, p.4070A.
5. **Deonandem, Kalowetie (1990),** "Religion and the struggle for hegemony in Nicaragua", Dissertation Abstract International, Vol. 52(11) May 1992, PP 4070 A.
6. **Dutt N.K (1965),** "Attitude of the University students towards religion", Journal of Psychological Research. 1965, Vol.9(3), pp.127-130.
7. **Francis, Leslie J(1993),** "Personality and Religion among college students in the U.K. Personality and Individual differences, April 1993 Vol.14 (4), pp.619-622.
8. **Freud (1955),** Analysis of phobia in a five year – old Boy. London: Hogarth Press, Vol.10.
9. **Gaston, J.E. and Broun, L.B.** Religion and Gender Proto type. Psychological abstracts 1993, Vol. 80, 9382.

10. **Green Celia (2004)** betters from Exile: Observations on a culture in decline, Oxford Forum, Chapter –I, xx.

11. **Greer J.E.** "Attitude to religion reconsidered", British Journal of Educational Students, Vol.31, No. 1, pp. 18-28.

12. **Gupta A. (1980),** "Personality and Mental consistent of Religiousness in the Tibetan Students in the Adolescent Age Group", Buch M.B., third survey of research in education.

13. **Hassan M.K. and Khalique (1981),** "Religiosity and its correlates in college students", Journal of Psychological Research, Vol.25 (3), pp.129-136.

14. **Helpburm, Lawrence R.** Religion in the social studies. The question of religious attitudes, Religious education, 1971, (May) Vol. 66 (3),172 – 179.

15. **Horne, E.P. & Stender, W.H.** Students Attitude to Religious practicies Journal of Social Psychology (21) 1945, p. 215.

16. **John Kottman E.** A semantic study of some selected dimensions of religious attitude, sociology and social research, 1968, 52(4), 430-437.

17. **Kapil, H.K. and Agarwal,** Susham, changing patterns of valves amongst women in modern Hindu Society. Psychological Research, 1967, 2(1-2), 29-32.

18. **Krause, Neal (1993),** "Measuring Religiosity in their life", Vol.15 (2), pp.170-197.

19. **Lester. D.Crow & Alice Crow,** "Educational Psychology", New Delhi: Publishers: Eurassa Publishing House Pvt. Ltd., Ramnagar, pp.241-242.

20. **Lewis, Robert E, Eraser Make W and Pecora, Peter J.** "religiosity among Indochinese Students in Utah", Journal for scientific study of religion, June, 1988, Vol. 27(2), pp. 272-283.

21. **Loewerthal, Kate M and Goldblatt, Vivienne,** "Family size and depressive symptoms in orthodox Jewish Women" Journal of Psychiatric research 1993 (Jan – Mar) Vol. 27(1), pp. 3-10.

22. **Maranell, Cary M.** Factor analytic study of some selected dimensions of religious attitude sociology and social research, 1968, 52(4) 430-437.

23. **Mary, R. (1950),** "The meaning of Anxiety", New York: Ronald.

24. **Medoof, M.H. & Skow, L. Lee,** Religion and behaviour, An empirical analysis Psychological Abstracts, 1993, Vol. 80, 13254.

25. **Misra S.L (1970),** "A Comparative study of religion – caste difference in concept formation ability of young adult", Psychological annual Vol.4, pp.10-12.

26. **Nagarajan K. (1994),** "Research methodology in Education Chennai: Sterling Publishers Pvt.Ltd., pp.354-355.

27. **Pang, Henry,** Religious attitude of students, Psychological reports, 1968, 22(2), 344.

28. **Ponton, Marcel.O, and Gorsuch, Richer.L (1995),** "Prejudice and religion revisited; A cross-cultural investigation with a venezuelan sample", Journal for the scientific study of religion Vol.27 92), pp.260-271.

29. **Prizyna, Wlady Slaw.** Religious attitude and personality traits analyzed on the basis of dear supplied by RB cattel's 16 factor questionnaire. Rocniki Filozoficzne: Anaales de philosophie, 1969, Vol. 17(4), 99-124.

30. **Rajamanickam (1966),** "A psychological study of religious and related attitudes of the students and professional groups in South India", Annamalai: Annamalai University.

31. **Rizvi S.A.H. (1986),** "A study of attitude towards religion education in relation to certain valve orientations Buch. M.B. Forth Survey of research in education, 1991, pp. 190.

32. **Roquiya Zainuddin (1994),** "Religiosity and Spirituality as related to some personality needs", Journal of community and research, Vol.2(2), pp.105-114.

33. **Sayed Firoj and Karananidhi S.,** "A study of religiosity and valves, Journal of Psychological research, 1995, Vol. 39 (3), pp. 30-34.

34. **Seetharam G.K.N.,** "It is time to act to the values," Yojana 30(1-2) 1986 pp.73-76.

35. **Seligman, M.E.P., Walker, E.F. & Rosenhan, D.L. (2001)** Abnormal Psychology, (4th end) New York, W.W. Norton & Company, Inc.

36. **Spielberger, C.D. (1966),** The effects of Anxiety on complex learning is academic achievement", New York: Academic Press.

37. **Swami Nikhilanda** "Inter – religious attitude; Rama Krishna Vivekandnada Centre, New York.

38. **Tandom B.K (1967)** "A study of attitude towards religion of Higher Secondary School students in Utterpradesh towns", Buch M.B. A survey of research in education, pp. 132.

39. **Telford, C.W.** A study of religious attitude: Journal of social Psychology 31, 1950, p. 217-230.

40. **Thomas Thai. V.** An investigation of religious attitudes, ideals, and personality trafts of the four groups of Catholic College Student Dissertational Abstract International, 1969, 30 (4-4), 1441.

41. **Tritter, - Jonathan (1992),** "An Educated change in; Moral Values some Effects of Religious and State Schools on their Students," Oxford – Review-of-Education; Vol.18, No.1, pp.29-43.

42. **Wiema, J.** Authoritarianism, religious Conservatism and Socio centric attitudes in Roman Catholic groups. Human relations, 1965, 18(3), 231 – 239.

43. **Woods J.H., Winger G (1995)** Current benzodia zepine issues, Pshycho pharmacology 118(2): 107-15.

4. Personality Disorder of College Students

1

The Problem and its Perspective

INTRODUCTION

Personality disorders often lack distinguishable characteristics related to an individual's behavior or mannerisms. They can be interpreted as reactions to the problems an individual experiences in everyday life. However, if a person is exhibiting abnormal personality characteristics on a regular basis, without any presence of extraordinary pressure in their day to day existence, the characteristics can be indicative of a personality disorder.

An individual's personality takes shape over the course of one's life. The average person experiments with a multitude of behaviors and expressed characteristics, until they arrive at a predictable pattern of personality expression. A personality disorder, describes consistent behavior by a person that indicates that they have made a poor adjustment to the adaptation of normal, socially acceptable behaviors. These patterns of behavior can result in functional impairment and a distressing alienation from normal society.

The perception an individual with antisocial personality has of society leans toward a dark view, that there is little kindness or social order to be found in day to day life. They believe that aggression and manipulation are skills one needs to succeed in this world. Individuals with this disorder are quick to argue, quickly to anger, and have a need to exert control over their environment and the people in it. These individuals often create a personal appearance of congeniality, that masks their mistrust of others and lack of concern for the welfare of other people. When antisocial people are brought into a counseling environment with others, they learn that other people share their experiences, difficulties, and frustrations. The art of sharing their experiences with others helps them to find social acceptance. This coupled with an increased responsibility for their actions are major steps on the road to recovery for those with antisocial behavior disorder.

People with avoidant personality disorder are very uncomfortable with the notion of developing relationships with others. An avoidant is usually shy, quiet and unassuming. They have anxiety around others and have trouble asserting themselves in group settings. They usually have very low self-esteem, which creates a self concept that they are unworthy of being accepted and admired by others.

People afflicted with borderline personality disorder experience a pattern of instability of self-image, interpersonal relationships and mood. Someone with borderline personality experiences mood swings and can alternately exhibit hostile behaviors or withdraw into sullen, depressed states of mind. Their relationships are marked by inconsistency, because the sufferer swings between an over idealized viewpoint of the situation at hand, or they undervalue the significance of the relationships or people in their lives. In the case of the borderline personality, stress can trigger dysphasia, a combination of anxiety, depression, and anger that can rapidly intensify. The borderlines unconventional behavior is a result of their effort to relieve the inner state of distress that is symptomatic of dysphasia.

Individuals with dependant personality disorder cling to those they have relationships with, and subordinate themselves to the people they are involved with. They need instruction from their relationship partners, on even actions and behaviors as individualistic and basic as how to dress, groom themselves, communicate, and their choice of hobbies, interests, and other friends. They also need constant reassurance that their actions are appropriate and acceptable.

Dependent people usually arrange their lives in a way that their lives in a way that their decisions are made for them by parents, spouses, bosses, or friends. They even tend to choose careers that fit into the employment choice recommendations of others. Having excessive dependence on others limits these individuals when it comes time to express their opinion or show initiative.

Individuals with histrionic personality disorder have an acute deep seated need to gain approval from others. They display an insincere and excessive emotionality and their friendships are short-lived in duration. Friends distance themselves from the histrionic person, because they tire of the conceited and manipulative behavior of the person suffering from the disorder.

The histrionic person often has a faulty self-image. They can consider themselves generous and trustworthy when the opposite is true. Their incorrect self-concept is related in many cases to an upbringing characterized by parental physical abuse and emotional neglect. The individual learns to perform for the benefit of others in an effort to win their attention and approval. In the meantime they lose their true sense of self.

The Narcissistic person exemplifies another personality disorder, characterized by the manipulation of others by insincere behaviors intended to win acceptance or praise. The disorder differs from the histrionic in that rather than appearing warm and sociable, the individual evokes a cold and aloof social prescience.

They tend to have delusions of grandeur which they incorporate into their self-concept. While maintaining this exaggerated self-concept, they anticipate a public reception appropriate to this deluded sense of personal status. Sometimes the narcissistic person is merely someone who has been hurt in past relationships, and has a need to maintain a self-generating from of self-love. This self-love may be necessary because of a lack of love based relationships in their lives. However, an individual needs to embrace a true self-concept and a high level of unconditional self-love in order to avoid a semblance of narcissistic behavior in the eyes of someone mental health care providers.

Family relationship is a key factor to develop individual's personality. If the home relation is not conducive to the students naturally personality deviation will be accepted. The sample taken for this study in Engineering College Students. In this scenario the investigator has made an attempt to study the influence of family relationship on their personality disorder.

THE CONCEPT OF PERSONALITY

Woodworth (1958) defines personality as the total quality of an individual's behavior as it is revealed in his habits of thought and expression, his attitudes and interest, his manner of acting and his personal philosophy of life. Haggard defines personality, as the configuration of individual characteristics and ways of behaving which describes as individuals unique adjustment to his environment. Freedom (1918) defines personality as the product of the dynamic and characteristic organization within the individual of psycho-biological structures or systems and their interaction with the environment". An often quoted definition of personality calls it the dynamic organization within the individual of those psycho-physical systems that determine his unique adjustment to his environment. Allport, (1937). Developing further, he proposed that trait model of personality for the first time.

According to Cattell (1961) "Personality is concerned with all the behavior of the individual both overt and under the skin". Trait formulations have provided a prevalent vehicle for psychologists attempts to describe individual differences and to incorporate person variables in the prediction of human behavior. That is the assumption that personality can be construed as a set of central traits or relatively enduring behavioral predispositions, has largely structured traditional non-psychodynamic personality theory, measurement and research.

Jung, attempted to classify human beings on two behavioral dimensions: extrovert and introvert. His typology is widely known and is most influential among professional workers. The major characteristics of the two types are as follows:

i. INTROVERT

A person who tends to withdraw into himself, especially, when faced by emotional conflicts and stress in his environment. Introvert individual is shy, avoids people and enjoys being alone. Scientists and philosophers may be termed as introvert.

ii. EXTROVERT

In contrast to the introvert type, extrovert person's orientation is towards the external world. He deals people intelligently in social situations. He is conventional, outgoing, social, friendly, and free from worries. Social workers, politicians, business executive may be types as extrovert. These two broad categories have been further classified on the basis of rational and irrational process.

This classification has been criticized on the ground that in general, the different types or classes as suggested by Jung do not exist. On the basis of typical characteristics prescribed for the extrovert and introvert, most of us may belong to both categories at different times and any may be called ambient. This introduces a complication and hence the type approach does not give a clear classification or description of personality.

THEORIES OF PERSONALITY

In our day-to-day conversation we ascribe traits to our friends and near one's as being honest, shy, aggressive, lazy, dull, dependent etc. Traits may be defined as relatively permanent and relatively consistent general behavior patterns that an

i. PERSONALITY TRAITS

Personality trait refers to those elements that help in the formation of personality. Good defines a trait as a "a characteristic and relatively permanent mode of behavior, the outcome of heredity and environment".

Garrett defines personality trait as, "distinctive ways of behaving more or less permanent for given individual."

Sociability, submission and persistence are some of the personality traits. The personality traits are expressed in ones behavior. The personality traits are unstable in nature. The expression of a trait depends on the situation. Some of the personality traits are as given below:

a. Honesty

In the presence of this personality trait, one behaves honestly, is sincere in his work.

b. Emotional stability

This personality enables the individual to maintain equilibrium and mental state even in adverse situations.

G.W.Allport (1961), defined a trait, "as a generalized and focalized neuropsychic system with the capacity to render many stimuli functionally equivalent and to imitate and guide consistent forms of adoptive and expressive behavior."

The definition given by Allport (1961) is a comprehensive one. Traits according to him are general and enduring in nature. They are not linked with a small of stimuli. He classified human traits as cardinal traits, central trait, and secondary disposition. Traits differ in intensity and magnitude from individual to individual. They operate in their own environment in a unique manner.

The traits have certain properties. There are some traits which can be measured quantitatively. They are not static in nature. During childhood days they are flexible. With the attainment of maturity they become stable. Even then some variables continue throughout life. Trait is also a mental set. They are organized frames of reference. In the interaction of individual with the environment traits are learned. The personality of an individual consists of the traits like physical, mental, intellectual, social, emotional and spiritual The reaction of this "patterns of traits" to stimuli may not be the same for different personalities in the same situation or even for the same personality in different situations. Consider the variations in emotional response to a frustrating situation such as this a person is waiting to meet a friend, but the friend fails to appear. In this situation, one person is amused, another angry and a third annoyed, and perhaps a fourth indifferent. Furthermore, in the same situation an individual may react in different ways on different days, depending on such factors as his physical well being, his general emotional tone, and his most recent experiences. In short, even if the stimulus is apparently the same, the individual's response to it on different occasions may be highly variable on account of the uniqueness of each personality, or the uniqueness of the pattern of traits in each individual.

The personality of each individual is most of the time determined by many factors the biological, sociological and psychological. All the factors sometime determine an individual to develop certain specific qualities. Leadership qualities could also be one among them. The origin of leaderships drawn from different classifications, they can be seen, as executive, elected and self-emerging.

EYSENCK'S THEORY OF PERSONALITY

Eysenck provides a hierarchical type approach to personality. He describes three basic categories of personality at the top of the hierarchy.

Extroversion ”! introversion, neuroticism ”! stability, psychotism ”! normality.

These have been ultimately reduced to two dimensions namely, stable ”! unstable and introversion ”! extroversion. Each of these categories involves certain qualities at the next lower of trait level. For example, the traits of an introvert would include such qualities as persistence, rigidity of approach, subjectivity etc. These traits in turn are associated with the next habitual response level.

For example, we may except an introvert to be persistent in tasks like problem solve etc. Generally, the last is the specific response level, which applies to specific tasks in which also the traits involved in the categories would be expressed in diverse degrees. Eysenck's approach is hierarchical with the top indicating types and the lower indicating traits.

EXTROVERSION, NEUTROTICISM AND PSYCHOISM

Eysenck evaluates both structure and dynamic of personality. Structure consists in the organization of specific responses into habits, habits into traits and traits into type dimensions. The main two dimensions are neuroticism and extraversion. Neuroticism was first established as a dimension in large sample of mental patients and then extended to the normal population. Highly neurotic persons are, likely to be dependent poorly organized nervous system, touchy, suggestible and lacking in persistence and so on. Extroversion was also established as a dimension along with neuroticism. Highly extroverted persons are likely to be sociable and lively and to have a good sense of human.

NEUROTICISM AND THE AUTOMATIC NERVOUS SYSTEM

Eysenck has proposed that neuroticisms also reflect emotionality. Neuroticism is a manifestation of certain characteristics of the autonomous nervous system. From a review of numerous pertinent studies, he concludes that these are a close relationship between neuroticism and liable activity of the autonomous nervous system. If such was the case, neuroticism could also be expected to be inheritable some extent inheritable. Neurotic deviations are mild in nature and could be curable. The personality disorders are very much related to psychotic deviation.

DIFFERNET TYPES OF PERSONALITY DISORDER

i. PARANOID DISORDER

In paranoid disorder which has an actuate onset and carries a good prognosis. The duration of illness is usually less than 6 months. The common etiology is abrupt change in environment in immigrants paranoia is a disorder with an insidious onset and relatively stable, chronic course. It is characterized by welt systematized delusions. The emotional response and behavior is understandable in the height of paranoid disorder.

Also called delusional disorder, this disorder is characterized by:Persistent delusions, Persecution, Grandeur, Jealousy.

A hallucination is commonly found among them. As personality disturbance will happen in the area of delusions. In this type of disorder, absence of schizophrenia and mood disorder is common.

ii. DEPRESSION

Depression in elderly patients may present as dementia clinically. It is called depressive pseudo dementia. Identification of depression is very important as it is treatable. These patients themselves complain of memory impairment, difficulty is sustaining attention and concentration and reduced intellectual capacity. In contrast a patient of dementia does not complain of these disturbances. Infact when confronted of these disturbances. Infact when confronted with memory testing him often confabulates. As depression may often be superimposed on dementia it is at time necessary to give a therapeutic trial with antidepressants.

The number of conditions which can cause dementia is large. But a majority of causes are due to a few common causes namely Alzheimer's diseases, multi-infarct dementia and hypothyroidism.

iii. MANIC

One percent of the population is affected by Manic disorder. This disorder tends to occur in episodes lasting usually 3-4 months, followed by complete recovery. The elevated mood can pass through following four stages depending on the severity of manic episode. The euphoria characterized by increased sense of psychological well being and happiness not in keeping with ongoing events. This is seen in hypomania. The elation moderate elevation of mood or feeling of confidence and enjoyment along with increased psychomotor activity. This is classical of manic. The exaltation or severe elevation of mood intense elation with delusions of grandeur. The ecstasy or very severe elevation of mood, seen in delirious or stupor us manic.

Along with these variations in elevation of mood expensive mood may be present, which is unceasing and unselective enthusiasm for interacting with people and surrounding environment. There may be rapid, short lasting shifts from euphoria to depression or anger.

There is increased psychomotor activity ranging from over activeness and restlessness to manic excitement where the person is on the – toe –on –the- go, (i.e., involved in ceaseless a activity). The activity is usually goal oriented and based on external environmental cues. The person is more talkative than usual describes thoughts racing in mind develops pressure of speech uses playful language with punning, rhyming, joking and testing and speaks loudly.

In manic there is marked increase in activity with excessive planning and at times execution of multiple activities. Due to being involved in so many activities and distractibility there is decrease in functioning ability in later stages. There is named increase in sociability even with previously unknown people. Gradually this sociability leads to an interfering behavior though the person does not recognize it as abnormal at that time.

Due to grandiose ideation, increased sociability over activity and poor judgement the manic person is involved in high risk activities like buying sprees reckless driving foolish business investments distributing money and or articles to unknown persons. He is usually dressed up in gaudy and flamboyant clothes although in serve manic these may be poor self-care.

Sleep is usually reduced with a decreased need for sleep Appetite may be increased but later these is usually decreased food intake, due to marked over activity. Insight into the illness is absent.

iv. ANXIETY

Anxiety is the commonest psychiatric symptom in clinical practice and anxiety disorders are one of the commonest psychiatric disorders.

Anxiety is a normal phenomenon which is characterized by a state of apprehension or unease arising out of anticipation of danger. Anxiety is differentiated from fear as fear is an apprehension in response to an external danger while in anxiety the danger is largely unknown normal anxiety becomes pathological when it causes significant subjective distress and (or) impairment in functioning trait anxiety is a habitual tendency to be anxious in general and is exemplified by " I often feel anxious". State anxiety is the anxiety felt at the present moment exemplified by 'I feel anxious now'. Persons with trait anxiety often have episodes of state anxiety.

The symptoms of anxiety can be broadly classified in two groups:

THE PSYCHIC SYMPTOMS OF ANXIETY ARE

Apprehension, poor concentration, inability to relax, irritability, initial insomnia, when severe, felling of impending doom depersonalization and desealization and exaggerated startle response.

THE PHYSICAL SYMPTOMS OF ANXIETY ARE

Motor tension live trembling, body aches, restlessness, twitching, fatigue, Autonomic palpitations, dysprea, tachycardia, dry mouth, frequency of micturition, dizziness, lump in the throat.

v. SCHIZOPHRENIA

One percent of the population suffers from schizophrenia. Although this disorder has puzzled philosophers, physicians and general public for centuries, systematic study of schizophrenia is but a century old. To understand what schizophrenia is, it is important to have a brief look at the history of evolution of the concept of schizophrenia.

vi. THE SYMPTONS OF SCHIZOPHRENIA ARE

a) HALLUCINATIONS, audible thoughts leaving of voice or hallucinatory voices.

Also thought withdrawal, thought insertion, Thought diffusion or broad casting, Made feeling or affect. Made impulses, and Made volition or acts.

These symptoms have been described in detail as they have very often been used for diagnosis of schizophrenia and have influenced future classifications significantly. As mentioned earlier, they are not specific for schizophrenia and may be seen in other psychiatric disorders like mood disorders, organic psychiatric disorders.

Schizophrenia is characterized by disturbance in thought and verbal behavior, perception, affect, motor behavior and relationship to external world. The diagnosis is entirely clinical.

Autistic thinking is one of the most important features of schizophrenia. Here thinking is governed by private and illogical rules.

A pattern of spontaneous speech in which things said in juxtaposition lack a meaningful relationship or there is idiosyncratic shifting from one frame of reference to another. The speech is often described as being 'disjointed'. Thought blocking is a characteristic feature of schizophrenia, although can also be seen in complex partiel seizures (temporal lobe epilepsy).

vii. HYSTERIC

The word hysteric has been used in so many contexts by psychiatrists, physicians and non-professionals that it no longer has any one meaning. These various contexts are:

1. Impulsive, uncontrolled behavior.
2. Manipulative, dramatic, exhibitionistic emotional and (or) seductive behavior.
3. Hypochondriasis.

DEFINITION OF FAMILY

In a time when sociologists at least in the western world-contend that disintegration and deinstitutionalization of the family has led to a growing pluralization of family forms, defining the family is not an easy task. They range from conceiving of the family as a legalized two generational unit of co-residing persons related by blood and or adoption to viewing it as a widely unspecified constellation of persons who of their own volition call themselves a family.

FAMILY RELATIONSHIP

The number of possible relationships within a family increases exponentially with the number of individual family members. In a four-person family, for example these are 11 groupings of family members (six dyads, four triads and one tetrad). These complex patterns of relationships should be kept in mind as some of the major types of relationships should be investigated.

"Home, a centre of love and affection, is the best place for education and the first school of the child". He regarded home as the one indispensable factor in the young child's training, and the mother as the fountain head of all true education. A child sees the high of the day in the home. Family is the first social environment.

THE IMPORTANCE OF HOME

A successful system of education must harness them all to meet the all around educational needs of man. "Home is the eternal school of life". It is one of the important units of society.

IMPORTANT FUNCTIONS OF HOME OR FAMILY

It is often said that home is the first institution of education and the mother is the first teacher of child. Family as the first teacher educates the child in his health habit, speech pattern, basic ideas and the money fold attitudes towards himself and associates. Intact, family provides the foundation on which the future superstructure of the child education in constructed.

As long as the child is depended on his parents they have to work for satisfying his economic needs. They have to provide for his food, clothing, education, recreation and various other needs, where he needs money. Not only this, they have to train him for some vocation or occupation in life. It clearly reveals that home or family has great educational potentialities.

SPECIFIC EDUCATIONAL FUNCTIONS OF HOME

Physical care of the child is the first important educational responsibility of the family. The home provides such necessities as food, clothing, shelter and the medical care to the child. Thus he maintains good health. Physical health also depends upon good health habits such as regular brushing of teeth, proper sleep etc. The family gives early training in these health rules to enable the child to develop sound physical health.

"Sound mind in a sound body" is an age old maximum. Within the home, the family helps the child in his early intellectual development. Language is the most important activity which the child develops in the family.

FAMILY AS AN EDUCATIONAL AGENCY

The family can play a significant role as an educational agency. Since the whole educative influence proceeds from the parents, it is desirable that there should be healthy relationships between parents and other elders in the family. Moreover, the child-parents relationship also matters a lot in the educative process that goes on within the home.

Crow and Crow have rigidly pointed out: "unfortunate is the educational influence of the home in which parents disagree in the parents of the child concerning what constitutes desirable child behavior. The young child should not be led to discover that if one present denies him a desired privilege, he can get it act of the other parents. Relatives should not become a source of comfort for the undisciplined child. In that case the whole education becomes a force and the family cannot achieve anything constructive". They should become models of desirable behavior for the children and should not indulge in anything which may be vicious of anti-educative.

Raymont warns that the division of responsibility must in no way be taken in imply "a rigid separation" of the two. He adds, "The wise parent and teacher will, however, seek to understand

Each others aims and to second each other's efforts, so that the child's education will form an organic whole. Nothing can be more demoralizing to child than lack of unity and harmony in his home life and his school life".

This it is through complementary nature of the home and the school that education of the child becomes or shared responsibility and a joint enterprise. It is an this senses that the teacher is the only true parent and the only true teacher.

WAYS AND MEANS ADOPTED TO SEEK ACTIVE CO-OPERATION BETWEEN THE HOME AND SCHOOL

The first essential thing in the home-school relationship is the parent's interest in their child's education. Crow and Crow have rightly pointed out that the beginning months at school, "constitute an important milestone an a child's life". During this period the parents should take pride in the fact that their son or daughter is now big enough to go to school. At home, the child should be given the feeling that his teacher will be as much interested in his welfare as his own parents are. In fact, during the child's whole school life this feeling should continue and parents should show a sincere interest in the child's activities at school. Parental reports about their children count a lot towards the teacher understands of the child. A complete case history of the child will be of immense use.

All wise parents are interested in their child's work at school. The school can enlist the faith and co-operation of the parents by sending detailed reports of the work of the child to his parents. These reports will invite parents opinion and advice in the well-being of the child. The school can also make suggestions about the child's home, conditions of work, play, rest and food and about his relations with his elders and friends.

Parents visit to the school is an essential condition for co-ordinate effort of the home and the school. The visit will provide occasions and opportunities for home-school co-operation.

ROLE OF PARENT'S EDUCATION

It is a platitude and also a truth that it can be one of the easiest things in the world, to become, and one of the hardest things in the world to be a parent. Sensible parents gave proper replies to children's questions and contribute, to the development of their powers of expression, understanding, conversation and discussion. "The hand that rocks the cradle rules the world" bears a testimony to the fact that any education is misnomer if there is no pertinent sharing of parents. There is no denying the fact that education does not commence with the alphabet, it begins with a mother's look, with a fathers and of approbation or a sign of reproof, with sister's gentle pressure of the hand or a brother's noble act of forbearance. Hence the starting point of all education is the early life of the child curved out by the genius with the child's need. Parents who themselves are in conflict with their quarrels and tragic scenes are bad company for the child considered mother as a true nurse.

The mother plays an important role in promoting the forward looking tendencies in the growing child. The moral tone and the emotional-atmosphere of the life may have equal reaction on the child's school work. Thus if the home and mother supply the right environment of study, love and affection and provide the child with the opportunity to express himself in freedom, then like a plant, given good soil and sunlight, the child will flourish.

The foundation for education is laid in the home of the child. That is home is the eternal school or in other words, home is a school away from school and school of the parents under the bracing environments of parental proof.

Education is a careless process of modification and corrections. Mother educates children to develop them in to a potential parent. Thus the seed of parenthood at the adult stage. The lamp lighted by another lamp shines lack to the previous one. It is abundantly clear now that parenthood pervades the entire life of the child. To make the life rich and fuller, the image of an ideal home must be visualized. If one has to prepare the list of educators participating in the task of education parents will primarily top the list.

The loving mother and intelligent father have to play their roll in complete harmony and accordance is a home away from home. Home is the base and school forms that future construction. "Home is a place on which the sun shines and home is a place in which the sun stains". The first lesson of citizenship is being learnt at home. There cannot be water light compartments between home and school.

STATEMENT OF PROBLEM

Personality Disorders and Family Relationship among Engineering College Students.

OPERATIONAL DEFINITION

1. PERSONALITY DISORDERS: By this the investigator means the scores obtained from Multiphase Personality Questionnaire constructed and standardized by H.N. Murthy.

2. FAMILY RELATIONSHIP: By this the investigator means the scores obtained from Index of Family Relationship by Walter W Hudson.

3. ENGINEERING COLLEGE STUDENTS: By this the investigator means the students who are studying the Bachelor of Engineering after completion of their Higher Secondary education.

DEFINITION OF TECHNICAL TERM USED

1. PERSONALITY DISORDERS: Personality Disorders often lack distinguishable characteristics related to an individual's behavior or mannerisms. A Personality disorders, describes consistent behavior by a person, that indicates that they have made a poor adjustment to the adaptation of normal, socially acceptable behaviors.

2. FAMILY RELATIONSHIP: Family, broadly speaking is a single unit of people who live together and share life's basic day-by-day functions. Humanity has demonstrated the need for such a core group, and the need for each individual to grow. These dual, sometimes, contrasting, human needs create the paradox of the family unit, in which exist struggle for separateness and togetherness, difference and similarity, protection and freedom, support and independence.

OBJECTIVES OF THE STUDY

1. To find out the significant difference between boys and girls of Engineering College Students on their personality disorders.
2. To find out the significant difference between personality disorders and Family Relationship of Engineering College Students.
3. To find out the significant difference between boys and girls of Engineering College Students belonging to nuclear and joint family on their personality disorders
4. To find out the significant difference between the students belonging to nuclear and joint family on their Family Relationship.
5. To find out the significant difference on the personality disorders of engineering college students based on their mother's occupation.
6. To find out the significant difference on the Family Relationship of engineering college students based on their mother's occupation.
7. To find out the significant difference of personality disorders among engineering college students based on their parental income.
8. To find out the significant difference of Family Relationship among Engineering College Students based on their parental income.
9. To find out the significant difference on the type of personality disorders of Engineering College Students based on their father's occupations.

10. To find out the significant difference on the type of Family Relationship of Engineering College Students based on their Father's occupation.
11. To find out the significant relationship between home relation and personality disorders of Engineering College Students.

LIMITATIONS

1. This study is limited to investigate among the Engineering College Students
2. A sample of 250 is selected for this study.
3. This study is taken only one college named Thandhai Periyar Engineering College in Vellore District.

CONCLUSION

Family is the first place of education of the child. It plays a vital role in the Personality development of the child. Children of same parents vary in personality and respond to stimuli and environment in different ways. This chapter deals with the overview of the problem, objectives and limitation of the study. The next chapter concerns with the review of related literature.

2

Review of Related Literature

INTRODUCTION

Review of related literature is an important prerequisite to actual Planning and then the execution of any research work. Best (1963) writes "A familiarity with the literature in any problem area helps the students to discover what is already known, attempted methods promising and disappointing, and problems that remain to be solved"

The investigator feels that the study of related literature in acquiring information about the studies done in the field protects against unnecessary duplication, guides in carrying out the investigation successfully and makes him familiar with the steps. In the following pages, a review is made on the studies conducted in India and abroad related to the present study.

NEED FOR SURVEY OF RELATED LITERATURE

Extensive initial reading in a field makes the investigator familiar with the accumulated facts in this field. Study of related literature sensitizes the individual to new avenues in research. It furnished the researcher with indispensable suggestions about comparative data, good procedures, likely methods.

Barg says that review of literature is an important part of the scientific approach and is carried out in all areas of scientific research. It gives scholars the understanding of previous work that has been done. It also provides the means of getting to the frontiers in the particular field of knowledge.

So the investigator has attempted on relevant information related to his work. A number of studies conducted on family relationship and academic achievement are presented in this chapter.

STUDIES RELATED TO PERSONALITY DISORDERS

Johnson and Jeffrey-G. 1996 conducted a study on Psychiatric Symptomatology and Substance Use in Adolescents with Personality Disorders.

The extent to which adolescents diagnosed with one or more Personality Disorders through the Personality Diagnostic Questionnaire-Revised were at an elevated risk of substance abuse was studied with 441 undergraduates. Those with one or more Personality Disorders showed higher levels of psychiatric Symptomatology and substance use.

Hardy and Gillian-E.(1995) conducted a study on Impact of Cluster C Personality Disorders on Outcomes of Contrasting Brief Psychotherapies for Depression.

Study compares 27 depressed clients diagnosed with Cluster C Personality Disorder (PD) with 87 depressed clients without the diagnosis. All clients completed cognitive-behavioral or psychodynamic-interpersonal psychotherapy. Treatment length did not influence outcome for PD clients. PD clients whose depression was also relatively severe showed significantly less improvement after treatment than either PD clients with less severe depression or non-PD clients.

Mills and Anne (1995) conducted a study on a Survey of Current Practice.

Report's findings of a 1993 questionnaire complcted by 46 North American art therapists that focuses on the outpatient treatment of multiple Personality Disorder. Includes information on role in diagnosing, fees and third-party payment, and therapeutic activities. Treatment issues include pacing and containment, and managing the client's chronic suicidality.

Fong and Margaret-L. (1995) conducted a study on a Primer for Counselors.

The DSM-IV categorizes 10 Personality Disorders, long-term patterns of personality traits that result in impairment of social and occupational functioning. The author details steps in the recognition and diagnosis of Personality Disorders, with emphasis on using the DSM-IV diagnostic framework.

Kjos and Diane (1995) conducted a study on Linking Career Counseling to Personality Disorders.

Relates Personality Disorders to career development issues and counseling interventions. Case examples suggesting career-focused treatment interventions for dependent, borderline, obsessive-compulsive, and passive-aggressive Personality Disorders are presented.

Morris and Maureen-Batza (1995) conducted a study on the Diagnostic Drawing Series and the Tree Rating Scale: An Isomorphic Representation of Multiple Personality Disorder, Major Depression, and Schizophrenic Populations.

The tree drawings of 80 subjects, who were diagnosed with either multiple Personality Disorder, schizophrenia, or major depression, and a control group, were rated. Patterns were examined and graphs were used to depict results. Certain features were found to distinguish each category. The descriptive statistical findings were both consistent and inconsistent with earlier Diagnostic Drawing Series research findings.

Baltaxe and Christiane (1995) conducted a study on Discourse Cohesion in the Verbal Interactions of Individuals Diagnosed with Autistic Disorder or Schizotypal Personality Disorder.

This study compared high functioning adolescents and young adults with autism (n=8) or schizotypal Personality Disorder (n=9) in use of social language referencing. Both groups had similar rates, types, and patterns of cohesive reference errors, though subjects with schizotypal disorder used cohesive ties of reference more often and more correctly than did subjects with autism.

Trull and Timothy-J. (1995) conducted a study on Borderline Personality Disorder Features in Non clinical Young Adults. Identification and Validation.

Two studies involving approximately 3,500 college students were conducted to establish and validate a self-report method of identifying non clinical young adults with significant borderline Personality Disorder features and to evaluate clinical correlates of this classification across relevant areas of functioning. Results support the validity of the self-report method.

Schroeder and Marsha-L (1992) conducted a study on Dimensions of Personality Disorder and Their Relationships to the Big Five Dimensions of Personality.

Dimensional measures of aspects of Personality Disorders (PD) were developed. Convergence of these measures with the "Big Five" personality factors was studied in 300 general population subjects. Results suggest substantial similarity between the five factors and PD measures, though the latter cannot be entirely subsumed by the Big Five model.

Stevens and Gail-Flint (1994) conducted a study on Prison Clinicians' Perceptions of Antisocial Personality Disorder as a Formal Diagnosis.

Surveyed and interviewed 53 clinicians who work with prison inmates. Results indicated that clinicians used diagnosis of antisocial Personality Disorder liberally among inmates and felt majority of inmates could be so diagnosed. Large minority of clinicians went beyond Diagnostic and Statistical Manual of Mental Disorders criteria and reported looking for characteristics associated with concept of psychopathy.

Waller and Glenn (1994) conducted a study on childhood Sexual Abuse and Borderline Personality Disorder in the Eating Disorders.

Examination of 115 women with eating disorders revealed a secondary diagnosis of borderline Personality Disorder associated with a history of childhood sexual abuse. A model involving background features, precipitants, and immediate and long-term psychological consequences is suggested to explain the link to childhood abuse, and implications for treatment of eating disorders are considered.

Clarkin and John-F (1993) conducted a study on a Comparison of SCID - II BPD and NEO-PI.

Hospitalized female patients with borderline Personality Disorder were assessed for Axis II disorders by the Structured Clinical Inventory for the Diagnostic and Statistical Manual of Mental Disorders (SCID-II) and for personality traits with the NEO Personality Inventory. The relationship of results to social adjustment and the utility of information on pathology and personality traits are discussed.

Weaver,-Terri-L. and Clum,-George-A. (1993) conducted a study on Early Family Environments and Traumatic Experiences Associated with Borderline Personality Disorder.

Assessed childhood trauma experiences (sexual abuse, physical abuse, witnessed violence, early separation) and family environment characteristics of 17 depressed female patients with borderline Personality Disorder (BPD) and 19 without BPD. Significantly, more BPD subjects reported histories of sexual abuse, physical abuse, and witnessed violence. Sexual abuse emerged as only significant predictor of dimensional BPD score.

STUDIES RELATED TO FAMILY RELATIONSHIP

Peters and Scott-Ryan (1995) conducted a study on Family Relations and Writing: Using One to Improve the Other—an Annotated Bibliography.

Presents a 25-item annotated bibliography of journal articles (published between 1991 and 1994) describing writing and research exercises and approaches for helping students becomes aware of their own families and others.

Lawson and David-M. (1994) conducted a study on Counselor Trainee Early Family Structure and Current Intergenerational Family Relationships Implications for Training.

Investigated counselor trainee's recollections of early family structure and current intergenerational relationships. Found trainees who remained relatively free from "triangling" patterns with parents reported significantly greater spousal intimacy, more individuation from parents, and less triangulation with children and spouses. Reports other results and implications.

Kashubeck,-Susan and Christensen,-Sue-A. (1995) conducted a study on Parental Alcohol Use, Family Relationship Quality, Self-Esteem, and Depression in College Students.

Family relationship quality, not parental alcohol use, predicted levels of depression and self-esteem in 201 college students. Witnessing spousal abuse related to increased depression in adult children of alcoholics, whole poorer family relationship quality was associated with lower self-esteem, suggesting the experience of paternal alcoholism is not uniform among offspring.

Kister and Joanna (1995) conducted a study on Family Relations Resource Guide. A Resource for Teaching the Family Relations Core Course Area of Ohio's Work and Family Life Program.

This resource guide provides those teaching the Family Relations course of the Ohio Work and Family Life Program an overview of the course content, teacher background information, learning activities, and assessment ideas. It has one teaching module for each process competency and each content competency in the Family Relations and Process Competency units of the Occupational Competency Analysis Profile (OCAP). These modules appear in this guide in the same order in which the competencies are listed in the OCAP. The learning activities are written from the students' perspective, but teacher notes are included to assist teachers in conducting activities. The four process modules are as follows: managing work and family responsibilities, solving personal and family problems, relating to others, and assuming a leadership role. The eight content modules cover the following subjects: analyzing the significance of families; nurturing human development; forming one's own family; building and maintaining healthy family relationships; developing family communication patterns; dealing with stress, conflicts, and crises; managing work and family roles and responsibilities; and analyzing social forces affecting families. Each module consists of these components: module overview, including practical problem, process competency, competency builders, and supporting concepts; teacher background information with rationale, background, and list of references; learning activities; assessment (paper and pencil, classroom experiences, and application to real-life settings); and handouts.

McHale and Susan-M. (1995) conducted a study on Links with Family Relations and Children's Well-Being.

Examined patterns of mothers' and fathers' differential treatment of first-born and second-born school-age siblings in 110 families and the links between parents' differential treatment and children's well-being and dyadic family relationships. Found that parental patterns were linked to differences between the siblings' well-being and that younger siblings exhibited greater vulnerability to differential treatment.

Brody and Gene-H. (1994) conducted a study on Family Process in Rural, Two-Parent African American Families.

Examined hypothesis that parental religiosity contributes to organization of rural African American family relationships among sample of 90 African American youths and their married parents. Religiosity was linked with higher levels of marital interaction quality and co caregiver conflict. Associations between religiosity and parent-youth relationship quality were mediated by marital and co caregiver relationships.

Mortimer,-Jeylan-T and Shanahan,-Michael-J (1994) conducted a study on Adolescent Work Experience and Family Relationships.

A 3-year study of 1,000 adolescents and their parents found that student employment has significant effects on family relationships. It fosters separation and individuation, of which parents approve, and diminished family time did not affect the quality of relationships. Boys' work had more positive effects than did girls' work.

Larson and Jeffry-H. (1994) conducted a study on the Impact of Job Insecurity on Marital and Family Relationships.

Examined relationship between perceived stress resulting from job insecurity and marital and family functioning. Data from 111 married couples in which at least 1 spouse was working in insecure job environment showed that job insecurity stress was related in systematic way to marital and family dysfunction and number of family problems reported.

Gentry and Deborah (1994) conducted a study on 1993—Twenty - Fifth Annual National Council on Family Relations Videotape Competition.

Lists and annotates winning entries in 1993 National Council on Family Relations Videotape Competition in categories of substance abuse, aging, social issues, divorce/remarriage, families with special needs, family violence, human development, reproduction and family planning, marital/family issues, mental health, nontraditional families, parenting, sexuality, teenage pregnancy, sexually transmitted disease and Acquired Immune Deficiency Syndrome, and others.

McGuire,-Jacqueline and Earls,-Felton (1993) conducted a study on Exploring the Reliability of Measures of Family Relations, Parental

Attitudes, and Parent-Child Relationships in a Disadvantaged Minority Population.

Forty mothers, living in economically disadvantaged inner-city locations completed four parenting questionnaires (Parental Attitudes to Childrearing, Parental Acceptance Rejection Questionnaire, Raising Children, and Conflict Tactics Scale) from two to four weeks apart. Significant test-retest reliability was established for all four measures and internal consistency was similar to published reports.

Whitbeck and Les-B. (1993) conducted a study on Family Relationship History, Contemporary Parent-Grandparent Relationship Quality, and the Grandparent-Grandchild Relationship.

Investigated effects of early family experiences on mediating role of parents for grandparent-grandchild relationship. Findings from parents' and ninth graders' reports regarding 1,138 grandparents revealed that recalled non optimal parent-child relationships between parents and grandparents negatively affected the contemporary parent-grandparent relationship and subsequently affected contact and relationship quality for grandchildren and their grandparents.

Cook,-William-L. and Goldstein,-Michael-J. (1993) conducted a study on Multiple Perspectives on Family Relationships: A Latent Variables Model.

Tested the assumption that social desirability and other factors bias familial self-reports, through the use of a latent variables modeling approach that evaluated rater reliability and bias in mother, father, and child ratings of parent-child negativity. Results based on 78 families demonstrated that family member ratings contained a significant "true score" component that correlated with observer ratings.

CONCLUSION

The chapter mainly concerns with the study of related literature. The next chapter deals with the design and methodology used in this study.

3

Design of the Study and the Method of Investigation

INTRODUCTION

This chapter describes in detail, the design of the study, nature and selection of sample and a brief description of the tools of investigation. It also gives a description of the procedure adopted for the collection of data, for its scoring and classification and finally the proposed statistical treatment of the data for testing the hypotheses that were formulated are explained.

HYPOTHESES

1. There is no significant difference between boys and girls of Engineering College Students on their personality disorders.
2. There is significant difference between personality disorders and family relationship of Engineering College Students.
3. There is no significant difference between boys and girls of Engineering College Students belonging to nuclear and joint family on their personality disorders.
4. There is significant difference between the students belonging to nuclear and joint family on their family relationship.

5. There is significant difference on the personality disorders of Engineering College Students based on their mother's occupation.
6. There is significant difference on the family relationship of Engineering College Students based on their mother's occupation.
7. There is significant difference of personality disorders among Engineering College Students based on their parental income.
8. There is significant difference of family relationship among Engineering College Students based on their parental income.
9. There is significant difference on the type of personality disorders of Engineering College Students based on their father's occupations.
10. There is significant difference on the type of family relationship of Engineering College Students based on their Father's occupation.
11. There is significant relation between home relation and personality disorders of Engineering College Students.

TOOLS AND TECHNIQUES

To test the hypotheses the following tools have been used.

1. Index of family Relations by Walter W. Hudson
2. Multiphasic Personality Questionnaire by H.N.Murthy

INDEX OF FAMILY RELATIONS

DESCRIPTION

The English poet John Donne wrote, "No man is an island; every man is a piece of the continent, a part of the main". For many of us, that continent is our family, those people with whom we share ourselves each day. The family can be a source of great positive energy, encouraging us to try new things and supporting us when our attempts fall short. But for some, the family situation is a source of stress and frustration, pulling energy away from us rather than feeding our needs. These needs that are not met belong to all the family members, for no one is immune to the effects of a stressful family life. Children may show it through physical complaints or school problems, while mom and dad may show the pressure in martial conflicts or behaviors which remove them from home. Both the individual family members and their interview relation rise or fall on the health of the family unit.

For more than thirty years, family researchers have been concerned with the evaluation of the family process. As with any other complex process, attempts have been made to specify what it is in family relationships that can cause problems. Some of the other tests are the results of that work such as martial roles and sexual compatibility, but Dr. Walter Hudson saw the need for a global measure of family satisfaction - an index that went directly to the question, "How do you feel about being a member of this family?" In 1977, he developed the Index of Family Relations as part of his series of tests for use in psychological and social work treatment. It has included because of its straight forward way of evaluating family satisfaction.

TABLE 1

SHOWING THE NATURE OF STATEMENTS IN THE INDEX OF FAMILY RELATIONS

Sl.No.	Nature of Statements	Item Numbers	*Marks* Never	Very Rarely	Sometime	Often	Always
1.	Positive	1, 4, 5, 8, 14,15,17, 18,20,21, 23	1	2	3	4	5
2.	Negative	2,3,6,7,9, 10,11,12, 13,16,19, 22,24,25	5	4	3	2	1

ADMINISTRATION

The test is administered to those students who had been randomly chosen from the Engineering College Students. The following instruction was given:

- Given below are twenty-five statements regarding family relations
- Five answers are given beside every statement
  1. Never
  2. Very rarely
  3. Some time
  4. Often
  5. Always

- Put a tick mark of the answer which is most suitable in your opinion.

Each statement was read clearly and distinctly so as to enable the students to respond to them with ease. The students were found to be cooperative.

i. SCORING PROCEDURE

The index of Family Relations contains both positive and negative statements. The positive items are those which indicate comfortable family relations among the students. They are the following items: 1, 4, 5, 8, 14, 15, 17, 18, 20, 21 and 23. For the positive statements those who marked NEVER will score one; VERY RARELY will score two; SOME TIME will score three; OFTEN will score four; and ALWAYS will score five.

On the other hand the negative statements indicate difficult family relations. The following items are negative: 2, 3, 6, 7, 9, 10, 11, 12, 13, 16, 19, 22, 24 and 25. For these items those who marked NEVER will score five; VERY RARELY will score four; SOME TIME will score three; OFTEN will score two; and ALWAYS will score one.

To find total score, the total points of positive items and the total points of negative items are added. From this sum, twenty-five points are subtracted. The result is the final score.

ii. INTERPRETING THE SCORE

Students who score between 30-100 are comfortable with their present Family Relations. A high score on this test indicate a low level of family satisfaction. Students who score from 0 to 29 often report significant problems in relating to their family relations.

MULTIPHASIC PERSONALITY QUESTIONNAIRE

i. DESCRIPTION

Multiphase Personality Questionnaire was constructed and standardized by Dr. H.N.Murthy. This Inventory can use for the normal category of people, to assess their degree of Personality Disorder because it is assumed that each person has lesser degree of Personality Disorder. It comprise of 100 statements with their response of True or False. The different areas of Personality Disorder like Paranoid, Depression, Manic,

Anxiety, Schizophrenia, Hysteric, and Psychopathic can be measured using this inventory. In this inventory high score indicate there is every chance of Personality Disorder and low score indicate less degree of Personality Disorder.

ii. SCORING PROCEDURE

The inventory is scored based on the scoring key given by the Author as for as paranoid is concerned if as person is scores 6 and above the person is having the particular disorder. For Schizophrenia and Depression if a person score 5 and above the person may have Schizophrenia and Depression disorder. For Hysteric the score 4 and above indicate Hysteric disorder. In the same manner for manic also 6 and above scores indicated the person is having the manic problem. Also for the Psychopathic deviation the score 17 and above scores the Psychopathic disorder.

In Anxiety disorder the scores 11 and above shows Anxiety disorder.

PILOT STUDY

A pilot study was conducted to determine the suitability of the tools used in the present investigation. A random sample of 50 students was selected for the study for establishing the reliability and validity.

ESTABLISHING RELIABILITY OF MULTIPHASIC PERSONALITY QUESTIONNAIRE

The reliability of a test may be defined as the degree of consistency with which the test measures what it measures. A test score is called reliable, when we have a reason to believe it to be stable and trustworthy.

RELIABILITY OF MULTIPHASIC PERSONALITY QUESTIONNAIRE

To compute the reliability of Personality Disorder for the sample shown, the Spearman Brown Reliability Formula Method was used. The reliability was computed it was found to be 0.64, showing that the tool is highly reliable.

ESTABLISHING VALIDITY

Validity means ability to produce findings that are in agreement with conceptual or theoretical values. It refers to the success of the scale in measuring what it meant to measure. A test is valid, when it measures truly and accurately the ability or quality one wants to measure. Thus, validity means truthfulness of the test.

i. VALIDITY OF MULTIPHASIC PERSONALITY QUESTIONNAIRE

The validity of Index of Personality Disorder was found out by computing the square root of the reliability co-efficient which worked out to be 0.81, clearly reveals that the tool is highly valid in nature.

ii. ESTABLISHING RELIABILITY OF FAMILY RELATIONS

The reliability of a test may be defined as the degree of consistency with which the test measures what it measures. A test score is called reliable, when we have a reason to believe it to be stable and trustworthy.

iii. RELIABILITY OF FAMILY RELATIONS

To compute the reliability of Family Relations for the sample shown, the Spearman Brown Reliability Formula Method was used. The reliability was computed it was found to be 0.83, clearly reveals that the tool is highly reliable in nature.

ESTABLISHING VALIDITY

Validity means ability to produce findings that are in agreement with conceptual or theoretical values. It refers to the success of the scale in measuring what it meant to measure. A test is valid, when it measures truly and accurately the ability or quality one wants to measure. Thus, validity means truthfulness of the test. Intrinsic validity computed by calculating the square root of reliability and it was found as 0.91, clearly reveals that the tool is valid in nature.

STATISTICAL TECHNIQUES

Suitable descriptive and inferential statistical techniques were used in the interpretation of the date to draw out a more meaningful picture of results from the collected data. In the present study the following statistical measures were used:

- Mean
- Standard Deviation
- Critical Ratio
- ANOVA
- Correlation

CONCLUSION

This chapter outlines the design of the present study, the procedure followed and the nature of the sample. It describes the hypotheses to be tested, the tools to be used and the methods of administration and scoring. The method of investigation designed was found to be quite appropriate and effective for the study.

4

Analysis of the Data

INTRODUCTION

This chapter presents the results obtained from the analysis of data collected from the Engineering Colleges in Vellore District of TamilNadu, on two variables, namely Personality Disorders and Family Relationship. The data has been subjected to statistically treat and are given in the tabular form.

ANALYSIS OF THE DATA FOR PERSONALITY DISORDERS AND FAMILY RELATIONSHIP

HYPOTHESIS-I

There is no significant difference between boys and girls of Engineering College Students on their Personality Disorders.

TABLE 1

Showing Mean, S.D and Critical Ratio of boys and girls of Engineering College Students on their Personality Disorders

Type of personality	Gender	N	Mean	S.D.	SEMD	CR	LS
Paranoid	Male	200	6.70	1.74	0.12	2.29	0.05
	Female	50	6.17	1.35	0.19		
Depression	Male	200	4.22	0.98	0.69	2.89	0.01
	Female	50	3.82	0.85	0.12		
Manic	Male	200	6.20	1.27	0.09	0.45	N S
	Female	50	6.28	0.99	0.14		
Schizophrenia	Male	200	6.94	2.19	0.15	3.87	0.01
	Female	50	6.02	1.27	0.18		
Psychopathic	Male	200	13.43	2.35	0.167	0.19	N S
	Female	50	13.36	2.38	0.383		
Hysteric	Male	200	4.87	1.22	0.08	3.50	0.01
	Female	50	4.40	0.72	0.10		
Anxiety	Male	200	9.10	1.93	0.147	2.22	0.05
	Female	50	9.76	1.86	0.26		

From the above table 1 it is observed that the mean scores obtained by the male students in Paranoid, Depression, Schizophrenia, Hysteric tendency and Anxiety are higher than the female students and it is statistically proved. All the other Personality Disorders there is no significant difference occurred Hence hypothesis is partially accepted.

HYPOTHESIS-II

There is significant between boys and girls on the Family Relationship of Engineering College Students.

TABLE 2

Showing Mean, S.D and Critical Ratio of boys and girls of Engineering College Students on their Personality Disorders

Gender	N	Mean	SD	SEMD	CR	LS
Male	200	72.01	7.61	0.539	1.08	NS
Female	50	70.68	7.88	1.114		

From the above table 2 it is observed that the mean scores obtained by the male students are having better attachment to their family than the female students. But it is not statistically proved hence the empirical hypothesis rejected.

HYPOTHESIS- III

There is no significant difference between boys and girls of Engineering College Students belonging to nuclear and joint family on their Personality Disorders.

TABLE 3

Showing Mean, S.D and Critical Ratio of Engineering College Students

Type of personality	Type of Family	N	Mean	S.D.	SEMD	CR	LS
Paranoid	Nuclear	129	6.57	1.76	0.155	0.29	NS
	Joint	121	6.63	1.59	0.145		
Depression	Nuclear	129	4.13	0.99	0.087	0.01	NS
	Joint	121	4.14	0.94	0.086		
Manic	Nuclear	129	6.20	1.23	0.109	0.25	N S
	Joint	121	6.23	1.21	0.111		
Anxiety	Nuclear	129	9.05	1.97	0.174	1.50	NS
	Joint	121	9.42	1.88	0.172		
Schizophrenia	Nuclear	129	6.58	2.04	0.100	1.31	N S
	Joint	121	6.93	2.10	0.191		
Hysteric	Nuclear	129	4.80	1.14	0.101	0.43	NS
	Joint	121	4.74	1.15	0.105		
Psychopathic	Nuclear	129	13.51	2.25	0.198	0.66	NS
	Joint	121	13.31	2.47	0.225		

From the above table 3 it is observed that type of family has no influence on their Personality Disorders. Hence the empirical hypothesis rejected.

HYPOTHESIS-IV

There is significant influence between the students belonging to nuclear and joint family on their family relationship.

TABLE 4

Showing Mean, S.D and Critical Ratio of Engineering College Students

Type of Family	N	Mean	SD	SEMD	CR	LS
N	129	71.62	7.55	0.539	0.27	NS
J	121	71.88	7.84	1.114		

It is observed from the table 4 the students belonging to nuclear and joint family has no significant difference on their family relationship and hence the empirical hypothesis rejected.

HYPOTHESIS-V

There is significant difference on the type of Personality Disorders of engineering college students based on their mother occupations.

TABLE 5

Showing Mean, S.D and Critical Ratio of Engineering College Students

Type of personality	Type of Family	N	Mean	S.D.	SEMD	CR	LS
Paranoid	Housewife	186	6.51	1.64	0.121	1.32	NS
	Employed	64	6.84	1.76	0.221		
Depression	Housewife	186	4.06	0.95	0.070	2.11	NS
	Employed	64	4.35	0.96	0.121		
Manic	Housewife	186	6.25	1.25	0.092	0.88	N S
	Employed	64	6.10	1.12	0.141		
Anxiety	Housewife	186	9.29	1.95	0.143	0.82	NS
	Employed	64	9.06	1.90	0.238		
Schizophrenia	Housewife	186	6.72	2.03	0.149	0.37	N S
	Employed	64	6.84	2.22	0.277		
Hysteric	Housewife	186	4.80	1.18	0.087	0.63	NS
	Employed	64	4.70	1.03	0.129		
Psychopathic	Housewife	186	13.34	2.29	0.168	0.78	NS
	Employed	64	13.62	2.54	0.318		

From the above table 5 it is observe that mother's occupation has no influence on their Personality Disorders. Hence the empirical hypothesis rejected.

HYPOTHESIS-VI

There is significant difference on the type of family relationship of engineering college students based on their mother occupations.

TABLE 6

Showing Mean, S.D and Critical Ratio of Engineering College Students

	N	Mean	SD	SEMD	CR	LS
HW	186	71.88	7.87	0.578	0.49	NS
EM	64	7.35	7.09	0.887		

From the above table 6 it is observe that there is no significant difference occurred among the students studying in Engineering colleges based on their mother's occupations in their family relationship. So the empirical hypothesis rejected.

HYPOTHESIS-VII

There is significant difference of Personality Disorders among engineering college students based on their parental income.

TABLE 7

ANOVA for the different areas of Personality Disorders of Engineering College Students based on Parental Income

Type of personality	Source of Variance	Sum of Squares	Df	Sum of Mean Squares	F-ratio	LS
Paranoid	BSS	1.55	2	0.78	0.27	NS
	WSS	700.64	247	2.83		
	TSS	702.19	249			
Depression	BSS	2.37	2	1.18	1.27	NS
	WSS	229.72	247	0.93		
	TSS	232.10	249			
Manic	BSS	24.09	2	12.04	8.53	0.01
	WSS	348.80	247	1.41		
	TSS	372.90	249			
Anxiety	BSS	1.66	2	0.83	0.21	NS
	WSS	934.88	247	3.78		
	TSS	936.54	249			
Schizophrenia	BSS	2.82	2	1.412	0.32	NS
	WSS	1071.29	247	4.337		
	TSS	1074.11	249			
Hysteric	BSS	6.29	2	3.14	2.40	0.05
	WSS	323.16	247	1.30		
	TSS	329.45	249			
Psychopathic	BSS	20.55	2	10.27	1.85	NS
	WSS	1366.18	247	5.53		
	TSS	1389.73	246			

It is observed that from the above table 7 Manic and Hysteric tendency have significant difference have been acquired, but all the other Personality Disorders there is no significant difference based on their parental income. Thus Empirical hypothesis is accepted for manic and hypothesis tendency and rejected for other areas of Personality Disorders.

Further analysis is done to find out the income group difference for Manic and Hysteric Disorders.

HYPOTHESIS-VIII

There is significant difference of family relationship among Engineering College Students based on their parental income.

TABLE 8

ANOVA for the different areas of Family Relationship of Engineering College Students based on Parental Income

Source of Variances	Sum of Squares	Df	Mean of Squares	F-ratio	LS
BSS	93.31	2	46.65	0.791	NS
WSS	14569.80	247	58.98		
TSS	14663.12	249			

It is observed that from the above table 8 that there is no significant difference between parental income groups on their family relationship of Engineering College Students. Thus empirical hypothesis rejected.

HYPOTHESIS-IX

There is significant difference on the type of Personality Disorders of engineering college students based on their father's occupations.

TABLE 9

ANOVA for the different areas of Personality Disorders of Engineering College Students based on Father's Occupation

Type of personality	Source of Variance	Sum of Squares	Df	Sum of Mean Squares	F-ratio	LS
Paranoid	BSS	15.70	3	5.235	1.87	NS
	WSS	686.48	246	2.790		
	TSS	702.19	249			
Depression	BSS	0.871	3	0.290	0.30	NS
	WSS	231.22	246	0.940		
	TSS	232.100	249			
Manic	BSS	20.08	3	6.69	4.66	0.01
	WSS	352.81	246	1.43		
	TSS	372.90	249			
Anxiety	BSS	5.89	3	1.966	0.51	NS
	WSS	930.64	246	3.783		
	TSS	936.54	249			
Schizophrenia	BSS	6.694	3	2.23	0.51	NS
	WSS	1067.42	246	4.33		
	TSS	1074.11	249			
Hysteric	BSS	2.599	3	0.86	0.65	NS
	WSS	326.85	246	1.32		
	TSS	329.45	249			
Psychopathic	BSS	21.71	3	7.23	1.30	NS
	WSS	1365.02	246	5.54		
	TSS	1386.73	249			

It is observed that from the above table 9 for the Personality Disorders areas Manic has occupied a significant difference between the students belonging to fathers who are employed. All the other areas Personality Disorders no significant difference has been required. Thus the empirical hypothesis is accepted for manic area and rejected for other of Personality Disorders.

HYPOTHESIS-X

There is significant difference on the type of family relationship of engineering college students based on their Father's occupation.

TABLE 10

ANOVA for the different areas of Family Relationship of Engineering College Students based on Father's Occupation

Source of Variances	Sum of Squares	Df	Mean of Squares	F-ratio	LS
BSS	227.46	3	75.82	1.29	NS
WSS	14435.65	246	58.68		
TSS	14663.12	249			

It is observed that from the above table 10 there is no significant difference acquired among the students studying in engineering colleges based on their father's occupations in their family relation. Thus the empirical hypothesis rejected.

HYPOTHESIS-XI

TABLE 11

Showing Correlation Co-efficient of Personality disorders and Family Relationship of Engineering College Students

Type of Personality	Family Relationship	L.S.
Paranoid	0.098	N S
Depression	0.028	N S
Manic	0.111	N S
Anxiety	0.084	N S
Schizophrenia	-0.074	N S
Hysteric	-0.045	N S
Psychopathic	0.036	N S

From the above table 11 it is observe that the computed correction coefficient between Personality Disorders and family relationship show no relationship. From this we can conclude family relation may not show any significant relation with the various type of Personality Disorders.

TABLE 12

Showing Correlation Matrix for the Personality Disorders scores

	Paranoid	**Depression**	**Manic**	**Anxiety**	**Schizophrenia**	**Hysteric**	**Psychopathic**
Paranoid	-						
Depression	0.3694xx						
Manic	0.2643xx	0.2458xx					
Anxiety	0.0425	-0.03460	0.0359	0.0425			
Schizophrenia	0.0776	0.1152	0.0591	-0.1175	0.0776		
Hysteric	0.0070	0.1296x	0.0466	-0.2413xx	0.3317xx		
Psychopathic	0.0020	0.2193xx	0.1212	0.1210	0.1560x	0.1055	-

Inter correlation between various Personality Disorders have been Personality Disorders have been computed and it is given in the above table 11. It is observe from the table 12. Correlation between paranoid Vs depression, paranoid Vs Manic, Depression Vs Manic, Schizophrenia Vs Hysteric showed significant relation between these variables positive on the other hand Anxiety and Hysteric shows negative relation. This categories show 0.01 level of significant. The variables Hysteric Vs Depression, Psychopathic Vs Schizophrenia shows positive correlation it is significant level 0.05 level.

CONCLUSION

A brief report of the research study together with interpretation is given here. The conclusion arrived at, along with their educational implications have been presented in the succeeding chapter.

5

Summary, Findings and Conclusion

INTRODUCTION

A brief summary of the study, stating the problem, the objective, the methodology and the major findings are presented in this chapter. The implications of the study are then discussed, suggesting a few areas for further.

STATEMENT OF THE PROBLEM

Personality Disorders and Family Relationship among Engineering College Students.

OBJECTIVES OF THE STUDY

1. To find out the significant difference between boys and girls of Engineering College Students on their Personality Disorders.
2. To find out the significant difference between Personality Disorders and Family Relationship of Engineering College Students.
3. To find out the significant difference between boys and girls of Engineering College Students belonging to nuclear and joint family on their Personality Disorders.

4. To find out the significant difference between the students belonging to nuclear and joint family on their Family Relationship.
5. To find out the significant difference on the Personality Disorders of Engineering College Students based on their mother's occupation.
6. To find out the significant difference on the Family Relationship of Engineering College Students based on their mother's occupation.
7. To find out the significant difference of Personality Disorders among Engineering College Students based on their parental income.
8. To find out the significant difference of Family Relationship among Engineering College Students based on their parental income.
9. To find out the significant difference on the type of Personality Disorders of Engineering College Students based on their father's occupations.
10. To find out the significant difference on the type of Family Relationship of Engineering College Students based on their Father's occupation.
11. To find out the significant relationship between home relation and Personality Disorders of Engineering College Students.

HYPOTHESIS

1. There is no significant difference between boys and girls of Engineering College Students on their Personality Disorders.
2. There is significant difference between Personality Disorders and Family Relationship of Engineering College Students.
3. There is no significant difference between boys and girls of Engineering College Students belonging to nuclear and joint family on their Personality Disorders
4. There is significant difference between the students belonging to nuclear and joint family on their Family Relationship.
5. There is significant difference on the Personality Disorders of Engineering College Students based on their mother's occupation.

6. There is significant difference on the Family Relationship of Engineering College Students based on their mother's occupation.
7. There is significant difference of Personality Disorders among Engineering College Students based on their parental income.
8. There is significant difference of Family Relationship among Engineering College Students based on their parental income.
9. There is significant difference on the type of Personality Disorders of Engineering College Students based on their father's occupations.
10. There is significant difference on the type of Family Relationship of Engineering College Students based on their Father's occupation.
11. There is significant relation between home relation and Personality Disorders of Engineering College Students.

METHODOLOGY

To Verify the hypothesis the following tools were used

1. Multiphase Personality Questionnaire by H.N.Murthy
2. Index of Family Relations by Walter W.Hudson

These tools were administrated among 250 Engineering College Students.

MAJOR FINDINGS

1. It is observed that the mean scores obtained by the male students in Paranoid, Depression, Schizophrenia, Hysteric tendency and Anxiety are higher than the female students and it is statistically proved table 1.
2. It reveals that the mean scores obtained by the male students are having better attachment to their family than the female students. But it is not statistically proved table 2
3. It is concluded that type of family has no influence on their Personality Disorders table 3.
4. It is observed that students belonging to nuclear and joint family have no significant difference on their Family Relationship table 4.

5. It is reveals that mothers occupation has no influence on their Personality Disorders table 5.
6. It is found that there is no significant difference occurred among the students studying in Engineering colleges based on their mother's occupations in their Family Relationship table 6.
7. It is concluded that Manic and Hysteric tendency have significant difference have been acquired, but all the other Personality Disorders there is no significant difference based on their parental income table 7
8. Family income has no influence on the home relation of Engineering College Students table 8.
9. It is inferred that from the above table 4.9 for the Personality Disorders areas manic has occupied a significant difference between the students belonging to father's who are employed. All the other areas Personality Disorders no significant difference have been required table 9.
10. It is concluded that from the above table 4.10 there is no significant difference acquired among the students studying in Engineering Colleges based on their father's occupations in their Family Relationship table 10
11. It is found that the computed correction coefficient between Personality Disorders and Family Relationship show no relation table 11
12. Inter correlation between various Personality Disorders have been Personality Disorders have been computed and it is given in the table 11. It is observe from the table 12. Correlation between paranoid Vs depression, paranoid Vs Manic, Depression Vs Manic, Schizophrenia Vs Hysteric showed significant relation between this variables positive on the other hand Anxiety and Hysteric shows negative relation. This categories show 0.01 level of significant. The variables Hysteric Vs Depression, Psychopathic Vs Schizophrenia shows positive correlation it is significant level 0.05 level.

EDUCATIONAL IMPLICATIONS

Personality refers to the total quality of an individual our education institution or very much involved to development integrity personality. The curricular and co-curricular activities are focused on developing good relationship with the family as well as different social groups. If there is any quality development of personality it create certain Personality Disorders as well as Psychotic deviation as for as this study is concerned main Engineering College Students shows Depression Anxiety, Paranoid and Hysteric tendency, it denotes that these people should have given proper Psychotic guidance. Otherwise their personality development attachment with the family other social groups and community will be effected. Ultimately the society will suffer a lot also Engineering colleges which gives counseling will not be an effective one. So the education as well as Psychologist should take effective necessary steps to develop good relationship as well as integrated personality.

SUGGESTIONS FOR FURTHER RESEARCH

1. This study may be conducted among arts and science students.
2. A cross cultural study may be conducted taking the variables personality adjustment behavior among self concept and Family Relationship among women students may be conducted.
3. Personality level of aspiration and Anxiety youngest at the school level may be conduct.

CONCLUSION

The purpose of the present investigation was to study Personality Disorders and Family Relationship among Engineering College Students. The study is sure find some usefulness in the field of education and findings of the study can serve as a database for further research.

5. Self Acceptance and Locus of Control

1

Introduction

Education is a lifelong process that begins at birth and continues throughout our life. Knowledge or information is nothing but the experiences based on the sense of perception. The bodily faculties that give an ability to gain experience in this universe are called senses, viz. the senses of sight, hearing, smell, taste and touch. It is during this educational life many of the adolescents face different problem. To lead a secure life everyone needs to adjust with the present environment and have the ability to control effectively. In order to arrive at such a level of positive interaction the individual needs to possess a positive self acceptance of himself during their educational period requires their ability of accepting himself as he is in order to live effectively and dynamically with the environment.

Adolescence is a period when the students need proper motivation to reach the goals set in the academic field. Thus motivation is closely related to locus of control. The focus on the two types of locus of control would enable the adolescence to develop the right mode of thinking leads to positive self-acceptance.

Adolescence is generally regarded as a period of great stress and strain. It is so because of the nature of the physical and mental development during the period. Adolescence is normally a period between 13 and 19 or 20 years of age. Some psychologists are of the view that it starts from twelfth year and stretches up to 21 or 23 years of age. Mostly the students between the age 14 to 16 or 17 are called teenagers and the educational system categories them as High school students ranging from VIII, IX and X standard. Some adolescents talk amongst themselves about their need of earning money. One will say 'he have no love for school'. The other will reply 'he deeply love school'. It indicates that their tastes, interests and aptitudes vary. The main problem of adolescents are overzealous, idealists and fame-hungry, impatient behavior, adverse effect of elders policy of double standard. But posing the factors of their failure on others especially on fate is high among the High school students.

DEFINITION OF SELF ACCEPTANCE

According to **Wayne Dyer,** "Self Acceptance means liking the entire physical you, and eliminating those cultural impositions to be proper or to merely tolerate your body when it behaves other than in a cosmetic fashion".

According to **Jersild (1963),** the sum total of a person's view of what he wishes he were or think he ought to be, as distinguished from what he is generally is called **self acceptance**. The adolescent's self acceptance has many facts, It includes aspirations he is vigorously striving to attain, or hopes dimly some day to relays.

According to **Roger** (1951), self-acceptance comprises what the person would like to be or holds out as a goal for individual development and achievement.

Garrison et al, (1967) says the term self acceptance has been shown to be valuable in determining the relationship between how the child sees himself and what he thinks he should be like. The self acceptance begins when the child identifies with as parental figure. During middle childhood and early adolescence it moves through a stage of romantics and glamour and culminates in the late adolescence as a composite of desirable characteristics which may be symbolized by an attractive, real and visible young adult or perhaps even an imaginary person.

Hilgar (1971) expressed that the self consists of all the ideas, perceptions and values that characterize 'I' and 'me' It includes the awareness of ' what I am and what can do'.

Garrison et al (1967) says that the person who accepts himself is guided by his own standard. He has insight and understanding in relation to his ability, worth and in relation to others. In order to be able to accept himself, a person must have a Self Concept which is realistic and which is not too different from his ideal of what he should be the Self Accepting person is familiar with his weakness. He recognizes those that he cannot change, those he must accept and live with. Such a person approves himself with his deficiencies and self acceptance promotes self evaluations. Such a person can be critical about himself and has sense of responsibility for his actions. He don't blame others or destiny for his condition. Nor does he strive to put up a show in order to win the approval of others.

Sheerer (1949) in his study on the acceptance in the following manner.

(a) To perceive one's self as a person of worth, worthy of respect rather than condemnation

(b) To perceive one's standards as being based upon his own experience rather than the attitudes or desires of others.

(c) To perceive one's own feelings, motives and personal experience without distraction of the sensory data. It is found that if an individual thinks well of himself, he is likely to think well of others and a person who is highly Self Accepting also accepts others ideas and guidance.

THE CONCEPT OF SELF-ACCEPTANCE

Self-Acceptance is love and happy with who you are now. Some call it **self-esteem**, others **self-love**, but whatever you call it, you'll know when you are accepting yourself cause it feels great. It's an agreement with yourself to appreciate, validate, accept and support who you are this very moment, even those parts you'd like to eventually change.

Self Acceptance is one of the influencing factors of personality to determine the quality of one's behavior. Self-Acceptance is the fullest description of oneself of which a person is capable of at one time.

No one, not even the greatest in any field, in the wildest imagination possible is born with a Self Acceptance. Self Acceptance is something that is developed through countless learning experiences as the child interacts with others and with his environment, as he discovers himself, a he becomes aware of what he is capable of doing and what he cannot do.

PROCESS OF ACCEPTANCE

Acceptance exists at the care of your being. It is your default status. In order to reach this base level of acceptance, you need only remove the items lying on top. To do this you must first identify all the things you do not accept about yourself. Then one by one eliminate them by examining and questioning your beliefs around the issue.

* Know yourself and your beliefs.
* Take a good hard look at your honesty level.
* Know you are doing the best you can.
* Relax your value judgments.
* Examine guilt.
* Understand your motivations.
* Ask yourself questions about what you don't accept.

SELF ACCEPTANCE AND ADOLESCENTS

Adolescence is the period when one thinks about one's own identity physical, intellectual, emotional and moral aspects that influence the development of one's self.

It is more difficult for girls to formulate a clear and accepting view of their feminine identity than it is for boys, to accept their masculinity. In their upbringing there is more incentive for boys to prefer to be boys than for girls to prefer to be girls. Boys have more privileges they are less strictly supervised, they are not judged as severely as girls for misconduct, they move in to a man's world very smoothly.

The masculine gender looks forward to an occupation and financial independence as a necessity in life than the feminine gender. As girls reach and advance through adolescence, the major occupation many of them look forward to his marriage and motherhood. It has been found that with increasing age boys become more secure in their masculine role whereas the girls become less firmly identified with their feminine role. This paves the way for the masculine and feminine gender to develop a positive self-acceptance.

MOTIVATION BEHIND THE ACCEPTANCE

Acceptance is a concept that sounds positive and also provides opportunities for positive development within an individual, but generally acceptance of self becomes difficult as adolescence do not look at themselves with a positive approach. The necessity for motivation becomes a driving force behind the concept of self acceptance.

The high school level of the student population requires a positive self acceptance to improve their achievement motivation. Motivation directs the Self Acceptance of the students. The Locus of Control, level of aspiration and their strength of need freely influence it. Internal locus of control may not improve their Self Acceptance but on the other hand. External locus of control has a direct influence on their self acceptance. Self acceptance plays a key role on academic achievement.

LOCUS OF CONTROL

Originally developed within the framework of **Rotter's (1954)** Social learning theory, the Locus of Control construct refers to the degree to which an individual believes the occurrence of reinforcement is contingent on his or her own behavior. The factors involved with reinforcement expectancy are labeled "external" and "Internal" control. In short, internal locus of control refers to the perception of positive or negative events as being a consequence of one's own actions and thereby under one's own personal control. In contrast, external locus of control believes that her behavior is guided by fate, luck. A locus of control orientation is a belief about whether the outcome of our actions is contingent on what we do (internal control orientation) or on events outside our personal control (external control orientation) **(Zimloardo, 1985)**.

Thus the locus of control is conceptualized as referring to a undimensional continuum ranging from external to internal.

INTERNAL LOCUS OF CONTROL

Individual bclicvcs that his/her behavior is guided by his/her personal decisions and efforts.

EXTERNAL LOCUS IF CONTROL

Individual believes that his/her behavior is guided by fate, luck, or other external circumstances.

The locus of control is a concept in psychology, originally developed by **Julian Rotter** in the **1950's**.The Locus of Control represents how a person's decision-making ability is influenced, essentially those who make choices primarily on their own are considered to have internal locus of control. People with external locus of control are generally more apt to be stressed and suffered due to depression as they are more aware of work situations since those who make decisions based more on what others think are said to have external locus of control. Women tend to have more external locus of control than men. Having an internal locus of control can also be referred to as "Personal control" or "Self - determination".

HISTORY OF LOCUS OF CONTROL

The locus of control construct originated from social learning theory, though the groundwork for his theory was laid by **Fritz Heider (1958).** According to social learning theory, the potential for any given behavior to occur is function of the individual's expectancy that the behavior will be effective in securing a desired end or reinforcement.

Social learning theory attempts to explain the person's selection of specific responses from a larger repertoire in predicting behavior in social settings. Although social learning theory evolved from associationistics and instrumental conditioning theories, it encompasses a wide range of behavior determinants including personality, motivation and situational context. Within this frame work, Rotter developed the concept of Locus of control.

Heider's speculations were refined and formalized also by Weiner, Frieze, Reed, Rest and Rosenbaum (1971). Weiner described the elements in the kinds of explanations individuals use to account for their performance. The internal versus external dimension of behaviors is known as locus of control orientation.

Internals believe that the reinforcements they receive are primarily a result of their own behavior, ability, effort or characteristics. Individuals at the external end of the locus of control continuum attribute the control of their reinforcements to force outside themselves, such as luck, chance, fate or powerful others.

Individuals may learn to attribute to themselves greater control over their own behavior and view themselves as agents who can affect the world, rather than as passive objects being victimized by environmental commands. This fact is one of the focal issues of the **Bandura's (1977)** self-efficiency theory. Self-efficiency is one's perceived capacity to meet some challenge or perform a particular response.

According to **Rose (1981),** teachers with a generalized expectancy of internal control perceive classroom events as being a consequence of their own actions and under their personal control. Teachers with an expectancy of external control perceive little contingency between their actions in the class room and student behavioral outcomes. The degree of contingency expected by individuals between their behavior and its effect has been conceptualized by Rotter as the personality dimension Internal - External (I-E) Locus of Control.

According to **Brown Autry and Langenback (1985),** the Locus of Control construct is an element of attribution theory. Attribution theory is associated with the investigation of the perception of causality, the judgment of why a particular incident occurred.

THE CONCEPT OF LOCUS OF CONTROL

The essence of the Locus of Control concept is that each of us located the controlling elements in our lives either inside or outside ourselves. The person who believes that he can decide for himself what he will do or be that he is the 'captain of the soul'. Locates his control internally and the person who believes that what happens to him is largely a matter of luck or who depends on the decisions of other is locating his control externally. The Locus of Control construct originated from **Rotter's (1966)** social learning theory. So the concept of Locus of control is rather a recent origin. Many of the Psychologists are interested in this idea and a number of studies are going on in this new field.

DEFINITIONS OF LOCUS OF CONTROL

According to **Roddin** Considerable attention has been devoted to this construct since the **1980**s, because many mental and physical outcome variables have been identified that depend largely on the extent to which the individuals actually are and even more importantly - perceive themselves to be in control of their lives and of the resources needed to make meaningful decisions about their life circumstances **(Rodin et al.,)** It has been argued that as adults age they experience an increasing number of life events over which they have little or no control.

TYPES OF LOCUS OF CONTROL

A number of researches have been conducted to find out whether Locus of Control is a too broad term. They have suggested that it might be better to breakdown the concepts internal and external into component parts. **Levenson (1973)** for instance, maintains that externals may be of two different sorts, people who believe the world as disordered (that things happen by chance) and people who believe the world as ordered but luck decides the fate or result.

Researchers have developed a test that distinguishes between the internals who take responsibility primarily for his success and the internals who blame himself for his failures. These two types have been shown to follow different developmental courses and to have differences in the classroom situation.

INTERNAL LOCUS OF CONTROL

If one person perceives that an event or achievement is contingent on his own behaviors or his own relatively permanent characteristics, he is termed to have internal control.

Here he assumes that he is the master of his fate and the captain of his soul. He thinks he can do what he wants to do and achieve results by his own efforts. Such people have internal locus of control.

CHARACTERISTICS OF INTERNAL LOCUS OF CONTROL

1. Internals are more likely to seek information
2. They are more sensitive and alert
3. Internals pay more attention to relevant cues, when there are uncertainties in the situation.
4. They show more incidental learning
5. They are more responsive to information requirements.
6. Internals pursue goals by paying careful attention to demands of the taste.
7. They sct realistic goals and take responsibility for their actions.

EXTERNAL LOCUS OF CONTROL

When the subject as following some action of his own, but not being entirely perceives reinforcement contingent on his action, then it is typically perceived as the result of luck, fate, etc. When the events are interpreted or attributed in this way by an individual, this signifies the belief in external control.

If one believes that his ability and his skill would not make much difference because luck and other people will govern the outcome of his efforts. He is said to have external locus of control.

CHARACTERISTICS OF EXTERNAL LOCUS OF CONTROL

1. Externals are more suspicions to social influences and social demands.
2. They pursue goals by relying more on behavior-oriented outcomes towards the social agent in the situation.
3. They are not ready to take the responsibility of their actions.

LOCUS OF CONTROL Vs EDUCATION

It has often been said that obtaining a good education is the key to being successful in the world. Many things may contribute to school achievement and one variable that is over looked is locus of control. In the context of education, locus of control refers to the types of attributions are makes for reaching success and/or failure in school tasks. If someone believes that his or her successes and failures are due to the factors within their own control such as effort or ability, then that person is said to have an internal locus of control. On the other hand if someone believes that his or her successes and failure are due to factors outside of their own control, such as fate, luck, then person is said to have an external locus of control.

MODIFICATION OF STUDENTS LOCUS OF CONTROL

Attribution training, which concentrates on strengthening the students' internal locus of control **(Deshler, Schumacher & Lenz, 1984)** may be helpful in increasing motivation. Attribution training has been shown to increase internal locus of control and improve task persistence **(Shelton, Anastopoulos & Linden, 1985).** Usually the implementation of attribution training utilizes some form of self instructional set of statements. Students are trained to say positive things to themselves, first out loud, then in a whisper, then silently to themselves. This type of training is easy to implement & requires no special materials. For some students, attribution training can have a considerable impact on their overall efforts at school. When students are struggling or not putting forth much effort, it would be wise to consider locus of control as a possible contributor to the problem. A teacher's effort to motivate a student may prove futile, the child has external locus of control. Teaching children from a young age that hard work can pay off would be beneficial. If they were taught to believe in their own ability to control their lives and the reinforcements in their lives, they would be more likely to succeed in school.

DEVELOPMENT OF LOCUS OF CONTROL

Generally, the development of locus of control stems from family, culture and past experiences leading to rewards. Most internals have been shown to come from families that focused on effort, education, and responsibility. On the other hand, most externals come from families of a low socioeconomic status where there is a lack of life control.

NEED AND SIGNIFICANCE OF THE STUDY

The study of self acceptance and locus of control among high school students is very important. This study may help us to diagnose the psychological problem faced by the students. Mostly the students are lack in their personality. Self acceptance is one of the main variable of personality which is taken for this study. And every person especially the students need some type of motivation to reinforce their attitude. Hence locus of control is one of the main variable of motivation which is also considered for this study. Our present society shows positive signs of self-empowerment. Our adolescent population have also empowered themselves to meet the exclusive challenges in the Society.

Viewing the state of their self acceptance the adolescent needs to be encouraged in the educational field, to think for themselves, act rationally and reach the goals they have set. The adolescents of our present time need to face problems and demand which needs to be tackled effectively. The school and the family provide the support and Guidance for there. The individual himself should learn to acquire self-confidence and self-acceptance.

Adolescence is the most crucial and significant period of an individual's life. It represents the culmination of childhood and an initiation of the adult who is to be. In this stage, human personality develops new dimensions. It is the period to learn new things. It is the period of anxiety and worries. Adolescents are tightly ambitions. They will develop so many desires and ambitions to be filled. Despite their best planning and efforts they may not get the desired success. At times they find themselves in a state of utter confusion and bewilderment. All the paths for face repeated failures that lead them to distances. The main significant of Self Acceptance is once you truly accept yourself, you will waste no energy or time on self deception or deceiving others and you will develop clarity as to just what needs improving.

As everyone know, generally in an educational setting knowledge flows from the teacher to the student. This type of environment could cause students to withdrawn. It is suggested that students take more of an active control in the learning process. It is also important to take into consideration whether each student has an external or internal locus of control.

STATEMENT OF THE PROBLEM

Self Acceptance and Locus of control among High School students in Tiruvallur District.

DEFINITION OF THE TERMS

a) Self acceptance

Self acceptance is one of the influencing factors of personality as it governs the individual's reaction towards people and situations and determines the quality of one's behavior.

Self-Acceptance as measured through this inventory in an assessment of factors such as sense of personal worth and satisfaction with self.

b) Locus of Control

Locus of control refers to an individual's generalized expectations concerning where control over subsequent event resides. In other words, who or what is responsible for what happens.

OPERATIONAL DEFINITIONS

a) Self Acceptation

Self Acceptance scores are obtained by administering self acceptance inventory constructed and standardized by **Kakkar, Patiala, 1984.**

b) Locus Control

Locus of control scores are obtained by administering Locus of control Scale constructed and standardized by **Stephen Nowicki, Strickland in 1973.**

OBJECTIVES OF THE STUDY

1. To study the level of self acceptance among High School students.
2. To Study the level locus of control among High School students
3. To find out the significant difference between boys and girls of High School students in their self Acceptance.
4. To find out the significant difference between boys and girls of High School students in their locus of control.
5. To find out the significant difference between different ages among High School students in their self acceptance.
6. To find out the significant difference between different ages among High School students in their locus of control.
7. To find out the Significant difference between the high School students studying in different management in their self acceptance.
8. To find out the Significant difference between the high School students studying in different management in their locus of control.
9. To find out the significant difference between joint and nuclear family of High School students in their self Acceptance.
10. To find out the significant difference between joint and nuclear family of High School students in their locus of control.
11. To find out the significant difference between rural and urban area High School students in their self acceptance.
12. To find out the significant difference between rural and urban area High School students in their locus of control.
13. To find out the Significant difference between English and Tamil Medium of High School students in their self acceptance.
14. To find out the Significant difference between English and Tamil Medium of High School students in their locus of control.
15. To find out the Significant Relationship of Self Acceptance and Locus of Control among High School students.

LIMITATIONS OF THE STUDY

* The sample is restricted to 300 students
* The study is restricted to High School students
* The study is limited to 5 Schools of Tiruvallur District.

CONCLUSION

The first chapter highlights the overview of the problem and the statement of the problem, need and significance of the study, objectives and limitations of the study.

A review of related literature is dealt in the chapter that follows.

2

Review of Related Literature

INTRODUCTION

The purpose of present investigation is to study the effect of Locus of control and Self Acceptance. A large number of studies have been carried out in the field of Locus of control. The research literature is reviewed under the following captions.

STUDIES RELATED TO SELF ACCEPTANCE

STUDIES ABROAD

Fuster's (1964) A Study on the relationship between Self Acceptance and acceptance of others among College Students.

According to Fuster, Self Acceptance implies the formation of a realistic Self concept which includes one's strength and weakness. Self Acceptance flows from that inner craving of waiting to be that person which is truly oneself. A fine feeling of being in this world for a propose which is fully within his reach and which is achieving gradually as the years roll by Self Acceptance should be developed in Children because it makes a person like comfortably with himself. Self Accepted Child adopts a realistic approach to life situation. Such a Child can develop a positive attitude towards life.

BAKER (1977) Studied the influence of psychological education to enhance Self-understanding and Self Acceptance in College Students.

The result shows that there is no demonstrated effect of the course on the participants Self Acceptance because these Students were the kind of people who improve without participating in this course. Baker's Study also emphasizes the need for psychological education to improve Self Acceptance in Adolescents.

HURLEY (1990) Studied the "Constructive thinking and elevated ratings of Self in interpersonal groups".

First they conducted the constructive thinking inventory (CTI) for one hundred and three university students. Results shows that constructive thinking and rating one's self above peers, especially, for acceptance of Self consistently correlated positively, suggesting an underlying sense of independence, From this study it is clear that constructive thinking can be inculcated in Children by proper Self Acceptance programme.

Fraley-Stephen-E. (1992) From Self-Blame to Self-Acceptance: Freeing Myself in a Prison Undergraduate Program.

A prison inmate who is a graduate psychology student reflects on how the study of social and behavioral sciences contributed to his moral and ethical growth.

Starn (1993) Studied Learning disabilities of male adolescents.

Thirty Seven 9th and 10th grade males from two suburban Midwestern School systems were administered the Californial psychological inventory (CPI) Self Acceptance taken as one of the variable. The data do not provide evidence that adolescents with learning disabilities experience greater dependence and greater isolation and loneliness than their non-learning disabled peers. Correlation showed that there is a significant relation between Self Acceptance and their disabilities.

Statman-Daniel (1993) Studied Self-Assessment, Self-Esteem, and Self-Acceptance.

Discusses students' self-esteem is best improved through self-acceptance rather than by comparisons with others. Argues that some comparisons are essential to the concept of self and therefore are important to self-esteem. Concludes that some students may have low self-esteem because they accurately assess their abilities with others.

Randolph, Elizabeth (1993) Developed Self-Awareness and Self-Acceptance in Emotionally Handicapped Students through the Bibliotherapeutic Process.

This practicum involved the development, implementation, and evaluation of a program which used a bibliotherapeutic approach to develop specific behaviors with three second graders and seven fifth graders, all in a resource program for students with emotional handicaps. A needs assessment survey of mainstream teachers identified needs in the following areas: responsibility, cooperation, conflict resolution, and truthfulness. Although projected goals were not met, individual students made gains in each area. Students experienced attitude changes, improved self-concepts, and more realistic awareness of objective areas. Items in the appendix include the student contract, target behavior survey, the data collection chart, and critical thinking questions.

Mills-Brett-D. (1993) studied the Rehabilitation Counseling for Athletes Prior to Retirement: A Preventative Approach Using Self-Acceptance To Enhance Performance before and after Retirement.

This study suggests that collegiate and professional athletes preparing to retire should be provided with pre retirement and postretirement rehabilitation counseling. The counseling should involve a preventative approach centered around self-acceptance, to enhance the athlete's performance before and after retirement. The development of self-acceptance in an athlete helps him or her to experience less competitive cognitive anxiety. Questions are presented that athletes can ask themselves to examine their level of self-acceptance and that coaches can ask themselves to determine their enhancement of athletes' self-acceptance. Counselors are encouraged to provide empathy and support, break the problem into manageable parts and develop a plan to tackle those parts, and determine the athlete's internal and external strengths and resources.

Yuan,-Frances (1994) studied that moving toward self-acceptance among Students with Learning Disabilities.

This study describes a course developed at Lesley College (Massachusetts) to help students with learning disabilities accept their disability and develop self-understanding and self-advocacy skills. It describes the course model and major tenets, highlights some course components, and summarizes results of a study of the courses impact.

CHROMIC (1996) Studied the level of acquisition of Self advocacy attribution within a group of High School students with learning disabilities after being exposed to an instructional unit developed to teach Self - advocacy skills.

The subjects were high school students (10th - 12th) with learning disabilities who were receiving services within transition resource classes. The conclusion was that seven week Self advocacy unit was not powerful enough to effect a change in the self advocacy attributes of the students as measured by the CPI qualitative data. Results indicated that most students were able to identify individual strengths and weakness, but were able to describe effectively the nature of their disability.

FREDERICK, VERDINE J (1997) Studied the relationship among acceptance of a learning disability grade level at diagnosis and achievement of students with learning disabilities.

The study sample consists of fifty high schools. Only students whose records indicated that they had been designated as learning disabled by a board of education, special education, team were considered for participation. The tools were given to each of the 50 learning disabled students in their schools. The findings demonstrate that lower the students grade level when a diagnosis of a learning disability is determined, the greater the students Self Acceptance of his or her learning disability.

BRILL (1999) Studied Self Acceptance and a heightened sense of emotional vulnerability.

The transition period from child to adult arrives the adolescents' intense need for emotional security in the form of acceptance by peers. Throughout life emotional needs and fear are interpreted differently. Helpless infants have a moral fear of living abandoned. At childhood, our emotional security requires contribute reassurance of our lovability and acceptability. In adolescence, this core emotional needs become Focused upon Self and social acceptance. The unbearable emotional distress leads the adolescence to a variety of destructive behavior patterns, some may become self-destructive, some may express in anger and violence. Self Acceptance makes a person emotionally balanced. Self accepted person can be well adjusted with the peers and society.

LEVON (2001) Studied Self Acceptance as the ability to see and recognize all aspects of self without judgment, either positive or negative.

Self Acceptance is not about living or approving one's self. It is simply about being aware of all of the parts of the self. It is about being awake and fully conscious. He also says that increase of self acceptance increase the raw material at disposal. It is about adding and expanding. It is the contrasts, conflicts, inconsistencies and polarities in life that make it interesting and awesome.

SIM T.N. (2003) Studied Father and mother linkage in relation to adolescent academic and athletic competence and self worth.

A total of 140 Singapore undergraduates reported on themselves and their parents. Results indicate that some adolescent attributes exist only when mother's characteristics are considered. The link between father's responsiveness and athletic competence existed only when mother's responsiveness was high and that link between father's acceptance of individualization and athletics competence existed only when mother's acceptance of individualization was moderate or high.

STUDIES IN INDIA

ARORA (1981) Studied the problems of students in professional courses of medicine, law, engineering and education in relation to personality factors.

In this study Self Acceptance was taken as one of the variable. A student's problem checklist consisting of 10 areas were administered to a sample of 800 boys & girls preparing for the first professional degree in medicine, law, engineering and education. Result shows that high problem students in general, found to have lower personality adjustment, lawer creative persons, and higher level of aspirations, and high Self Acceptance than low problem students.

WAHEEDA (1989) Studied the behavioral training in improving personality characteristics of juvenile delinquents in relation to Self Acceptance.

The sample was drawn from Government Special Home for boys at Chengelpet and Government special home for girls at Kilpauk, Madras, run by Government of Tamil Nadu. The samples were chosen by administering kakkar's Self Acceptance inventory to a group of 50 male and female delinquents. The samples were given Jerner's personality inventory to assess the personality characteristics of the juvenile delinquents. His major findings were that the high self acceptance experimental low acceptance group, no significant difference was found in both the high Self Acceptance and low self acceptance group among males and females and the high self acceptance group showed improvement in a social index whereas the low self acceptance group had no improvement.

Sunanda. Y. (1991) conducted a study of reaction of frustration as related to life satisfaction and self acceptance among the aged.

The objective is to relate frustration reaction to the acceptance of age- linked changes. The 'Sample comprised under middle age (40-49 years) advanced middle age (50-59 years) young old (60-69 years) and old age (70+ years). The tools used included frustrations reaction of life satisfaction. Scale, Jamuna and Ramamoorthy is Assessment of self acceptance and a bio-data schedule. The collected data was subjected to statistical analysis. Mean, S.D, 't' test, correlation and analysis of variance was calculated. He found that self acceptance among the aged was positively related to life satisfaction.

BHARADWAJ (1998) Studied Parental rejection, acceptance and adolescent value conflict.

In a sample of 500 adolescents by employing a two group design. Tools used were parenting scale constructed and standardized by Bharadwaj et al. and value conflicts scale constructed and standardised by Bharadwaj.

STUDIES RELATED TO LOCUS OF CONTROL

STUDIES ABROAD

Guss,-Thomas (1990) Studied Integrating Underemployment and Hardship: Using Locus of Control To Develop a Profile among Married Men. The role of marital issues and individual characteristics in hardship, and the emphasis in the literature of the traditional provider role, there is a need to explore the experience of underemployment among married men. only husbands were selected for this project. A random sample of a non-metropolitan northwest community produced 137 couples with a variety of incomes.. Husbands in hardship were more oriented to chance, while non hardship providers were more internal. Results suggest that locus of control is a distinguishing characteristic among married men.

Thompson,-Josephine-T.(1991) Established the Locus of Control among Ninth Graders: Using Peer Mentors To Reduce Student Disengagement, Absenteeism, and Failures.

An intervention program was implemented to reduce absences, stimulate responsibility for assignments, and increase participation in extracurricular activities among disengaged ninth-grade students (N=18). Mentors felt the greatest benefits were showing disengaged students that someone cares and that if attitudes toward school could be improved needless failures and dropouts could be prevented.

Martin,-Janice-E.; et. al . (1991) Studied the relationship among Internal-External Locus of Control and Rational-Irrational Beliefs.

The study investigated the relationship between Internal-External Locus of Control Scale and Irrational Beliefs Test (IBT) scores. The independent variable was locus of control, the dependent variables were IBT full-scale and subscale scores. Data were collected through administering these instruments to state human service agency employees (N=105). Statistical analyses indicated that there was a significant correlation between internal-external locus of control and IBT full-scale scores and that there were significant correlations between internal-external locus of control and 8 out of 10 IBT subscale scores. Internal locus of control subjects exhibited more rational beliefs. Likewise, external locus of control subjects maintained more irrational beliefs.

Hipps,-Elizabeth-Smith; Halpin,-Glennelle (1991) Studied Job Stress, Stress related to performance-based accreditation, Locus of Control, Age, and Gender As Related to Job Satisfaction and Burnout in Teachers and Principals.

The purpose of the study described here was to: (1) determine the amount of variance in burnout and job satisfaction in public school teachers and principals which could be accounted for by stress related to the state's performance-based accreditation standards; (2) examine the relationship between stress related to state standards and the age and gender of the educators; and (3) develop measures of educator job stress common to both teachers and principals and stress related to the state performance-based accreditation standards. Surveys were sent to teachers (N=445) and principals (N=128). Responses were received from 219 teachers and 58 principals.

Whitney,-Patricia (1991) Studied Children's Locus of Control and Intrinsically Motivated Reading.

Study investigated the relationship between locus of control and intrinsically motivated reading for children. To find the hypothesis that students with an internal locus of control would be more productive readers than those with an external locus of control, a matched sample was drawn. The t-test for matched samples and the Pearson product-moment both indicated non-significant differences between intrinsic motivation of internal and external subjects. The t-test for matched samples and the Pearson product-moment both indicated non-significant differences between intrinsic motivation of internal and external subjects. The most revealing factor was that the students felt they were "too busy" for free-choice reading. To find the hypothesis that students with an internal locus of control would be more productive readers than those with an external locus of control, a matched sample was drawn. The t-test for matched samples and the Pearson product-moment both indicated non-significant differences between intrinsic motivation of internal and external subjects.

Evans,-Jan-Holmgren (1991) Studied The Relationship between Internal Locus of Control and Rehabilitation Prognosis.

Studies involve the subject groups selected and the indexes of outcome, as well as the manipulation of treatment, structures cause limited general ability. Different studies contradict each other probably too frequently for strictly scientific purposes. The importance of internal locus of control on the rehabilitation process of any illness or disability tends to have numerous methodological problems. Questionnaires exist that measure a person's internal locus of control, however, that extra inner essence of a person defies scientific exploration and measurement.

Ayersman,-David-J. (1992) Studied the effect of a Summer Enrichment Program for At-Risk Youths on Locus of Control and the Relation to Motivational Orientation.

Examining locus of control, and showing an effective treatment program for transitioning from externality to internality, it may be possible to predict other behaviors and eliminate negative behaviors (drug use, low self-esteem, poor grades) associated with externality which will assist in keeping children in school. This study examined the relationship between locus of control and motivation. Statistical significance was also found by age and gender with younger females being the most external and older males being the most internal. A moderate negative correlation was found linking one of the five motivation subscales (independent judgment) with locus of control.

Thompson,-Bruce; et.al.(1992) Studied the Nature of Children's Health Locus of Control Beliefs.

The study was to explore the structure of the health locus of control beliefs of children, using the Multidimensional Health Locus of Control Scales. People's beliefs about the origins of their health, sometimes referred to as health locus of control, have been shown to influence a variety of important behaviors. Two samples of 4th- through 6th-grade students were utilized to allow for cross-validation of results. The first group had 780 subjects, the second group had 524 subjects. Confirmatory methods were employed in this study.

Martin,-Janice-E.; et.al (1992) Studied the effects of internal-external Locus of Control and Selected Demographic Variables on Rational-Irrational Beliefs.

This study evaluated whether or not locus of control mediates rational-irrational beliefs. Results support the view that internally oriented individuals maintain more rational beliefs than do externally oriented people. Nine tables present study data. Data were generated investigating the impact of an internal-external orientation and selected demographic variables (age, race, gender, education, and occupation) on rational-irrational beliefs. Independent variables were locus of control and demographic characteristics, and the dependent variable was beliefs. Data were collected by administering the Internal-External Locus of Control Scale and the Irrational Beliefs Test to 105 state human service agency employees (81 internals and 24 externals). A one-way analysis of variance uncovered significant differences in internal and external females. In addition, there were significant differences in beliefs between internal and external subjects at different educational levels.

Sisco,-Sharon-S. (**1992**) Using Goal Setting To Enhance Self Esteem and Create an Internal Locus of Control in the At Risk Elementary Student.

Study examined the effects of a program designed to enhance the self-esteem of at-risk students by developing an internal locus of control in the students. The Piers-Harris Children's Self-Concept Scale was administered as a pretest and posttest, providing the data from which the discrepancy gap for showing improvement in self-esteem was formulated. The program consisted of six major components: (1) a specified vocabulary and format; (2) goal identification and description by students; (3) student evaluation and selection of alternative actions to accomplish goals; (4) student journal writing showing reflective evaluation and identification of successful and unsuccessful behaviors; (5) a scale to evaluate student goals; and (6) peer encouragement through class meetings. Results indicated that students' self-esteem improved and fewer severe behavior referrals were necessary. However, attendance was not significantly affected. Related materials are appended.

Freedman,-Susan-A. (1992) Studied Sex, Gender and Locus of Control in College Students.

Study was undertaken to examine the relationship between locus of control and gender role. Locus of control has most frequently been measured using Internal versus External measures. A non significant trend for the interaction of sex by locus of control was found. Findings further indicated that Internal locus of control may be over-represented in some college populations.

Enger,-John-M.; et.al (1993) Studied Internal/External Locus of Control and Parental Verbal Interaction of At-Risk Adolescent Black Males.

The academic and discipline problems of young black male students in a small southern town, the Positive Impact Program (PIP) was developed for at-risk black males. Two possible at-risk factors, locus of control and the quality of parental verbal interaction, were studied for participants in the PIP. Locus of control and communications with parents were compared to those of previously normed groups. The Verbal Interaction Questionnaire (developed by P. C. Blake in 1991) scores were comparable to those for rural predominantly white male and female high school students. In general, students more internally controlled reported having more positive parental verbal communication, while those more externally controlled had more negative parental verbal communication. Eighteen of the 42 boys were in the PIP, but no significant differences were found for these students on either measure, and no locus of control scores were available from the period before PIP participation.

Bernhard,-Judith-K.; Siegel,-Linda-S. (1994) Increasing Internal Locus of Control for a Disadvantaged Group: A Computer Intervention.

Discussion of locus of control (LOC), gender, and mathematics and technical subjects focuses on a study of preschool girls and boys

Highlights include treatment of experimental and control groups; gender differences; parent questionnaires; and pretests and posttests.

Reeh,-H.-Elise; Reilly,-Karen-J. (1995) A Quasi Meta Analysis of the Health Locus of Control Construct.

The study about the Internal HEALTH LOCUS OF CONTROL (HLOC) is related to health-promoting behavior, positive health status, health knowledge, information-seeking, and treatment success. The results of this analysis indicate that HLOC research is primarily conducted in the United States by a fairly even distribution of male and female researchers, who are often members of psychology faculties. Studies are mostly published in psychology journals, with some research appearing in medical journals. These studies have included a wide variety of participants, including hospital patients, employees, school children, and university students. HLOC research is generally of an applied nature, and is most often correlational in design.

Fournier,-Genevieve; St-Onge,-Susan (1995) Studied about the Shaping Vocational Locus of Control through Beliefs.

Presents a survey of rudimentary results, and proposes a typology of vocational beliefs. Presents a synthesis of the theoretical foundations implemented in an investigation of the principal vocational beliefs of individuals having difficulty with their career choice. Suggests principles of intervention to help young adults facing difficulty in career decisions

Hawkes,-Brent-B (1995) Studied Locus of Control in Early Childhood Education This study discusses research on locus of control, particularly as it relates to early childhood education. Some measures of children's sense of locus of control are discussed, including the Optimism-Pessimism Test Instrument and the Stanford Preschool Internal-External Scale. Factors which inhibit the assessment of children's sense of locus of control are detailed, including: (1) lack of development of children's vocabulary and communication skills; (2) children's tendency to select the last possible answer offered in a structured interview situation; (3) children's tendency to respond "yes" to yes or no questions; and (4) the prevalence of a research bias which assumes that elementary school children do not have well-developed self-awareness. The review concludes by noting that locus of control appears to be an important element of children's experiences and potential success in school.

Tyler,-Doris-Kennedy; Vasu,-Ellen-Storey (1995) Studied Locus of Control, Self-Esteem, Achievement Motivation, and Problem-Solving Ability: LogoWriter and Simulations in the Fifth-Grade Classroom.

The effects of using LOGO, or problem-solving- oriented simulation software on locus of control, self-esteem, and achievement motivation for fifth-grade students. The importance of these variables in predicting LOGO mastery and far-transfer problem-solving ability was also examined.

Santa-Rita,-Emilio (1995) Studied the Effect of Computer-Assisted Student Development Programs on Entering Freshman Locus of Control Orientation.

To determine the effect of SUCCESS programs on students' perceived locus of control and empowerment study was conducted at New York's Bronx Community College of two entering freshmen classes in fall 1995 (n=35). The experimental class received six SUCCESS assignments over 14 weeks related to basic college survival information and calculations of grade point averages and financial aid data. The Nowicki-Strickland Internal-External Control Scale was administered to both groups at the beginning and again at the end of their first semester to determine differences in student sense of power versus helplessness, persistence with parents in achieving goals, and perception of luck as a determinant in obtaining goals. Comparison of pre- and post-test scores for both groups indicated that students who completed the SUCCESS assignments did not shift significantly with respect to overall perceived control of reinforcement and there were no significant differences between the experimental and control groups' sense of persistence with parents. The SUCCESS students did however perceive luck as having a considerably lesser effect on the attainment of desired outcomes than the control group

Cook,-Ann; Troike, Roger (1995) Studied Adolescent Parenting: Contrasts in Self-Esteem and Locus of Control.

Of the 17,051 women who become pregnant every day in America, 2,795 or 16% of them are adolescents. The self-esteem and locus of control of 85 pregnant and parenting teens enrolled in the Ohio Graduation, Reality, Dual Role Skills (GRADS) Program were measured and compared to the scores of 85 non-parenting peers. Self-esteem was measured using Rosenburg's Self-Esteem Scale. Locus of control was measured by Rotter's Internal-External Locus of Control

Scale. No significant differences in the mean scores were discovered. This supported the assumption that involvement in the GRADS Program allowed pregnant and parenting teens to retain a level of self-esteem and locus of control equivalent to their non-parenting peers. The results of this study substantiate the worth of in-school support groups for high risk adolescents.

STUDIES IN INDIA

PANI, MINA (1991) Studied the effect of culture and locus of control.

The performance among 40 tribal and 40 non-tribal Indian students in grade 3. Both tribal and non-tribal students were divided into internal Vs external locus of control groups. Reading task included both oral comprehension and several met linguistic tasks. The poorest performance was evidenced by tribal students and students with external locus of control.

SAEEDUZZAFAR AND SHARMA, RAMA (1991) Studied the effect of religion (Hinduism and Islam) on locus of control and dependence proneness among externally oriented and internally oriented individuals.

The results showed that Muslim students were more dependent prone than Hindu Students. Externally oriented students were more depended than internally oriented students. However, the interactional effect of religion and locus of control was insignificant.

CONCLUSION

The survey of the related literature has helped much to have a proper perspective of the problem chosen for the study. The review of related literature has enabled the investigator to formulate relevant literature also resulted in providing insight into the selection and use of effective methods of study, analysis and interpretation.

3

Design of the Study

INTRODUCTION

This chapter describes in detail, the design of the study, nature and selection of sample, a brief description of the tools of investigation and the criteria for their investigation. It also gives a description of the procedure adopted for the collection of data, for its scoring and classification, finally the proposed statistical treatment of the data for testing the hypothesis that were formulated are explained.

HYPOTHESIS

The following hypotheses have been set for the present study

1. The level of Self Acceptance among High School Student is Average.

2. The internal locus of Locus of Control is predominant among High School Student

3. There is a significant difference between boys and girls of High School students in their self acceptance.

4. There is a significant difference between boys and girls of High School students in their locus of control.

5. There is a significant difference between different ages among High School students in their self acceptance.

6. There is a significant difference between different ages among High School students in their locus of control.

7. There is a significant difference between the high School students studying in different management in their self acceptance.

8. There is a significant difference between the high School students studying in different management in their locus of control.

9. There is a significant difference between joint and nuclear family of High School students in their self Acceptance.

10. There is a significant difference between joint and nuclear family of High School students in their locus of control.

11. There is no significant difference between rural and urban area High School students in their self acceptance.

12. There is no significant difference between rural and urban area High School students in their locus of control.

13. There is a significant difference between English and Tamil Medium of High School students in their self acceptance.

14. There is a significant difference between English and Tamil Medium of High School students in their locus of control.

15. There is a significant relationship of self acceptance and locus of control among High School students.

Tools and materials used

To test the hypotheses, two inventories were used for the present investigation viz., Self Acceptance inventory and Locus of control inventory.

THE SELF ACCEPTANCE INVENTORY

The Self Acceptance inventory constructed and standardized by **Dr.Kakkar (Patiala, 1984)** was used in this study. It consists of 34 statements with positive and negative statements. The nature of items of Self Acceptance Inventory has been presented below.

TABLE 1

Showing the nature of the items of self acceptance inventory

S.NO	NATURE OF ITEM	ITEM NUMBER
1.	True	3,6,9,11,13,15,16,19,22,23,24,25,28, 30,33,34
2.	False	1,2,4,5,7,8,10,12,14,17,18,20,21,26,27

ADMINISTRATION

The following instructions were given to the students before administrating the inventory. The purposc of this questionnaire is to detect the type of Self Acceptance students have about themselves. There are 34 items in the questionnaire. The subjects were asked to read each statement carefully and respond by putting a tick on "True" column. If it is not applicable, put tick (x) on "False" column.

SCORING

For one correct answer, one score is provided according to key. Scoring through a template is also possible where circles which show through the template are counted and the total entered in the proper cell of the last page is treated as raw score.

LOCUS OF CONTROL INVENTORY

The Locus of Control Inventory constructed and standardized by **Stephen Nowicki and Strickland in 1973** was used in this study. It consists of 40 statements. The nature of items of Locus of Control has been presented below.

TABLE 2

Showing the nature of the items of locus of control inventory

ADMINISTRATION

S.no	Nature of item	Item number
1.	Yes	1,3,5,7,8,10,11,12,14,16,17,18,19,21,23,24, 27,29,31,33,35,36,37,39
2.	No	2,4,6,9,13,15,20,22,25,26,28,30,32,34,38,40

The following instructions were given to the students before administrating the inventory. The purpose of this questionnaire is to detect the type of Locus of Control students have about themselves.

There are 40 items in the questionnaire. The subjects were asked to read each statement carefully and respond by putting a tick on "Yes" or "No" in all the responses.

SCORING

For one correct answer, one score is provided according to the key. The total number of agreements between the answers and the ones on the key is a raw score.

PILOT STUDY

A pilot study was conducted to assess the reliability of the tools. Pilot study also helped in understanding the difficulties faced by the subject in answering the questionnaires. The pilot study was conducted on 50 students to assess the reliability and validity.

RELIABILITY OF THE TOOLS

The Reliability Coefficient of The Self Acceptance Inventory Has Been Computed by Using the Odd Even Method. The Reliability Coefficient was Computed by **Spearman Brown** Formula. Obtaining A Value f 0.747 Indicating, That the Tool was Highly Reliable.

The reliability coefficient of the Locus of Control has been computed by using the odd even method. The reliability coefficient was computed by **Spearman Brown** formula obtaining a value of 0.866 indicating, that the tool was highly reliable

VALIDITY OF THE TOOLS

The validity of the score was calculated by taking the square root of reliability. In the case of Self Acceptance inventory it is found to be 0.864, also suggesting that tool is valid. In the case of Locus of Control inventory it is found to be 0.93 indicating that the tool is valid.

SAMPLE

A stratified random sampling technique was adopted for the selection of sample. The school selected for this study is divided into different strata, namely Government, Aided and Private schools. 300 students were taken for the study.100 students were drawn from Government schools, 100 from Aided schools and 100 from Private schools.

TABLE 3

Showing The Composition Of The Sample Selected For The Study Of Gender, Type Of School, Medium Of Instruction And Locality Of School.

S. No	NAME OF THE SCHOOL	GENDER		TYPE OF SCHOOL			MEDIUM		LOCALITY OF SCHOOL	
		Boys	**Girls**	**Govt**	**Aided**	**Private**	**English**	Tamil	**Urban**	**Rural**
1.	**Govt. welfare boys Hr.Sec school, Sevvapet.**	47		47				47		47
2.	**Govt. welfare girls Hr.Sec school, Sevvapet**		53	53				53		53
3.	**Siddhartha Matriculation school, Sevvapet**	34	16			50	50			50
4.	**Gnana vidyalaya matric school, Tiruvallur**	12	38			50	50		50	
5.	**Goudie Hr.Sec school,Tiruvallur**	77	23		100		50	50	50	50
Total		**170**	**130**	**100**	**100**	**100**	**150**	**150**	**100**	**200**

MAIN STUDY

Permission was sought from the respective heads of the institution and explanation was given regarding the purpose and nature of the study. After having fixed the day and time for the distribution of questionnaire, the investigator administered the questionnaire to the sample of students selected standard VIII, IX and X.

The students were gathered in a classroom and the purpose of the investigation was explained to them. The nature of the questions and the method of answering were explained. Total confidentiality of views was assured in a bid to stimulate the students to answer freely. They were made to feel one with the purpose of the investigation. More instructions were given on the first page of the questionnaire.

STATISTICAL TECHNIQUES

Suitable descriptive and inferential statistical techniques were used in the interpretation of the data to draw more meaningful pictures of results from the collected data. In the present study the following statistical techniques were used.

- MEAN.
- STANDARD DEVIATION.
- CRITICAL RATIO.
- ANALYSIS OF VARIANCE.
- CORRELATON COEFFICIENT.
- QUARTILE DEVIATION.

CONCLUSION

This chapter outlines the design of the present study, the procedure followed and the nature of the sample. It describes the hypotheses to be tested, the tools used and method of administration and scoring.

4

Analysis and Interpretation of the Data

INTRODUCTION

Analysis of data means studying the tabulated material in order to determine the facts or meanings. The data, after collection has to be processed and analyzed in accordance with the outline laid down for the purpose at the time of developing the research plan. This is essential for a scientific study and for ensuring that we have all relevant data for making contemplated comparisons and analysis. After analyzing the data the researcher has to accomplish the task of drawing inferences followed by report writing.

ANALYSIS AND INTERPRETATION OF THE DATA:

The data collected was subjected to statistical calculations and the hypotheses formulated have been verified.

1. Descriptive statistics to understand the nature of Self Acceptance and Locus of control.
2. 't' test to find out the significant difference of Self Acceptance with respect to location, medium of instruction, gender. And same for the other variable Locus of control.

3. ANOVA to find out the significance of difference for self acceptance and Locus of control with respect to age, type of school.
4. Correlation to find out the relationship between Self Acceptance and Locus of control.

Hypothesis – I

The level of Self Acceptance among High School Student is Average.

TABLE 1

Shows the frequency and percentage for the variable self acceptance.

CATEGORY	*RANGE*	*FREQUENCY*	PERCENTAGE
Low self acceptance	Below 14	57	19 %
Moderate self acceptance	From 14- 18	191	63.36%
HIGH SELF ACCEPTANCE	Above 18	52	17.3%

From the above table, it is clear that more number of students lie in the category of moderate self acceptance (63.36%). So the level of self acceptance among high school students is moderate in nature. Hence the above hypothesis is accepted.

Hypothesis –II

The internal locus of Locus of Control is predominant among High School Student.

TABLE 2

Showing the frequency and percentage for the variable locus of control

CATEGORY	RANGE	FREQUENCY	PERCENTAGE
Average locus of control	Below 22	27	9%
High locus of control	Above 22	273	91%

From the above table, it is clear that more number of students lie in the category of high locus of control. So the level of locus of control among high school students is external in nature. Hence the above hypothesis is rejected.

Hypothesis –III

There is a significant difference between boys and girls of High School students in their self Acceptance

TABLE 3

Significance of difference in the self acceptance means scores of high school students based on their gender

VARIABLE	GENDER	N	MEAN	SD	C.R	L.S
Self	Male	170	17.10	2.72	1.221	N.S
Acceptance	Female	130	16.68	3.12		

From the above table, C.R value (1.22) which is lesser than the table value (1.96). Hence there is no significance difference between the male and female students of high school on their self acceptance. Therefore the above hypothesis is rejected.

Hypothesis–IV

There is a significant difference between boys and girls of High School students in their locus of control.

TABLE 4

Significance of difference in the self acceptance means scores of high school students based on their gender

VARIABLE	GENDER	N	MEAN	SD	C.R	L.S
Locus of	**Male**	170	21.30	3.01	3,487	0.01
control	Female	130	20.05	3.13		

From the above table, C.R value (3.487) is greater than the table value (2.58). Hence there is a significance difference between the male and female students of high school on their self acceptance. Therefore the above hypothesis is accepted.

Hypothesis–V

There is a significant difference between different ages among High School students in their self acceptance.

From the above table it is clear that self acceptance of high school students of different ages has significant difference. So it is consider for further analysis.

TABLE 5

Showing the significant difference of self acceptance with respect to their different ages among high school students.

VARIABLE		SUM OF SQUARES	DF	MEAN SQUARES	F value	L.S
Self Acceptance	Between groups	54.845	2	27.423		
	Within groups	2466.071	297	8.303	3.305	0.05
	Total	2520.917	299			

TABLE 6

Showing the significance difference of ages of high school students for self acceptance.

VARIABLE	AGE	N	MEAN	SD	SEM	C.R value	L.S
Self acceptance	14 yrs	115	16.86	2.91	0.37	0.832	N.S
	15 yrs	117	16.54	2.95			
Self acceptance	15 yrs	117	16.54	2.95	0.426	2.629	0.01
	16 yrs	68	17.66	2.71			
Self acceptance	14 yrs	115	16.86	2.91	0.426	1.877	N.S
	16 yrs	68	17.66	2.71			

From the above table, the C.R value is found to be significant difference in the Self Acceptance of high school students with respect to 15 and 16 years of age. So in these group only the hypothesis is accepted. In other groups table value shows no significance. So the hypothesis is partially accepted.

Hypothesis –VI

There is a significant difference between different ages among High School students in their locus of control.

TABLE 7

Showing the significant difference of locus of control with respect to their different ages among high school students.

VARIABLE		SUM OF SQUARES	DF	MEAN SQUARES	F value	L.S
Locus of control	Between groups	5.779	2	2.889		
	Within groups	2904.941	297	9.781	0.295	N.S
	Total	2910.917	299			

The above table value reveals that the obtained 'f' value is lesser than the table value indicating no significant difference of Locus of control with respect to ages. Hence the hypothesis is rejected.

Hypothesis –VII

There is a significant difference between the high School students studying in different management in their self acceptance.

TABLE 8

Showing the significant difference of self acceptance with respect to their type of management among high school students.

VARIABLE		SUM OF SQUARES	DF	MEAN SQUARES	F value	L.S
Self Acceptance	Between groups	30.427	2	15.213		
	Within groups	2490.490	297	8.385	1.814	N.S
	Total	2520.917	299			

The above table value reveals that the obtained 'f' value is lesser than the table value indicating that the type of schools has no significant difference of self acceptance. Hence the hypothesis is rejected.

Hypothesis –VIII

There is a significant difference between the high School students studying in different management in their locus of control.

TABLE 9

Showing the significant difference of locus of control with respect to their type of management among high school students.

VARIABLE		SUM OF SQUARES	DF	MEAN SQUARES	F value	L.S
Locus of control	Between groups	66.140	2	33.070		
	Within groups	2844.580	297	9.578	3.453	0.05
	Total	2910.720	299			

From the above table value it is clear that type of schools has significant difference in Locus of control of high school students. So it is considered for further analysis.

TABLE 10

Showing the significance difference between different type of management with respect to locus of control among high school students.

VARIABLE	TYPE OF SCHOOL	N	MEAN	SD	SEM	C.R value	L.S
Locus of control	Private	100	20.77	3.83	0.478	1.17	N.S
	Aided	100	21.33	2.87			
Locus of control	Aided	100	21.33	2.87	0.374	3.06	0.01
	Govt	100	20.18	2.41			
Locus of control	Private	100	20.77	3.83	0.451	1.30	N.S
	Govt	100	20.18	2.41			

From the above table, the C.R value is found to be significant indicating that there is significant difference in the Locus of control of high school students with respect to their Aided and Government schools. So in these groups only the hypothesis is accepted. In other groups table value shows no significance. So the hypothesis is partially accepted.

Hypothesis–IX

There is a significant difference between joint and nuclear family of High School students in their self Acceptance.

TABLE 11

Significance of difference between self acceptances means scores of high school students based on their type of family.

VARIABLE	TYPE OF FAMILY	N	MEAN	SD	C.R	L.S
Self Acceptance	**Joint**	139	16.83	2.23	0.47	N.S
	Nuclear	161	16.99	2.97		

From the above table, C.R value (0.47) is lesser than the table value (1.96). Hence there is no significance difference between the type of family of high school on their self acceptance. Therefore the above hypothesis is rejected.

Hypothesis –X

There is a significant difference between joint and nuclear family of High School students in their locus of control.

TABLE 12

Significance of difference between locus of control means scores of high school students based on their type of family.

VARIABLE	TYPE OF FAMILY	N	MEAN	SD	C.R	L.S
Locus of control	**Joint**	139	21.02	3.23	1.35	N.S
	Nuclear	161	20.53	3.02		

From the above table, C.R value (1.35) is lesser than the table value (1.96). Hence there is no significance difference between the type of family of high school on their locus of control. Therefore the above hypothesis is rejected.

Hypothesis –XI

There is no significant difference between rural and urban area high School students in their self acceptance.

TABLE 13

Significance of difference between self acceptance mean scores of high school students based on their location.

VARIABLE	LOCATION	N	MEAN	SD	C.R	L.S
Self Acceptance	Rural	200	16.68	2.42	1.78	N.S
	Urban	100	17.40	3.66		

From the above table, C.R value (1.78) is lesser than the table value (1.96). Hence there is no significance difference between the self acceptance of high school students on the basis of location. Therefore the above hypothesis is accepted.

Hypothesis –XII

There is no significant difference between rural and urban area High School students in their locus of control.

TABLE 14

Significance of difference between locus of control means scores of high school students based on their location.

VARIABLE	LOCATION	N	MEAN	SD	C.R	L.S
Locus of control	Rural	200	20.78	2.98	0.15	N.S
	Urban	100	20.72	3.40		

From the above table, C.R value (0.15) is lesser than the table value (1.96). Hence there is no significance difference between the locus of control of high school students on the basis of their location. Therefore the above hypothesis is accepted.

Hypothesis -XIII

There is a significant difference between English and Tamil Medium of High School students in their self acceptance.

TABLE 15

Significance of difference between self acceptance means scores of high school students based on their medium of instruction.

VARIABLE	MEDIUM	N	MEAN	SD	C.R	L.S
Self	**Tamil**	150	16.48	2.26	2.62	0.01
Acceptance	**English**	150	17.35	3.38		

From the above table, C.R value (2.62) is greater than the table value (2.58) at 0.01 level. Hence there is a significance difference between the English and Tamil medium high school students on their Self acceptance mean scores, English medium scores (17.35) being higher than Tamil medium scores (16.48). Therefore the above hypothesis is accepted.

Hypothesis -XIV

There is a significant difference between English and Tamil Medium of High School students in their locus of control.

TABLE 16

Significance of difference between locus of control mean scores of high school students based on their medium of instruction.

VARIABLE	MEDIUM	N	MEAN	SD	C.R	L.S
Locus of	**Tamil**	150	20.40	2.65	2.008	0.05
control	**English**	150	21.12	3.50		

From the above table, C.R value (2.008) is greater than the table value (1.96) at 0.05 level. Hence there is a significance difference between the English and Tamil medium high school students on their Locus of control mean scores. Therefore the above hypothesis is accepted.

Hypothesis -XV

There is a significant relationship of self acceptance and locus of control among High School students

TABLE 17

Shows the correlation between self acceptance and locus of control among high school students.

VARIABLE	N	CORRELATION COEFFICIENT	L.S
SELF ACCEPTANCE Locus of control	300	-0.0241	N.S

The above table shows that there is no significant relationship between self acceptance and locus of control. Hence the above hypothesis is rejected.

CONCLUSION

The above analysis clearly shows that there is no significant relationship between the self acceptance and locus of control. The analysis and interpretation of data represent the application of deductive and inductive logic to the research process. The data are often classified by division into subgroups and then analyzed and synthesized in such a way that hypotheses may be verified or rejected. The final result may be a new principle of generalization. Like interpretation of results, the formulation of conclusion and generalizations also demands keen observations, wide look and power of logical thinking. A brief report of the present research study together with major findings and conclusions has been presented in the succeeding chapter.

5

Summary, Findings and Conclusion

In this chapter we have tried to assimilate, what we have done so far in the previous chapter by reinstating the statement of the problem, tools used for investigation, about the samples and finally presenting the major findings of the study. In the light of the major findings some useful recommendations for improvements and suggestions for research are proposed.

STATEMENT OF THE PROBLEM

Self acceptance and locus of control among high school students in Tiruvallur district.

OBJECTIVES OF THE STUDY

1. To study the level of self acceptance among High School students.
2. To Study the level locus of control among High School students
3. To find out the significant difference between boys and girls of High School students in their self Acceptance.
4. To find out the significant difference between boys and girls of High School students in their locus of control.
5. To find out the significant difference between different ages among High School students in their self acceptance.

6. To find out the significant difference between different ages among High School students in their locus of control.
7. To find out the Significant difference between the high School students studying in different management in their self acceptance.
8. To find out the Significant difference between the high School students studying in different management in their locus of control.
9. To find out the significant difference between joint and nuclear family of High School students in their self Acceptance.
10. To find out the significant difference between joint and nuclear family of High School students in their locus of control.
11. To find out the significant difference between rural and urban area High School students in their self acceptance.
12. To find out the significant difference between rural and urban area High School students in their locus of control.
13. To find out the Significant difference between English and Tamil Medium of High School students in their self acceptance.
14. To find out the Significant difference between English and Tamil Medium of High School students in their locus of control.
15. To find out the Significant Relationship of Self Acceptance and Locus of Control among High School students.

HYPOTHESIS OF THE STUDY

1. The level of Self Acceptance among High School Student is Average.
2. The internal locus of Locus of Control is predominant among High School Student
3. There is a significant difference between boys and girls of High School students in their self Acceptance.
4. There is a significant difference between boys and girls of High School students in their locus of control.
5. There is a significant difference between different ages among High School students in their self acceptance.
6. There is a significant difference between different ages among High School students in their locus of control.

7. There is a significant difference between the high School students studying in different management in their self acceptance.
8. There is a significant difference between the high School students studying in different management in their locus of control.
9. There is a significant difference between joint and nuclear family of High School students in their self Acceptance.
10. There is a significant difference between joint and nuclear family of High School students in their locus of control.
11. There is no significant difference between rural and urban area High School students in their self acceptance.
12. There is no significant difference between rural and urban area High School students in their locus of control.
13. There is a significant difference between English and Tamil Medium of High School students in their self acceptance.
14. There is a significant difference between English and Tamil Medium of High School students in their locus of control.
15. There is a significant relationship of self acceptance and locus of control among High School students.

SAMPLE

The present study is concerned with High School Students. Random Sampling technique is used among the Government, Aided and Private Schools in Tiruvallur district. The investigator selected randomly two Government School, Two Private School and one Aided School. The sample composes of 300 High School students.

TOOLS USED

The following tools and techniques were used:

1. Self acceptance inventory. (Dr.Kakkar,Patiala, 1984)
2. Locus of control inventory. (Dr.Stephen Nowicki, Jr., and Dr.Strickland in 1973)

MAJOR FINDINGS

1. It is found that the level of self acceptance among High School students are average in nature.
2. It is found that the level of locus of control is high (external) in nature.

3. It is found that boys and girls of High School students has no significant difference in their self acceptance.
4. It is found that boys and girls of High School students has significant difference in their locus of control.
5. It is found that the different ages of High School students has significant difference in their self acceptance.
6. It is found that the different ages of High School students has no significant difference in their Locus of control.
7. It is found that the type of school of High School students has no significant difference in their self acceptance.
8. It is found that type of schools of high school students has significant difference in their locus control.
9. It is found that type of family of High School students has no significant difference in their self acceptance.
10. It is found that type of family of High School students has no significant difference in their local of control.
11. It is found that the locality of High School students has no significant difference in their self acceptance.
12. It is found that locality makes no significant difference in their locus of control
13. It is found that the medium of instruction of High School students has significant difference in their self acceptance.
14. It is found that the medium of instruction of High School students has significant difference in their locus of control.
15. It is found that self acceptance and locus control of High School students correlation is not significant.

EDUCATIONAL IMPLICATIONS

In the educational scenario it is found that the High School part of education in the schools are very significant milestone of a student. This is due to some psychological aspects like emotional, mental, physical changes of High School students. This change gives or paves the way for various problems. During the adolescent stage the students normally find it difficult to adjust with home, school, peer and social setting. They normally possess on unstable self-acceptance. Since the self acceptance is a personality variable the high school students must possess this in their behavior.

This study in self acceptance and locus of control of High School students will throw more light on the impact of self acceptance and locus of control in relation to their education. If the self acceptance is high locus of control also would be better and thus it is found that the students also learn and perform better in their school subjects. Further the students are well adjusted to the school and also develop good habits.

SUGGESTION FOR FURTHER RESEARCH

Some suggestions with regard to possibilities of the record in the field of education are offered with a view to stimulate prospective research works in this area. These are as follows:

1. Self-acceptance in relation to personality and different kinds of adjustment behavior such as personal adjustment, social adjustment etc., can be studied among High School students.
2. A study of self-acceptance and locus of control among the college students.
3. A study of self-acceptance and academic achievement could be conducted among higher secondary students.
4. A study of locus control and personality could be conducted among college students.
5. A study of self-acceptance and leadership behaviour of college students.

CONCLUSION

Self-acceptance plays a vital role in every human being. Self-acceptance requires consistency, stability, and tends to resist change. If self-acceptance changed readily, the individual would lack a consistent and dependable personality. Man is a social being thus self-acceptance helps him to understand the self and what other think about himself. When there is an available in self-acceptance it may tend to lead the locus of control. So they help man to live smoothly and at peace with one another. If the locus of control is not good then the person cannot live freely in the society especially in the present fast developing world. So it is extremely necessary to develop high self acceptance, which is turn, would positively complements locus of control.

References

1. **Arora R.K.,(1981)**, *"An investigation into the problems of study in professional courses of medicine law, engineering and education in relation to personality factors"*, Third survey of Research in Education, National Council of Educational Research and Training, p.105.

2. **Ayersman,-David-J. (1992)**, *" Effect of a Summer Enrichment Program for At-Risk Youths on Locus of Control and the Relation to Motivational Orientation"*.

3. **Baker, Eugene .M (1977)**, *" Psychological Education to enhance Self Understanding and Self Acceptance in college students"*, http://WWW.spd.org/sdp/diss

4. **Brill, Ronala .R,** *" Dealing with the hazards of adolescence'*,http://www.emotionalhonesty.com/arthazadoles.html

5. **Bharadwaj .R (1998)**, *" Perceived parenting of rejection – Acceptance and adolescents value conflicts"*, Indian psychological review, Vol L1 special issue p.256

6. **Bernhard,-Judith-K.; Siegel,-Linda-S. (1995)**, *" Increasing Internal Locus of Control for a Disadvantaged Group: A Computer Intervention"*.Journal: Computers-in-the-Schools; v11 n1 p59-77 1994

7. **Chromic Daria, Theresa (1996)**, *"The American Dream and Self advocacy for students with learning disabilities"*, Theory: Curriculum and Learner outcome, Dissertation Abstracts International DAI-A 57/08, p.3455.

8. **Chaube S.D, (1981)**, *"Adolescent Psychology"*, M/S Vikas Publishing house, New Delhi.

9. **Furnham, A. and Henry, J. (1980).** Cross-cultural locus of control studies: experiment and critique. Psychological Reports, 47, 23-29.

10. **Freud, S. (1900).** *The interpretation of dreams. In the complete psychological works of Sigmund Freud.* London: The Hogarth Press, 1962.

11. **Fraley,-Stephen-E. (1992)** From, *"Self-Blame to Self-Acceptance: Freeing Myself in a Prison Undergraduate Program"*. Journal-of-Correctional-Education; v43 n4 p178-81 Dec 1992

12. **Frederick, Veedine .j (1997)**, " *The relationship among acceptance of a learning disability, grade level of diagnosis and achievements of students with learning disabilities*", Dissertation abstract international, DAI –A 58/05, p.3083

13. **Garrison, Albert j, and Kingston (1976)**, Educational psychology, Bombay: Vakils, Feffer and Simons pvt. Ltd.,p.448

14. **Hurley, John .R (1990)**, " *Constructive thinking and elevated of self in interpersonal groups*", Journal of Psychology Vol. CXXIIV, No.5, pp.563-575.

15. **Jersild Arthur, (1963),** "*The Psychology of Adolescence*", New York, T.Macmillan company, p.63

16. **Kao, G. and Thompson, J. S. (2003).** Racial and ethnic stratification in educational achievement and attainment. In K.S. Cook and J. Hagan (Eds.), Annual Review of Sociology (Vol.29,pp.417-442). Palo Alto, CA: Annual Reviews.

17. **Krampen, G. and Weiberg, H. (1981**). Three aspects of locus of control in German, American, and Japanese university students. Journal of Social Psychology, 113, 133-134.

18. **Lynch, Shirley; Hurford, David P.; and Cole, AmyKay. (2002)** *Parental Enabling Attitudes and Locus of Control of At-Risk and Honors Students. Adolescence,* 37(147) 527- 549.

19. **Levon, Dirk (2001)**, "*Self Acceptance, Ace up your sleeve*", http://www.masermuse.com/columistsreylogs/archives/00000056

20. **Rotter, J.B. (1954).** Social learning and clinical psychology. Englewood Cliffs, NJ: Prentice Hall.

21. **Rotter, J. B. (1966).** Generalized expectancies for internal versus external control of reinforcement. Psychological Monographs: General and Applied, 80 (1, Whole No. 609).

22. **Rogers, C. R. (1947).** Some observations on the organization of personality. American Psychologist, 2, 358-368

23. **Randolph,-Elizabeth (1993)**, " *Developing Self-Awareness and Self-Acceptance in Emotionally Handicapped Students through the Bibliotherapeutic Process*".

24. **Reeh,-H.-Elise; Reilly,-Karen-J. (1995),** " *A Quasi Meta Analysis of the Health Locus of Control Construct*".

25. **Shelton, T. L., Anastopoulos, A. D., & Linden, J. D. (1985).** An attribution training program with learning disabled children. Journal of Learning Disabilities, 18, 261-265

26. **Sim T.N (2003)**, "The father – adolescent relationship in the context of the Mother – adolescent relationship, exploring moderating linkages in the late adolescent sample in Singapore", Journal of Adolescent Research,Vol XVIII, No.4, pp.383-403

27. **Sisco,-Sharon-S. (1992)**, "Goal Setting To Enhance Self Esteem and Create an Internal Locus of Control in the At Risk Elementary Student".

28. **Sheerer, Elizabeth (1949)**, "An analysis of the relationship between acceptance and respect for theself acceptance of and respect for others in ten counseling cases", Journal of counseling psychology, Volume XIII, pp.169-175.

29. **Sisco,-Sharon-S. (1992)**, *"Using Goal Setting To Enhance Self Esteem and Create an Internal Locus of Control in the At Risk Elementary Student"*.

30. **Sunanda Y (1991)**, *A study of reactions to frustration as related to life Satisfactions and self acceptance among the aged,* Ph.D Sri Venkateswara university IV survey, ii p.977

31. **Santa-Rita,-Emilio (1995)**, *" The Effect of Computer-Assisted Student Development Programs on Entering Freshman Locus of Control Orientation"*.CS: Bronx Community Coll., NY. Dept. of Student Development.

32. **Starn Richard Lic (1993),"***Californial Psychological inventory profiles of male adolescents with learning disabilities*", A comparison with norm group scores dissertation abstracts international DAI –A 54/04 p.296

33. **Statman,-Daniel (1993)**, *"Self-Assessment, Self-Esteem, and Self-Acceptance"*. Journal-of-Moral-Education; v22 n1 p55-62 1993

34. **Thompson,-Josephine-T. (1991)**, *" Establishing Locus of Control among Ninth Graders: Using Peer Mentors To Reduce Student Disengagement, Absenteeism, and Failures"*

35. **Thielker, V. et al**. *The relationship between positive reinforcement and locus of control.* [Electronic version]. Retrieved December 5, 2004, from

36. **Tyler,-Doris-Kennedy; Vasu,-Ellen-Storey (1995),** " *Locus of Control, Self-Esteem, Achievement Motivation, and Problem-Solving Ability: LogoWriter and Simulations in the Fifth-Grade Classroom*". Journal-of-Research-on-Computing-in-Education; v28 n1 p98-120

37. **Waheeda .M (1998)**, "*Behavioral Training in improving personality characteristics of Juvenile delinquents in relation to Self Acceptance*", M.Phil Thesis in Psychology, Madras University p.63.

38. **Whitney,-Patricia (1991),** " *Children's Locus of Control and Intrinsically Motivated Reading*".

6. Self-concept and Emotional Maturity

1

Problem and its Perspectives

INTRODUCTION

The best and most perfect creation of the Almighty is man. Shakespeare has described him as an angel, little lower than his creator. The main reason which makes him so, when biologically he does not differ much with monkeys or apes and other similar higher animals, lies in the fact that while the animal can only be trained, man can both be trained and educated. The man who does not have any education is no more different than an animal. It is the education which makes him the noblest and finest creation of the world.

Education is the process of living through a continuous reconstruction of experiences. It is the development of all those capacities in the individual which will enable him to control his environment and fulfil his possibilities.

Education of a human being should begin at birth and continue throughout his life. The main aim of education is to develop harmonious personality of the learner. Education is considered to be the most significant agent of basic change in the status of a human being besides occupation and economic status.

Education is as old as mankind. In every society ancient or modern, simple or complex, primitive or advanced, one finds provision for education. Without education, no society can last more than a generation. The function of education is considered to be the adjustment of man to his environment which means his adaptation and reconstruction of his surroundings for his own benefit and that of society.

So the school, as an agency of education is the training ground for the future citizen in the school. The student learns the process of creating new knowledge as an essential byproduct.

The aim of education is always two fold.

1. There is a collective aspect
2. There is an individual aspect

From the collectively point of view, education is expected to turn the individual into a good citizen, i.e., into a person who has harmonious relations with the other members of the community, who is useful to the society and who fulfils with zeal his obligation as a citizen.

Education will give to the individual a strong and healthy body, helps him in building up his character and attains self mastery and supply him with good opportunities of discovering and developing harmoniously his natural abilities.

Education must promote the well being of those being educated. Education brings out and develops the best in an individual. It leads to self - perfection or fulfillment and improvement of others. It seeks to develop an integrated holistic personality harmonising the head, hands and heart of a person each activated by the educational procedure. Thus the real development is the improvement of the self and the refinement of human perceptions.

Educational research is that activity which is directed towards development of a science of behaviour in educational situations. According to **Robert M.W. Travers** (1964), the ultimate aim of such a science is to provide knowledge that will permit the educator to achieve his goals by the most effective methods.

SELF-CONCEPT

Self is the conscious reflection of one's own being or identity, as an object separate from other or from the environment. Self-Concept is the cognitive thinking aspect of self and generally refers to "the totality of a complex, organised, and dynamic system of learned beliefs, attitudes and opinions that each person holds to be true about his or her personal existence" (**Purkey**, 1988).

HISTORY

A milestone in human reflection about the non - physical inner self came in 1644, when **Rene Descartes** wrote principles of philosophy. Descartes proposed that doubt was a principal tool of disciplined inquiry, yet he could not doubt that he doubted. He reasoned that if he doubted, he was thinking and therefore he must exist. Thus existence depended upon perception.

A second milestone in the development of Self-Concept theory was the writing of **Sigmund Freud** (1900) who gave us new understanding of internal mental processes. While Freud and many of his followers hesitated to make Self-Concept a primary psychological unit in their theories, **Anna** (1946) gave central importance to ego development and Self - interpretation.

Self-Concept theory has always had a strong influence on the emerging profession of counseling. **Prescott Lecky** (1945) contributed the notion that self - consistency is a primary motivating force in human behaviour. **Raimy** (1948) introduced measures of Self-Concept in counseling interviews and argued that psychotherapy is basically a process of altering the ways that individuals see themselves.

By far the most influential and eloquent voice in Self-Concept theory was that of **Carl Rogers** (1947) who introduced an entire system of helping built around the importance of the self. In Roger's view, the self is the central ingredient in human personality and personal adjustment. Rogers described the self as a social product, developing out of interpersonal relationships and striving for consistency. He maintained that there is a basic human need for positive regard both from others and from oneself. He also believed that in every person there is a tendency towards self - actualization and development so long as this is permitted and encouraged by an inviting environment (**Purkey and Schmidt,** 1987).

While most Self-Concept theorists continued to write and conduct research during the 1970s and 1980s, general interest in Self-Concept declined.

Fortunately, there is a new awareness on the part of both the public and professionals that Self-Concept cannot be ignored if we are to successfully address such nagging problems as drug and alcohol abuse, drop-out rates, dysfunctional families and other concerns. In addition to this growing awareness, new ways are being developed to strengthen Self-Concept. For example, research by cognitive theorists **McAdam,** (1986); **Ryan, Short and Weed,** (1986) are demonstrating that negative self-talk leads to irrational thinking regarding oneself and the world.

BASIC ASSUMPTIONS

Many of the successes and failures that people experience in many areas of life are closely related to the ways that they have learned to view themselves and their relationship with others. It is also becoming clear that Self-Concept has at least three major qualities of interest: (1) it is learned (2) it is organised and (3) it is dynamic.

Self-Concept is learned

As far as we know, no one is born with a Self-Concept. It gradually emerges in the early months of life and is shaped and reshaped through repeated perceived experiences, particularly with significant others. The fact that Self-Concept is learned has some important implications:-

* Because Self-Concept does not appear to be instinctive, but is a social product developed through experience, it possesses relatively boundless potential for development and actualization.
* Because of previous experiences and present perceptions, individuals may perceive themselves in ways different from the ways others see them.
* Individuals perceive different aspects of themselves at different times with varying degrees of clarity. Therefore, inner focusing is a valuable tool for counselling.
* Any experience which is inconsistent with one's Self-Concept may be perceived as a threat, and the more of these experiences, the more rigidly Self-Concept is organised to maintain and protect itself. When a person is unable to get rid of perceived inconsistencies, emotional problems arise.
* Faculty thinking patterns, such as dichotomous reasoning (dividing everything in terms of opposites or extremes) or over generalising (making sweeping conclusions based on little information) create negative interpretations of oneself.

Self-Concept is organised

Most researchers agree that Self-Concept has a generally stable quality that is characterized by orderliness and harmony. Each person maintains countless perceptions regarding one's personal existence, and each perception is orchestrated with all the others. It is this generally stable and organised quality of Self-Concept that gives consistency to the personality. This organised quality of Self-Concept has corollaries.

* Self-Concept requires consistency, stability, and tends to resist change. If Self-Concept changed readily, the individual would lack a consistent and dependable personality.
* The more central a particular belief is to one's Self-Concept the more resistant one is to changing that belief.
* At the heart of Self-Concept is the self - as - doer, the "I", which is distinct from the self - as object, the various "me's". This allows the person to reflect on past events, analyse present perceptions, and shape future experiences.
* Basic perceptions of oneself are quite stable, so change takes time.
* Perceived success and failure affect Self-Concept. Failure in a highly regarded area lowers evaluations in all other areas as well. Success in a prized area raises evaluations in other seemingly unrelated areas.

Self-Concept is dynamic

To understand the active nature of Self-Concept, it helps to imagine it as a gyrocompass: a continuously active system that dependably points to the "true north" of a person's perceived existence. This guidance system not only shapes the ways a person views oneself, others, and the world, but it also serves to direct action and enables each person to take a consistent "stance" in life. Rather than viewing Self-Concept as the cause of behaviour, it is better understood as the gyrocompass of human personality, providing consistency in personality and direction for behaviour.

* The world and the things in it are not just perceived, they are perceived in relation to one's Self-Concept.
* Self-Concept development is a continuous process. In the healthy personality there is constant assimilation of new ideas and expulsion of old ideas throughout life.

* Individuals strive to behave in ways that are in keeping with their Self-Concepts, no matter how helpful or hurtful to oneself or others.
* Self-Concept usually takes precedence over the physical body. Individuals will often sacrifice physical comfort and safety for emotional satisfaction.
* Self-Concept continuously guards itself against loss of self esteem, for it is this loss that produces feelings of anxiety.
* If Self-Concept must constantly defend itself from assault, growth opportunities are limited.

CONCEPTS AND DEFINITIONS

The social psychological conception of the self is based on the idea that people are reflexive, responding to themselves just as they respond to other "objects". Since reflexive thinking requires language, it is assumed that infants and nonhuman animals lack a Self-Concept.

While a number of philosophers and psychologists have addressed the idea that behaviour is influenced by the way people see themselves, investigation into the importance of Self-Concept is most closely associated with the writings and therapeutic practices of Carl Rogers. According to Rogers, one's Self-Concept influences how one regards both oneself and one's environment. The Self-Concept of a mentally healthy person is consistent with his or her thoughts, experiences and behaviour.

Social psychologists have pointed out that Self-Concept also plays an important role in social perception - the process by which we form impressions of others.

Self-Concept has been defined by several authors. **William James** (1890) *holds it to be all that a person is tempted to call by the name 'me' or 'mine'.* **Murphy** (1947) *it as the individual as known to the individual.* According to **Symonds** (1951), *it is the way or manner in which the individual reacts to himself. He spells out four aspects of self: (1) how a person perceives himself: (2) what he thinks of himself: (3) how he values himself; and (4) how he attempts through various actions to enhance or defend himself.*

Sherif and Cantril (1947)

It is the constellation of attitudes of the type "what I think of myself, what I value, what is mine, and what I identify with". According to them, their attitudes when activated, energise, direct and control the person's behaviour.

Franken (1994) states that

"there is a great deal of research which shows that the Self-Concept is, perhaps, the basis for all motivated behaviour. It is the Self-Concept that gives rise to possible selves, and it is the possible selves that create the motivation for behaviour (p.443).

This supports the idea that one's paradigm or world view and one's relationship to that view provide the boundaries and circumstances within which we develop our views about possibilities. This is one of the major issues facing children and youth today.

CONCEPT OF EMOTIONS

A good person, according to Aristotle must have right emotions. Emotion is a complete state of arousal associated with varying degrees of physiological activation, a conscious awareness of feeling with specific cognitive label and tendency to move the organism into action.

The word emotion is derived from a latin term 'Emovere' which means to stir up, to agitate or to excite. Emotions influence actions in many ways. The stronger the emotion, the greater the activity to which it will give rise to negative emotion like kicking, biting, scratching, bed wetting, thumb sucking, crying, trembling running away, irritation, resentment, refusal to eat and so on. Emotions like affection, amusement, curiosity happiness and joy are positive emotions which help in carrying out the activities smoothly and earily. Increase in heart rate, rise in blood pressure, changes in blood compensation, increase in respiration, increase in muscle tension, perspiration, dilation of eye pupil are signs of emotions.

Emotions can be considered as a feeling first noticed at the bodily level as arousal; then it is noticed by the mind which interprets and apprehends the world resulting in bodily feelings. Emotions are neither bad nor good as such. But their relation with the situations is that which makes them effective or ineffective.

In India, emotions have always been considered as energies, the vital being which can be constructive or destructive according to the individual's desires and goals.

Definitions of Emotions

David Hume (1711 - 1776), the emotions are simple unanalysable impression of a non - bodily variety, or in other words, a type of psychic feeling - Emotion is a psychic energy that can be put to use in either in a destructive or constructive manner.

According to Jean Paul - Satre, the French philosopher.

Emotion is a manner of apprehending the world. It is not an innocent perception but a conscious strategy of the subject person. It is an intentional social act.

According to **Crow and Crow** (1973) emotion is an effective experience that accompanies generalized inner adjustment and mental and psychological stirred up status in an individual and that shows itself in his own behaviour.

In **Kumball Young's** view, emotion is the aroused psychological state of the organism marked by increased bodily activity and strong feelings directed to some subject.

Categories of emotions

Harold Schools berg speaks of 3 basic dimensions of emotions.

i. Pleasantness - Unpleasantness

ii. Attention - Rejection

iii. Level of activation (sleep - tension)

Others add a fourth dimension to the above three degree of complexity. When these 4 bipolar dimensions are imposed upon the possible emotional states we get several categories of emotions.

a. Primary goal oriented emotions (anger, joy, fear and grief are also called PRIMARY or basic emotions).

b. Emotions triggered by sensory stimulation (pain, disgust and delight).

c. Emotions pertaining to self appraisal and related to one's level of aspiration (pride, shame and guilt).

d. Emotions related to others.

e. Appreciative emotions (wonder and awe)

All these increasingly varied and differentiated patterns of emotional expressions are gradually evolved in the course of development and learning from the initial single generalised emotional response of excitement of the new born infant.

EMOTIONAL MATURITY

Psychologists differ considerably in their emphasis on the role of maturation in the development of emotional behaviour. **Gessel** says that maturation is responsible for the gradual evolution of emotional expression in infants and children. He strongly disagreed with the view that emotional development is largely a phenomenon of social stimulation. According to **Gessel,** maturation influences the expression of emotion through the development of capacities, rather than through the ripening of a specific innate response pattern. **Jones** demonstrated that while visceral components of emotional response are not highly correlated with the vigour of vocal and motor components during the neonatal period, this correlation is increased in preschool children, indicating that the integration of various aspects of emotional development are dependent partially upon maturation.

For **Gessel**, as the individual becomes more adequate physically, intellectually and socially through the development of his capacities there is a concomitant emotional growth. Outside control gradually disappears as the child's emotions mature, and ultimately the emotionally mature individual is able to function on the basis of inner controls.

Emotional Maturity is always relative. A five year old child has Emotional Maturity, if he is capable of the emotional behaviour we judge fit for a five year old.

Emotional Maturity develops throughout life. It is also a form of maturity from which one can regress more quickly. The child becomes more emotionally mature as the parent permits him to accept responsibilities and becomes independent and self sufficient.

Emotional development, like other aspects of development, is gradual and both innate maturational factors as well as learning plays a part in the development. Emotional development is linked with other areas of human development like physical, intellectual and social. Any retardation, undue acceleration or abnormal deviation in these areas would inevitably influence normal emotional development resulting in frustration, conflicts and imbalance in behaviour. Frustration is caused by the accumulation of emotional tensions affecting the personality of the individual.

According to **Cole**, *"The most outstanding mark of Emotional Maturity is the ability to bear tension"*. Besides, an emotionally mature person persists the capacity for fun and recreation. He enjoys both play and responsibility and keeps them in proper balance.

Kaplon and **Baron** stated that an emotionally mature person has the capacity to withstand delay in the satisfaction of his needs. He has belief in long term planning and is capable of delaying or revising his expectations in terms of demands of situations. An emotionally mature individual has the capacity to make effective adjustment with himself, members of his family, his peers in school, society and culture.

The levels of Emotional Maturity

In the empirically derived hierarchy of emotions, it is observed that there are six fairly distinct behavioural categories which we refer to as 'levels of Emotional Maturity'. Each level composed of a number of discrete emotions, represents a different "attitude" or way of perceiving and responding or reacting to all human beings regardless of culture or personality differences. Although the expression of each level always has cultural and personality nuances and variations, the emotions and emotional levels themselves retain both their relationships to each other and their underlying messages.

How individuals deal with change and their effectiveness in making contributions to themselves, their loved ones, an organisation, or to society directly relates to their emotional level. The higher the level at which a person actually functions, the greater their potential for all its positive aspects, increases exponentially as one moves up the levels.

The higher the level, the greater one's ability to easily deal with change both positively and constructively.

Level 6 represents the essence of Emotional Maturity. At this level, an individual communicates and performs with integrity. Levels 5 through 1 reflect varying degrees of emotional immaturity and a corresponding lack of integrity with level 5 being the least immature.

As we move down the levels, manifestations of responsible, mature behaviour exponentially decline. As we move higher or lower within a level, we increasingly begin to see more characteristics common to the next higher or lower level.

LEVEL 6 - LEADER / MENTOR

At level 6, individuals are passionate and compassionate, live and demonstrate Emotional Maturity and integrity, and therefore have a positive, expansive effect on their environment. They are responsible leaders and compassionate mentors.

Leaders / Mentors are trustworthy and have forthright, honest communication. They manifest great patience. They have self - respect and respect the dignity of others. They strive for quality and excellence but do not get caught in insatiable demands for perfection. They desire and will honestly listen and be open to many view points, including those that differ from their own. They demonstrate, demand, and reward authenticity and responsibility as well as high performance. They do not tolerate irresponsibility, incompetence injustice, or dishonest behaviour, and they know how to communicate with people exhibiting such behaviour.

Emotionally mature individuals of Level 6 have the entire range of emotions at their disposal. They can and do feel and express the entire range of emotions. They do so without malice, honestly and responsibly.

LEVEL 5 - DOER

Doers have many positive characteristics. They are generally responsible and conscientious. They are open to positive ideas, provided the actions or changes do not upset what has been shown to be workable. Doers are interested enough in positive ideas to check them out thoroughly. Therefore though they are progressive and will move forward, they like things substantiated before doing so. Once enough data and documentation are provided, they will make a decision. If the decision is positive, they will tend to want to "pilot" it rather than commit to fully putting it into effect right away. They tend to be more conservative, and concerned with maintaining the status quo than the expansive, proactive people of Level 6.

Even so, by contemporary standards, the attitudes and behaviours of individuals functioning on Level 5 are above average. Nevertheless, these people demonstrate less than they are capable of and therefore show some signs of Emotional Maturity, rationalized though those signs may be.

LEVEL 4 - COPER

Copers do "just enough". They are not particularly responsible or irresponsible. Theirs attention and interest is mainly on making life easier for themselves. They tend to be observers rather than participants. Although not particularly dependable, they are generally likeable because they try to avoid disagreements and prefer the easier way of "going along". Copers are often described as being "mellow" and "easy going". They tend to be somewhat non chalant about details and commitments. Not much is a "big deal" at Level 4. However, if life is not made to be "comfortable enough", Level 4 individuals can fairly easily drop into the antagonism of Level 3 and be "testy".

LEVEL 3 ASSERTER

Level 3 is the first level at which an individual's net impact is more destructive than constructive, to both themselves and their environment. The person's certainty and security have gone from positive to negative. Individuals at this level are starting to feel noticeably over whelmed by their environment. Life and the environment are viewed as a threat. Their defense is to lash out, to attack, and oppose "the enemy". There people range from being "testy" about specific things to being outright bullies about everything.

An asserter's basic operating mode is to oppose or attack other view points. Asserters will exaggerate some element of truth to divert the attention of others from their goals and strengths onto their "weakness". Emotionally, asserters will be antagomstic or angry. They are good at pressuring others to the point that others will be concessions just to get the asserters to back off. If others buy into the Asserter's attempted intimidation, the Asserter has "won".

LEVEL 2 MANIPULATOR

Manipulators are hostile, insecure and afraid. Consequently, they are too afraid to directly express their fears and hostility. They hide their hostility and destructive intention by artful deceit and covert manipulations. Individuals on the manipulator level are the most dangerous because not only is their underlying hostility vicious, but they are expert at hiding their true intentions and thus different to spot and deal with.

Manipulators have no concept of exchange and little or no real concept of right and wrong. Their attitude is that they are only doing what they need to do to survive in this “obviously hostile world”. They regard others as their enemies, and thus any means to “do others in” are justified in their minds. Manipulators often are able to assume any social level that will meet their destructive, hostile and unscrupulous ends. Manipulators view people who act with comparison, honesty, and integrity as simpletons who deserve to be taken advantage of Manipulators do not take responsibility but instead subtly point fingers. Supervisors may find themselves getting angry with the manipulator but be unable to be precise about why. Everything will always appear to have its reasons, including the Manipulator’s subtlet put - downs.

LEVEL - 1 VICTIM

Victims have an overwhelming sense of power lessness. The Victim - level individual feels he or she is about to - or already has lost. Victims have the view point that the environment has done them in. They have little, if any, sense of responsibility for anything, and truth has little meaning for them. Victims have a very narrow, self centered, and selfish viewpoint. They cry, whine or attempt to appears. Victims often try to feebly gain some semblance of control by getting others to feel sympathetic toward them. Victims do not see solutions, only problems. If offered a solution, victims will have myriad excuses for how the solutions cannot or will not work. People chronically at the victim level always will have one or more “unsolvable” problems.

SUMMARY OF LEVEL BEHAVIOUR

Individuals or organizations operating chronically at levels 1, 2 and 3 are emotionally challenged and will manifest correspondingly limited viewpoints, attitudes, abilities and behaviours at level 4 this also will be true but less so. Levels 4 and above demonstrate increasing responsibility, integrity, trust worthiness and a win - win viewpoint. It is only sustained Levels 5 and 6 that we find individuals who and organizations that are capable of capitalizing on their true potential.

Level 6 offers the broadest perspective and most consistently responsible mature behaviours. It manifest rational certainly, costiveness and creativity. It represents the ideal of a win - win attitude.

Level 5 is mostly positive and action and results - oriented but with a provision that willingness to move, expand and try new things occurs after thoroughly testing examination and validation.

Level 4 is barely more positive than negative, it is characterized by doing enough things right to get by.

Levels 3 and below are indicative of a lose - lose situation in which individuals are perceiving themselves as being overwhelmed by their environment and are fighting back in the only ways they know how. At level 3 and below, honesty, responsibility and contribution become inverted, and their opposites become the dominant manifestation.

At level 3, individuals are still "strong" enough to overtly lash out at their environment in the form of opposition attack and intimidation, which are emotionally characterized by antagonism and anger. At this level, people are not only obviously hostile but also frightened, despite their bluster.

When individuals become too frightened even to outwardly express their hostility, they go covert. This is level 2, which is the most dangerous level. The underlying hostility is covered up with social necessities, subtle deceits, and invalidation's of others that are always destructive but difficult to spot.

At level 1, individuals feel as though they have already "lost". Their behaviour takes on pathetic forms of helplessness to gain sympathy or gross attempts at appeasement.

Knowing the levels of maturity and their manifestations allows us to more elegantly facilitate the most positive forms of change, helping to create personal satisfaction and organisational success.

STAGES OF DEVELOPMENT OF EMOTIONAL MATURITY

Jersild presents one of the most comprehensive lists of the stages involved in the child's moving toward maturity in the emotional area.

1. A change from being a creature who at first receives much gives little, to onc who is capable of giving as well as of receiving and capable of learning to get enjoyment from giving.
2. Development of capacity, to identify with a larger social group, and the ability, to participate emotionally in the fortunes of the larger group.

3. Development from the status of being the child of family to the status ultimately, of being able to have children of one's own and along with this development a capacity to exercise the feeling and attitudes involved in being a parent psychologically, whether or not one is a parent biologically.
4. Progressive sexual development and the capacity after puberty to enjoying mature sex experiences.
5. An increased capacity for bearing the inevitable sufferings and pains connected with life and growth without feeling abused.
6. An increased capacity for sympathy and compassion as one assimulates the meaning for self and others of the joys and vicissitudes of life.

Some of the characteristics of the person who has achieved maturity, emotionally are suggested here.

1. He accepts criticism gracefully, being honestly glad for an opportunity to improve.
2. He does not indulge in self pity. He has begun to feel the laws of compensation operating in all life.
3. He does not expect special consideration from anyone.
4. He controls his temper.
5. He meets emergencies with poise.
6. His feelings are not easily hurt.
7. He accepts the responsibility of his own actions without trying to 'alibi'.
8. He has outgrown the "all or nothing" stages. He recognises that no person or situation is wholly good or wholly bad, and he begins to appreciate the Golden Mean.
9. He is not impatient at reasonable delays. He has learned that he is not the arbiter of the universe and that he must often adjust himself to other people and their convenience.
10. He is a good loser. He can endure defeat and disappointment without whining or complaining.
11. He does not worry about things he cannot help.
12. He is not given to boasting or "showing off" in socially unacceptable ways.

13. He is honestly glad when others enjoy success or good fortune. He has outgrown envy and jealousy.
14. He is open - minded enough to listen thoughtfully to the opinions of others.
15. He is not a chronic "fault - finder".
16. He plans things in advance rather than trusting to the inspiration of the moment.

Last of all, in terms of spiritual maturity:

1. He has faith in a power greater than himself.
2. He feels himself as an organised part of mankind as a whole, contributing his part to each group of which he is a member.

STATEMENT OF THE PROBLEM

"A study of Self-Concept and Emotional Maturity among high school students.

OPERATIONAL DEFINITIONS

Self-Concept

Self-Concepts is the individual's way of looking at himself. It also signifies his way of thinking, feeling and behaving.

Self-Concept is the dominant element in the personality pattern, it governs the individual's characteristics reaction to people and situations and determines the quality of his behaviour.

Emotional Maturity

Emotional Maturity is a process in which the personality is continuously striving for greater sense of emotional health, both intra - physically and intra personally.

OBJECTIVES OF THE STUDY

1. To find out the level of Self-Concept among High School students.
2. To find out the level of Emotional Maturity among High School students.
3. To find out whether there is significant difference in the Total Self-Concept and its dimensions of High School students with respect to their.

a. Gender
b. Medium of instructions
c. Type of Management
d. Locality
e. Type of family
f. Birth Order

4. To find out whether there is significant difference in the Total Emotional Maturity and its dimensions of High School students with respect to their.
   a. Gender
   b. Medium of instructions
   c. Type of Management
   d. Locality
   e. Type of family
   f. Birth Order
5. To find out whether there is any significant association between Self-Concept of High School students and the following variables.
   a. Gender
   b. Medium of instructions
   c. Type of Management
   d. Locality
   e. Type of family
   f. Birth Order
6. To find out whether there is any significant association between Emotional Maturity of High School students and the following variables
   a. Gender
   b. Medium of instructions
   c. Type of Management
   d. Locality
   e. Type of family
   f. Birth Order

7. To find out the relationship between Self-Concept of High School students and their Emotional Maturity.

SIGNIFICANCE OF THE STUDY

In the present day circumstances, youth and children face difficulties in life. These difficulties may lead to many psychosomatic problems such as anxiety, tensions, frustrations and emotional disturbances in the day to day life. Hence the study of emotional life is now emerging as a descriptive science.

As Self-Concept seems to play a significant role in the growth and development of a person, a detailed knowledge about its nature and its relation to other factors of personality provides an objective and encouraging basis for the educators to work on. An emotionally matured person will have a healthy Self-Concept not thinking too highly or too lowly of oneself. Since Self-Concept has acceptably a significant influence of behaviour, it was felt that a knowledge of the relationship between Self-Concept and Emotional Maturity would be very enriching and useful.

DELIMITATIONS OF THE STUDY

The investigator is conscious of the circumstances given below that might to some extent exert influence on the findings of the research.

1. The study was limited to the schools located in Kerala.
2. The study was limited to high school students only.
3. The sample is restricted to 300 students.

CONCLUSION

The first chapter highlights the introduction to the problem and its statement, operational definitions of the terms, objectives and limitations of the study.

A review of related literature, design of the study, analysis and interpretation of the data and summary of the results are dealt with the chapters that follow.

2

Review of Related Literature

INTRODUCTION

"The review of literature promotes a greater understanding of the problem and its crucial aspects" **Mouly**, 1964).

A review of empirical studies in any area indicates not only the relevance and significance of the problem of study but also the appropriateness of the planned methodology and of the techniques of analysis of the research data. Review of the related literature gives a right perspective to understand as well as appreciate every aspect of the work and the procedure followed studying in the problem.

According to **Good** (1959) *In order to be truly creative and original, one must read intensively and critically as a stimulus of thinking.*

Therefore careful study is carried out and is presented in this chapter under the following headings.

a. Studies related to Self-Concept

b. Studied related to Emotional Maturity

STUDIES RELATED TO SELF-CONCEPT

Indian Studies on Self-Concept

Paul Bruece (1958) studied the relationship of self acceptance to other variables with sixth grade children oriented in self understanding has pointed out that the child who indicates a marked discrepancy between his Self-Concept and ideal self, feeling his need satisfaction blocked would show evidences of insecurity in his behavior and would yield responses indicating manifest anxiety.

Deo P. and Sharma Sagar (1971) studied the relationship of Self - Concept and Anxiety. Under this study, 700 adolescents from 13 urban higher secondary schools in North India were selected. From the calculated data, Self -Concept and Anxiety was found to be negatively correlated and increase in Self-Concept is accompanied by decrease in anxiety. It was also found that Self-ideal discrepancy increases, Anxiety also increases.

Walia D (1973) made an attempt to study the gifted adolescents and their Self-Concept was affected by intelligence and sex. The gifted have higher idea of self and better insight than the average. The gifted have higher perceived ideal discrepancies as compared to the average adolescence.

Lalithamma and Passi (1973) analysed the relationship of creativity and Self-Concept in terms of low, average and high achievement. No significant difference were found among the groups in Self-Concept but over achievers were more creative.

Mohan (1975) Traced the growth of Self-Concept over years of adolescence and its relationship with intelligence and achievement. The results showed that longitudinal and cross sectional analysis revealed increased trend of female perceived self. Females showed more stability of self than males during adolescence.

Jogawar (1976) conducted a study to find out how the Self-Concept of the adolescence change as a function of age, the relationship of these changes with some family factors and the relationship of sex with these changes. For studying, the significant difference between group analysis for variance was used. The findings showed that the developmental course of Self-Concept and social self stood at higher level at the beginning and at the end stage of adolescence were found to be considerably lower level at the middle of the adolescent period.

Narayanan and Ganesan (1978) developed a Self-Concept check list to measure Self-Concept of Palamalai in Tamil Nadu who are scheduled tribes of that area. The scale consisted of both open ended and closed ended questionnaire and had 44 items. This community people seem to be unaware of expression of self but considered themselves strong and healthy.

Prasad S. (1982) studied certain important factors of stability of the Self-Concept. The samples included 132 college and university tutors, the inventory used was Sharan's ideal Self-Concept, self-satisfaction and role performance. The major findings were social change had been identified as an independent factor of self-consistency and older and younger generation differed significantly on anxiety, insecurity self-role in congruence and self-satisfaction.

Dastoor, H.F. (1982) studied the different types of Self-Concept prevalent among the nurses, to assess the relationship between the types of Self-Concept and job performance and to compare the Self-Concept of the most efficient and the least efficient nurses. Under incidental sampling method 700 samples were collected. About 71% of nurses had high to very high Self -Concept and had little or no doubt about the profession. The nurses with low proficiency and low Self-Concept had definite doubts about their profession.

Pandit I. (1985) studied the psychological needs and Self-Concept of adolescents and their bearing on adjustment. The sample consisted of 640 adults and the tools employed in this study were socio-economic status inventory by Deo, Jogawar and Shekar and Bhagia's school adjustment inventory. The calculated data results that the difference between perceived self and social self was not significant and the results for Self-Concept of adolescent boys and girls showed that boys had a higher Self-Concept than girls.

Ghose P. and Khurana (1986) made a study which aims at assessing socio-economic status and sex on anxiety, adjustments and Self-Concept. The sample consisted of 100 students belonging to different colleges in Delhi. Significant differences were found between the high socio-economic status group and low socio- economic status group as well as males and females with respect to Self-Concept, the high Self-Concept and low Self-Concept groups on anxiety, between high Self-Concept and low Self-Concept groups on adjustment.

Karan, Patricia (1989) studied the relationship of peer group and the Self-Concept of adolescence. This analysis showed that there is a positive relationship existing between the peer group and Self-Concept.

Chanda, Sunanda (1990) conducted a study on Self-Concept, parental influence socio-economic status and sex in education to career choice attitude among high school students. Attitude scale of career maturity inventory and the Self-Concept inventory were used to collect the data from 60 girls and 60 boys of class X. The results showed that parental influence interacted with Self-Concept in the prediction of career choice attitude scores

Ramiah L. (1990) made a relational study involvement and Self - Concept of standard IX students in Devakottai educational district. The objectives of the study were

1. To assess the level of parental involvement and Self-Concept of standard IX students.
2. To determine if there is any significant relationship between parental involvement and Self-Concept of standard IX students.

The sample comprised of 303 students from higher secondary schools and 97 students from matriculation schools. Saraswat's tool on Self -Concept and the investigator's questionnaire on parental involvement were used to collect the data.

The major findings showed that there was significant relationship between parental involvement and Self-Concept of the students and the more parental involvement the better the Self-Concept.

Joseph Alexandar E and Rajendran K (1992) analysed the influence of Self-Concept, Sex, Area and Parents education on adjustment problems. Check list were used to collect the data from 671 students of 5 universities of Tamil Nadu. The results showed that students with high Self-Concept are better adjusted than students with low Self-Concept.

Chauhan, Sarita (1992) made a study on values, Self-Concept, creativity and anxiety among professional college students Self-Concept scale of Mukta Rastogi was used to find out the Self-Concept of the students of the colleges of engineering, medicine and teaching. The data was collected from the sample of 405 students. The findings revealed that there was no difference in Self-Concept between students of engineering colleges and medical colleges. There was a little difference in the value of engineering students and teachers – training students.

Barooah, S and Phukan.M. (1999) designed a comparative study of Self-Concept of orphan children and the children with natural parents. The sample comprised 45 children with natural parents from 3 schools in Guwahati of age group 10 to 15 years and 45 orphan children from

SOS children's village Azara. A Self-Concept questionnaire was prepared to collect the data. The results revealed that there is no significant difference in the physical, educational and moral Self-Concept of children from the two groups. Intellectual Self-Concept of children with natural parents was found to be higher than Orphan children and the social Self-Concept and the social Self-Concept of orphan children was found to be lower than that of children with natural parents.

Foreign studies Self-Concept

Cross (1991) made a study to investigate the Self-Concept of middle school students and to examine the extent to which selected variables predict the Self-Concept of 293 students in Dade country, Florida. Phase one examined the difference in Self-Concept between music participants and non-participants in music. The Self-Concept scores of these two groups were compared. Phase two involved only the 140 music participants. The data for the choral students responses on the six independent variables were analyzed using a step-wise multiple regression design.

Kloomok - Shauna; Cosden - Merith (1992) made a study of 72 elementary children with learning disabilities explored how children maintain a positive Self-Concept despite academic difficulties. Children with high global Self-Concept, compared to low global Self-Concept, perceived themselves as more intelligent, more competent in nonacademic domains, and receiving more special support. Subjects did not discount the importance of academics. (Author / JDD)

Buege – Carol (1993) studied that reverse mainstreaming, creative drama and social skills training used during an academic year with a class of fourth-grade students and emotionally disturbed (ED) students improved the fourth grades attitudes towards emotionally disturbed children and improved the Self-Concept of the ED students.

Sax – Linda (1994) investigated factors associated with development of mathematical Self-Concept in college students. Results showed that some students' background characteristic, college characteristic and student experiences contribute to an overall decline in Mathematics.

Rothman (1995) **et al.,** studied the relationship between self perception of learning disability (L.D.) and Self-Concept and social support among 56 elementary students with L.D. Children with less negative perceptions of their L.D. showed higher Math's achievement scores and perceived more positive Self-Concept, intellectual and behavioral competence and support from classmates and parents.

Kaisa Aunola, Esko Leshnein and Tina Onatsu (2002) studied on 3 methods for developmental changes in the case of reading skills and Self-Concept in the University of Finland on 105 samples 61 boys and 44 girls, 6-7 years from 4 first grade class, preschool shows a unconstructed Mathew effect for the development of their Self-Concept, but not for the reading skills. However the results showed there was a multi constructed cumulative cycle between children reading skills and their Self-Concept.

Gordon et al., (1995) studied the Self-Concept and motivational patterns of Resilient African American High School students and determined the role of Self-Concept and motivation in aiding resilient African American high school sophomores to obtain academic competence. Results from 138 students suggest resilient African American high school students different from their monresilient peers in the cognitive domain; cognitive ability, cognitive environmental support, cognitive control and cognitive importance.

Jackson et al., (1994) studied about the stereotypic differences and the role of gender attitudes. The gender differences in overall self - evaluation and in specific dimensions of Self-Concept were examined in 470 primarily white college. 501 high school students were examined and it was found that there are gender differences in overall self - evaluation that favour males and that there are differences in specific Self-Concept areas that are consistent with gender stereotypes.

Connolly et al., (1994) examined peer Self-Concept and its association with structural and qualitative features of peer experiences in high school students. Factor analysis supported a three - factor model that differentiated the peer - Self-Concept in terms of the peer group, close friendship, and romantic relationships and found that both peer network structure and friendship quality were significant predictors of Self-Concept.

Pyryt et al., (1994) conducted a comparitive study of gifted and average - ability adolescents. The four dimensions of Self-Concept (academic, social atbletic and evaluative) were evaluated with 97 junior high school students and the results indicated that the gifted students differed in Self-Concept from average ability students, particularly in the area of academic Self-Concept.

STUDIES RELATED TO EMOTIONAL MATURITY

Indian studies on Emotional Maturity

Siddiqui, M.M. (1976) conducted a study on social psychological study of students behaviour" with special reference to indiscipline. The objectives of the investigation was to study the psychological (Emotional Maturity, social maturity, ascendance – submission, security and aggression) and social factors (educational attainment, socio-economic status and rural or urban inhabitation) which affected student behaviour in general; discipline in particular. The measures of Emotional Maturity, social maturity, ascendance submission and social factors showed that disciplined students were emotionally and socially more mature than the indisciplined ones.

Sinha, A.K. and Bhan, R.W. (1978) of Kurukshetra University studied mental health of university students. The sample consisted of 259 male students and 118 female students of Kurukshetra University and 293 male engineering students. The major findings were that the boys and girls of the university did not differ on emotional insecurity. The engineering boys were significantly superior in mental health to the university boys. Emotional insecurity was more prominent among children from the agricultural community. Emotional insecurity was evenly spread among children from business community and service community.

Arya A (1984) conducted a study on "Emotional Maturity and the value of superior children in the family", A printed scale was administered to 300 superior children (150 males and 150 females) at random. The major findings were (a) superior intelligence showed high relationship with emotional maturity (v) Agewise there was no significant difference on Emotional Maturity(c) Boys to be more mature (d) Residence did not link with Emotional Maturity.

A study was conducted by Manral, Bheema (1988) of Kaumann University on "The impact of Emotional Maturity and prolonged deprivation on indisciplined behaviour among university students in relation to their academic achievement". The descriptive survey method was used in this study. Stratified random sampling was used to select 472 students. The major findings were (a) Emotional Maturity was related to disciplined behaviour (b) There was no significant difference between male and female students on Emotional Maturity (c) High deprived students differed from lower deprived students in Emotional Maturity.

Kapil Renu, (1992) investigated on nature and sources of emotional tensions of educated girls of Hindu Society in Agra region. He found that (a) significant difference was found in the level of emotional tensions of highly educated and lower educated girls (b) Higher age group and lower age group educated girls also differed in the levels of emotional tension. (c) parental levels of education had a significant relationship with different kinds of emotional tensions in educated girls of Hindu society.

Arora, R.K. (1992) studied international effect of creativity and intelligence on emotional stability, personality adjustment and academic achievement. The major findings were high creative/high intelligence group was significantly higher in emotional stability, than the remaining three creative/high intelligence group. Those possessing both high convergent and divergent abilities were by far the most accommodative persons among different creative intelligence groups.

Sandhu, Daya Singh (1992) studied "A child's mind in the adult's body". An investigation of perceptual difference between males and females towards Emotional Maturity. The major findings suggested that females seem to consider Emotional Maturity special problem for males, whereas males see it as a problem for both sexes.

Foreign Studies on Emotional Maturity

Allen Jaffe (1981) examined how Illinois state legislators' scores on Emotional Maturity – immaturity measure compared with a similar non political group. The study indicated a higher mean level of Emotional Maturity for the political group.

Bush, Kethryn.J. (1989) conducted research on level of Emotional Maturity in first, second, third grade teachers, investigation of group differences, teachers anxiety, achievement and classroom attitudes. The main purpose of this study and trait emotions before and after administration of standardized tests and to examine the relationship between teacher test Emotional Maturity and teachers anxiety, intelligence, classroom, attitudes and sex differences. The sample consisted of 240, first, second, and third grade teachers and their schools. It was found that the Third grade teachers emotions appeared more positively related to teachers achievement than the second and third grades. Although a casual influence between these occurrences and the administration of GRT cannot be assumed, results provide an impetus for further investigations. Teacher's Emotional Maturity, students Emotional Maturity and environmental variables appear associated with statement achievement.

A study was undertaken by Creamer - Don G (1992) on how to use a developmental model of maturity to enhance student centered teaching. The findings indicated that student – centered teaching must foster the whole student. It presented a developed model involving setting goals in courses and interactive teaching / learning strategies to create student centered classroom. It describe sample course goals for developing and evaluating students maturity, and argues for a model addressing self, values and attitudes.

Heyer, et al., (1993) conducted an investigation on the relationship between parental marital status and the development of identify and emotional autonomy in college students revealed that development approach was used to examine relationship between parental marital status and identity and emotional autonomy to examine relationship between parental marital status and emotional autonomy in 388 college students. Confidence and sexual identity scores revealed that students whose parents were divorced had higher scores than students from intact families. There were no difference in the autonomy scores.

Lawrence P. Michael D. (1993) conducted the study of enablement, alienation, and emotions in middle school classrooms. This study was designed to pursue the question of the relationship between alienation, and emotions in the seventh and eighth grade, subjects and 2,159 students taught by 19 teachers in 14 middle schools. There are strong relationship between the student perceptions of classroom structure and their emotions. If they see themselves as having a great deal of control of over events in the classroom, and are less alienated, they have a much better emotions. Boys feel empowered than girls and classes taught by male teachers report themselves to be less in control than those taught by females. Emotions of students with female teachers are more positive than those taught by males.

Gerdes and Hillary et al., (1994) conducted longitudinal study titled emotional, social and academic adjustment of college students. The major findings were new school children completed surveys on expectations about college adjustments; later completed survey of actual adjustments. Six years later, results indicated that two different sets of items best discriminated among good standing per sisters and leavers. Emotional and social adjustment items predicted attrition as well as better academic adjustment items.

Allan, Bradford Drake (1997) studied emotions and its influences on mathematical problem solved among 209 under graduates. The major finding stated that the emotions may be more differentiated because psychological responses are stronger for better problem solvers.

Kellner et al., (1995) studied a school based Anger Management program for developmentally and emotionally disabled high school students and described a group program designed for high school students with cognitive, emotional and behavioural disturbances using Novaco's cognitive conceptualization of anger. Multiple techniques allowed multiply handicapped students to learn the physiology, triggers, and consequences of anger as well as to develop coping strategies for managing their anger and to reduce acting out.

Benge et al., (1996) studied the emotional development of twice exceptional rural students and case studies were developed over a 3 years period. The data were interpreted using Kazimierz Dabrowski's Theory of positive Disintegration, in which progressive conflicts and contradictions arise from life experience and become a fundamental and positive factor of development. The study revealed four general categories of behavioural and motivational themes. The students provided evidence of Level - 1 egocentrism, over excitabilities, and asynchronous development, three areas informed by Dabrowski's theory. In addition a fourth theme emerged called acute awareness of manipulation.

CONCLUSION

The survey of related literature has helped the investigator to have a clear perspective of the problem chosen for the present investigation. The review of the related literature has enabled the investigator to formulate the relevant hypotheses for the present study. Based on this review, a suitable methodology and well planned procedure for present investigation is adopted and it is explained in the next chapter.

3

Research Design and Methods

INTRODUCTION

The main aim of research is to provide knowledge that will allow the educator to achieve his goal by the most effective methods. The selection of the method depends upon the nature of the problem, the objectives of study and the population to be studied.

In any research Endeavour, methodology occupies a crucial position. Methodology is the art of applying the most suitable procedure to a particular activity. By methodology, we mean the philosophy of research process. This includes the assumption and values that serve as a rational for research and the standard criteria the researcher uses for interpretation, data and conclusion. Research design is a logical and systematic plan prepared for directing a research study. It specifies the objectives of the study, the methodology, and techniques to be allotted.

This chapter gives an overall picture of the design of the study, hypotheses, the psychological tools used for study, nature and selection of the sample, a brief description of the procedure adopted for the collection of data, its scoring and classification.

A research design (**Bryman**, 2001) provides a framework for the collection and analysis of data. A choice of research design reflects decisions about the priority being given to a range of dimensions of the research process. This include the importance attached to

a) Expressing casual connections between variables
b) Generalizing to larger groups of individuals than those actually forming part of the investigation.
c) Understanding behaviour and the meaning of the behaviour in its specific social context.
d) Having a temporal (i.e. overtime) appreciation of social phenomena and their interconnections.

HYPOTHESES

1. The level of Self-Concept among high school students is moderate in nature.
2. The level of Emotional Maturity among high school students is low in nature.
3. There is no significant difference in the total Self-Concept and its dimensions of high school students with respect to their
   a) Gender
   b) Medium of instructions
   c) Type of management
   d) Locality
   e) Type of family
   f) Birth order
4. There is no significant difference in the Total Emotional Maturity and its dimensions of High School students with respect to their.
   a) Gender
   b) Medium of instructions
   c) Type of management
   d) Locality
   e) Type of family
   f) Birth order
5. There is significant association between Self-Concept of High School students and the following variables.

a) Gender
b) Medium of instructions
c) Type of management
d) Locality
e) Type of family
f) Birth order

6. There is significant association between Emotional Maturity of high school students and the following variables.

a) Gender
b) Medium of instructions
c) Type of management
d) Locality
e) Type of family
f) Birth order

7. There is no significant relationship between Self-Concept of high school students and their Emotional Maturity.

DESCRIPTION OF THE TOOLS USED

To verify the framed hypotheses the following tools and techniques were used in the present investigation.

1. Self-Concept Questionnaire
2. Emotional Maturity Scale

SELF-CONCEPT QUESTIONNAIRE

Description

The Self-Concept inventory provides six separate dimensions of Self-Concept viz. Physical, Social, Intellectual, Moral, Educational and Temperamental.

1. Physical Self-Concept measures individuals view of their body, health, physical appearance and strength.,
2. Social Self-Concept measures individual's sense of worth in social interactions.

3. Temperamental Self-Concept measures individual's view of their prevailing emotional state or predominance of a particular kind of emotional reaction
4. Educational Self-Concept measures individuals view of themselves in relation to school, teachers and extracurricular activities.
5. Moral Self-Concept measures individual's estimation of their moral worth; right and wrong activities.
6. Intellectual Self-Concept measures individual's awareness of their intelligence and capacity of problem solving and judgments.

The following table indicates item numbers included in different Self-Concept dimensions.

Table - 1

Self-Concept dimensions along with their item numbers

Self-Concept Dimensions	Code Number	Item Numbers
Physical	A	2,3,9,20,22,27,29,31
Social	B	1,8,21,37,40,43,46,48
Temperamental	C	4,10,14,16,19,23,24,28
Educational	D	5,13,15,17,25,26,30,32
Moral	E	6,34,35,41,42,44,45,47
Intellectual	F	7,11,12,18,33,36,38,39

Administration of the test

The following instructions were given to students before administering the inventory. The purpose of the inventory is to detect the Self-Concept of the students. The inventory contains 48 items Each dimension contains eight items. Each is provided with five alternatives. Responses are obtained on the test booklet itself. The students have to read each item carefully and respond to it by marking a tick (√) on any one of the five responses given against that item. There is no time limit but generally 20 minutes have been found sufficient for answering all the items. In the event of the subjects raising any doubts, it must be made clear by the administrator. However the respondent is expected to independently decide and complete the test.

Scoring method

The sample is provided with five alternatives to give his/her responses ranging from most acceptable to least acceptable description of his/her Self-Concept. The alternatives or responses are arranged in such a way that the scoring system for all the items will remain the same i.e 5,4,3,2,1 whether the items are positive or negative. If the subject put (√) mark for first alternative the score is one. The summated score of all the forty-eight items provide the total Self-Concept score of an individual. A high score on this inventory indicates a higher Self-Concept, while a low score shows low Self-Concept. The score of each item on the front page is transferred against that item. All the scores of eight items given in that column is added. The score obtained is taken as the score for that particular dimension.

EMOTIONAL MATURITY SCALE

Description

Emotional Maturity Scale (Appendix -1) Standardised by Dr.Yashvir Singh and Dr.Mahesh Bhargava (Head, Department of Psychology, St.John's College, AGRA and Dr.Mahesh Bhargava, Director N.P.C. AGRA).

Emotional Maturity is assessed by evaluating the following five aspects of an individual namely.

a) Emotional unstability

b) Emotional regression

c) Social Maladjustment

d) Personality disintegration

e) Lack of independence.

a)Emotional Unstability

This is a broad factor representing syndrome of lack of capacity to dispose of problems, irritability needs, constant help for one's day to day work, vulnerability, stubbornness and temper tantrums.

b)Emotional Regression

Emotional regression is also a broad group of factors representing such syndromes as feeling of inferiority, restlessness, hostility, aggressiveness and self-centeredness.

c)Social maladjustment

Such a person shows lack of social adaptability and possess hatred, reclusiveness boasting and will be a lire and shirker.

d)Personality disintegration

It includes all those symptoms, which represent disintegration of personality, life reaction, phobia formation, rationalization, pessimism, immorality etc. Such a person suffers from inferiorities and hence reacts to environment through aggressiveness, destruction and has distorted sense of reality.

e)Lack of Independence

Such a person shows parasitic dependence on others is erotic and lack 'Objective Interests'. People think of him an unreliable person.

There are 48 positive statements in the Emotional Maturity Scale. Of these, statements 1-10 measure emotional unstability, statements 11-20 evaluate emotional regression, statements 21-30 assess social maladjustment statement 31-40 indicate personality disintegration while statements 41-48 determines the level of independence. The total score of items 1-48 attribute to the total Emotional Maturity of an individual.

The higher the score on the Emotional Maturity scale, lower is the Emotional Maturity and vice versa.

Administration of the test

The scale for psychological investigation consists of statements about what the students feel about emotional unstability, emotional regression, social maladjustment, personal disintegration and lack of independence in various situations. The students were required to select any one of the given five responses to indicate the extent to which they agree or disagree with each statement to describe their own feelings about Emotional Maturity. The students are requested to give their responses frankly and they were told that it would be kept confidential.

Scoring method

The weight age of 5,4,3,2 and 1 are given for the categories 'Very much', 'Undecided', 'Probably' and 'Never respectively. The net score of an individual with respect to Emotional Maturity is the sum of all scores in each of the 48 items.

Sample for the study

The sample of the study is mainly concerned with high school students studying in Thiruvananthapuram district in Kerala. A sample of 300 were chosen at random from Government, Aided and Private schools.

PILOT STUDY

Before finalizing the final structure of the questionnaires and collection of data for the main study a pilot study was attempted. It was conducted in the month of September 2006 on high school students drawn from each school selected randomly from the whole sample to establish reliability and validity of various tools used in the study.

STABLISHING RELIABILITY AND VALIDITY OF TOOLS USED

Self-Concept

Reliability

In order to establish the reliability of Self-Concept inventory, odd-even method of correlation was used. The correlation between the two parts of odd-even question score was calculated by using karl Pearson's Product moment formula and the co-efficient of reliability so obtained is 0.8241 showing that the tool is reliable.

Validity

In the case of Self-Concept inventory, it is found to be 0.9077 suggesting that the tool is valid.

Emotional Maturity

Reliability

This Emotional Maturity scale is a standardized tool. The reliability of the tool in the present study has been found by test-retest method. The obtained reliability coefficient is 0.8647 revealing that the tool is reliable.

Validity

In the present study the validity coefficient is computed as the square root of the reliability coefficient which is 0.9298 revealing that the tool is highly valid.

MAIN STUDY

The tools described below

a) Self-Concept inventory

b) Emotional Maturity Scale

are used to collect the information from the samples for the main study following the procedures mentioned for the administration of the tests. The tests were administrated on the samples of High School students in November 2006.

Table:2

Showing the time schedule of administered

Sl.No	Name of the Tool	Time Taken
1.	Self-Concept	45 minutes
2.	Emotional Maturity Scale	60 minutes

CONCLUSION

This chapter outlines the design of the present study, the procedure followed and the nature of the sample. It also describes the hypotheses to be tested, the tools used and methods of administration and scoring. The collected data were analyzed using appropriate statistical techniques described above to study the Self-Concept and Emotional Maturity among the High School students.

4

Analysis and Interpretation of the Data

INTRODUCTION

The collected data have to be processed so that intelligible conclusions may be drawn. Statistical analysis is of great use in this regard. *"Analysis of the data is as important as any other component of the research process"* **Gay** (1976). According to **Mouly** *"Research data becomes meaningful in the process of being analysed and interpreted"*. The purpose of analysis is to summarise the completed observations in such a manner that they yield answers to the research questions. Regardless of how well the study is conducted, an inappropriate analysis can lead to in appropriate conclusions.

In this chapter, an attempt is made to analyse and interpret the collected data. It deals with the statistical analysis of the data with reference to the hypotheses that were formulated. Interpretations are also made to account for the results obtained. The choice of statistical techniques for data analysis was largely determined by the research hypotheses.

Descriptive Analysis

The following table shows the sample under the following variables.

Table - 1

Showing the categories and percentage of the sample.

Variables	Categories	N	Percentage
Gender	Boys	150	50
	Girls	150	50
Medium of instruction	Malayalam	150	50
	English	150	50
Type of management	Private	100	33.33
	Aided	100	33.33
	Government	100	33.33
Locale	Rural	150	50
	Urban	150	50
Type of family	Nuclear	279	93
	Joint	21	7
Birth order	First	149	49.66
	Second	132	44
	Third and Above	19	633

INFERENTIAL ANALYSIS

Descriptive analysis

The following table explains the different dimensions of Self-Concept of High School students.

Self-Concept and its dimensions of High School students.

Table - 2

Mean and standard deviation of high school students for Self-Concept and its dimensions - total sample

Self-Concept and its dimensions	Mean Score	Standard deviation	Percentage
Physical	28.12	3.60	70.3
Social	28.44	4.23	71.1
Temperamental	28.22	3.99	70.55
Educational	28.81	4.44	72.02
Moral	29.30	4.48	73.25
Intellectual	25.84	3.86	64.6
Total Self-Concept	168.73	17.30	70.30

From table 2 it is observed that the total Self-Concept of high school students was 168.73 (70.30%). The Moral Self-Concept had the highest percentage of mean score (73.25%) and the Intellectual Self-Concept had the lowest percentage of mean score (64.4).

Table - 3

Emotional Maturity and its dimensions of high school students-total sample

Emotional Maturity and its dimensions	Mean	Standard deviation	Percentage
Emotional unstability	25.81	6.90	51.62
Emotional regression	22.59	6.50	45.18
Social maladjustment	22.36	5.85	44.72
Personality disintegration	20.25	5.77	40.5
Lack of independence	18.93	4.76	47.32
Total Emotional Maturity	109.94	23.05	45.80

It is observed from table 3 that the total Emotional Maturity mean score is 109.94. The dimension emotional unstability had a mean score of 25.81 which was found to be highest and the dimension lack of independence was found to have the least score (18.93).

(i)Self-Concept of high school students

The variable Self-Concept has been classified into three groups based on quartiles and the frequency and percentage of students in each category is given in table 4.

Table 4

Showing the criteria for classifying the sample into three groups based on Self-Concept

	SELF-CONCEPT	
Level	Frequency	Percentage
Low	101	33.67
Moderate	97	32.33
High	102	34.00

It is observed from the above table that (102) students of high school show a high level of Self-Concept indicating that the Self-Concept of high school students is high in nature.

(ii)Emotional Maturity of high school students

The variable Emotional Maturity has been classified into three groups based on quartiles and the frequency and percentage of students in each category is given in table 5.

Table - 5

Showing the criteria for classifying the sample into three groups based on Emotional Maturity

EMOTIONAL MATURITY		
Level	**Frequency**	**Percentage**
Low	103	34.33
Moderate	97	32.33
High	100	33.33

It is observed from the above table that (103) students of high school show a low level of Emotional Maturity indicating that the Emotional Maturity of high school students is low in nature.

Differential analysis

(i)Self-Concept with respect to gender

The mean, standard deviation and t value have been calculated for Self-Concept and its dimensions with respect to gender and the results are given in table 6.

Table - 6

Mean, Standard Deviation and t value for the scores of Self-Concept and its dimensions with respect to Gender

Self-Concept and its dimensions	Boys		Girls		t-value	Level of significance e
	Mean	SD	Mean	SD		
Physical	28.80	3.81	27.45	3.24	3.312	P<0.05
Social	28.97	4.24	27.90	4.17	2.209	P<0.05
Temperamental	29.18	3.68	27.25	4.07	4.302	P<0.05
Educational	29.37	4.36	28.25	4.46	2.185	P<0.05
Moral	29.15	4.19	29.45	4.76	-0.580	P>0.05
Intellectual	26.34	4.20	25.35	3.41	2.247	P<0.05
Total Self-Concept	171.81	17.86	165.65	16.21	3.128	P<0.05

From table 6, it is found that the total Self-Concept score was higher for boys (171.81) than for girls (165.65).

The 't' value calculated for the Self-Concept and its 6 dimensions with respect to gender revealed that boys and girls differed significantly in the Total Self-Concept and its dimensions namely Physical Self-Concept, Social Self-Concept, Temperamental Self-Concept, Educational Self-Concept and intellectual Self-Concept at 0.05 level except Moral Self-Concept.

(ii)Self-Concept with respect to medium of instruction

The mean standard deviation and t value were calculated for Self-Concept and its dimensions with respect to their Medium of Instruction and the same are given in the table 7.

Table - 7

Mean, Standard Deviation and 't' value for the scores on students Self-Concept with respect to Medium of Instruction

Self-Concept and its dimensions	Malayalam		English		t-value	Level of significance
	Mean	SD	Mean	SD		
Physical	27.43	3.33	28.81	3.73	3.380	P<0.05
Social	27.24	4.48	29.63	3.61	5.095	P<0.05
Temperamental	27.59	4.36	28.84	3.49	2.735	P<0.05
Educational	28.41	4.37	29.21	4.49	1.551	P>0.05
Moral	27.38	4.47	31.21	3.58	8.195	P<0.05
Intellectual	25.44	4.30	26.25	3.32	1.819	P>0.05
Total Self-Concept	163.50	19.42	173.95	12.99	5.479	P<0.05

From the above table, it is observed that the total Self-Concept is more (173.95) for the students who are studying in English medium schools than the students studying in Malayalam Medium Schools (163.50).

The 't' value calculated for the total Self-Concept and its 6 dimensions with respect to the Medium of Instruction revealed that the students from English medium and Malayalam Medium Schools differed significantly in the total Self-Concept and its dimensions such as Physical Self-Concept, Social Self-Concept, Temperamental Self-Concept and Moral Self-Concept at 0.05 level. The dimensions of Self-Concept such as Educational Self-Concept and Intellectual Self-Concept did not differ significantly even at 0.05 level with respect to Medium of Instruction.

(iii)Self-Concept with respect to type of management

The mean standard deviation and F-ratio were calculated for student's Self-Concept and its dimensions with respect to the Type of Management of the schools where they are studying and the results are tabulated in the table 8.

Table - 8

Mean, Standard Deviation and 't' value for the scores on Self-Concept with respect to the type of Management of School

Self-Concept and its dimensions	Private (1)		Aided (2)		Govt (3)		F ratio	L.S	Groups differed significantly
	Mean	SD	Mean	SD	Mean	SD			
Physical	28.80	3.85	27.33	3.35	28.24	3.46	4.350	P<0.05	(1,2)
Social	29.53	3.28	26.99	4.65	28.79	4.28	10.095	P<0.05	(1,2) (2,3)
Temperamental	28.88	3.28	26.99	4.05	28.78	4.32	7.408	P<0.05	(1,2) (2,3)
Educational	29.07	4.45	27.73	4.12	29.63	4.57	4.960	P<0.05	(2,3)
Moral	31.30	3.75	27.83	4.55	28.76	4.39	17.919	P<0.05	(1,2) (1,3)
Intellectual	26.75	3.10	24.02	3.85	26.76	3.92	18.772	P<0.05	(1,2) (2,3)
Total Self-Concept	174.33	12.95	160.89	16.83	170.96	18.83	18.209	P<0.05	(1,2) (2,3)

From table 8, it is found that the Total Self-Concept was high for the students studying in Private schools (174.33) and the same was low (160.89) for those who are studying in Aided schools.

The F-ratio calculated for the Total Self-Concept and its dimensions with respect to the type of management revealed that students studying in Private, Aided and Government Schools differed significantly in their total Self-Concept and all its dimensions namely Physical, Self-Concept, Social Self-Concept, Temperamental Self-Concept, Educational Self-Concept, Moral Self-Concept and intellectual Self-Concept at 0.05 level.

Further analysis of differences between the age groups through Turkey HSD revealed that in the total Self-Concept, the pupils who are studying in the Aided schools differed significantly from those who are studying in the Private Schools and Government Schools. The same is found to be true for the Social, Temperamental and Intellectual Self-Concept.

With regard to the Physical dimension of Self-Concept, students from Private Schools show significant difference from that of the students of Aided Schools. The pupils from Private Schools showed more Physical Self-Concept (28.80) when compared to those from Aided and Government Schools.

In the case of Educational dimension of Self-Concept, students from Aided Schools showed significant difference from the students of Government School.

It is observed from the table that in Moral dimension of Self-Concept, students from Aided Schools showed significant difference to both the Government School students and the private school students. Here the Private School students scored, more (31.30) than that of Government and Aided School students.

(iv)Self-Concept with respect to locality

Mean, Standard Deviation and 't' value for Self-Concept and its dimensions were calculated with respect to locality and the results are given in table 9.

Table - 9

Mean, Standard Deviation and 't' value for the scores of Self-Concept and its dimensions with respect to locality

Self-Concept and its dimensions	Rural		Urban		t-value	Level of significance
	Mean	SD	Mean	SD		
Physical	27.43	3.33	28.81	3.73	3.380	P<0.05
Social	27.24	4.48	29.63	3.61	5.095	P<0.05
Temperamental	27.59	4.36	28.84	3.49	2.735	P<0.05
Educational	28.41	4.37	29.21	4.49	1.551	P<0.05
Moral	27.38	4.47	31.21	3.58	8.195	P<0.05
Intellectual	25.44	4.30	26.25	3.32	1.819	P>0.05
Total Self-Concept	163.50	19.42	173.95	12.99	5.479	P<0.05

From the above table it is found that the Total Self-Concept is more for students from urban area (173.95) than those from the rural area (163.50).

The t value calculated for the Self-Concept and its 6 dimensions with respect to locality revealed that students from rural and urban area differed significantly in the Total Self-Concept and its dimensions such as Physical Self-Concept, Social Self-Concept, Temperamental Self-Concept, Educational Self-Concept and Moral Self-Concept at 0.05 level except intellectual Self-Concept where it did not show any significant difference even at 0.05 level.

(v)Self-Concept with respect to type of family.

The Mean, Standard Deviation and t value have been calculated for Self-Concept and its dimensions with respect to the Type of Family and the results are given in table 10.

Table - 10

Mean, Standard Deviation and 't' value for the scores of Self-Concept and its dimensions with respect to type of family

Self-Concept and its dimensions	Nuclear Mean	Nuclear SD	Joint Mean	Joint SD	t-value	Level of significance
Physical	28.13	3.55	28.00	4.28	0.139	P>0.05
Social	28.47	4.25	28.05	4.09	0.451	P>0.05
Temperamental	28.20	3.98	28.38	4.20	-0.186	P>0.05
Educational	28.86	4.46	28.19	4.20	0.697	P>0.05
Moral	29.28	4.49	29.52	4.38	-0.246	P>0.05
Intellectual	25.88	3.86	25.33	3.84	0.631	P>0.05
Total Self-Concept	168.82	17.54	167.48	0.414	0.414	P>0.05

From the above table, it is observed that the Total Self-Concept is more for students who come from Nuclear family (168.82) than that of those from Joint family (167.48).

The 't' value calculated for Self-Concept and its dimensions with respect to type of family revealed that the students coming from Nuclear and Joint family did not differ significantly in any of the dimensions of Self-Concept and in the total Self-Concept even at 0.05 level.

(vi)Self-Concept with respect to Birth order

The Mean, Standard Deviation and t value have been calculated for the total Self-Concept and its dimensions with respect to birth order and the results are given in table 11.

Table - 11

Mean, Standard Deviation and 'F' ratio for the scores on Self-Concept with respect to Birth Order

Self-Concept and its dimensions	First (1) Mean	First (1) SD	Second (2) Mean	Second (2) SD	Third (3) Mean	Third (3) SD	F value	L.S	Groups differed significantly
Physical	27.66	3.60	28.42	3.53	29.63	3.61	3.399	P<0.05	(1,3)
Social	28.19	3.92	28.58	4.39	29.37	5.43	0.773	P>0.05	N.S
Temperamental	27.93	3.97	28.39	3.84	29.26	5.05	1.151	P>0.05	N.S
Educational	28.69	4.55	28.76	4.37	30.11	4.15	0.870	P>0.05	N.S
Moral	29.56	4.23	29.03	4.67	29.11	5.07	0.501	P>0.05	N.S
Intellectual	25.46	3.66	26.15	3.98	26.74	4.32	1.691	P>0.05	N.S
Total Self-Concept	167.50	16.72	169.33	17.39	174.21	20.64	1.413	P>0.05	N.S

From table 11, it is observed that the total Self-Concept was highest (174.21) for the students whose Birth Order is third and above when compared to those whose birth order is first or second.

The F ratio calculated for the total Self-Concept and its dimensions with respect to the Birth Order, revealed that there is no significant difference between the groups based on their Birth Orders except physical dimension Self-Concept where the pupils whose birth order is 'one' differed significantly from those whose Birth Order is 'third' and above.

(vii) Emotional Maturity with respect to Gender.

The Mean, Standard Deviation and t-value have been calculated for the total Emotional Maturity and its dimensions with respect to Gender and the results are given in table 12.

Table - 12

Mean, Standard Deviation and 'F' ratio for the scores on Emotional Maturity with respect to Gender

Emotional Maturity and its dimensions	Boys Mean	Boys SD	Girls Mean	Girls SD	t-value	Level of significance
Emotional Unstability	25.16	6.88	26.47	6.87	1.645	P>0.05
Emotional regression	22.16	6.54	23.01	6.45	1.138	P>0.05
Social malajustment	22.57	5.98	22.16	5.73	0.601	P>0.05
Personality disintegration	20.77	5.80	19.73	5.71	1.575	P>0.05
Lack of independence	19.11	5.17	18.75	4.32	0.667	P>0.05
Total Emotional Maturity	109.77	23.94	110.11	22.20	-0.128	P>0.05

From the t values shown in table 12 it is revealed that boys and girls did not differ significantly in their total Emotional Maturity and in any of its dimensions.

(viii)Emotional Maturity with respect to Medium of Instruction

The Mean, Standard Deviation and t value have been calculated for the total Emotional Maturity and its dimensions with respect to medium of instruction and the results are given in table 13.

From table 13, it is found that the total Emotional Maturity score is high (112.78) for malayalam medium students indicating that they have less Emotional Maturity than the English medium students.

The 't' value calculated for the total Emotional Maturity and its dimensions with respect to medium of instruction revealed that the students from Malayalam and English medium differ significantly in the scores of their Total Emotional Maturity and its dimensions such as emotional unstability, social maladjustment and personality disintegration. In dimensions such as emotional regression and lack of independence, students from both the medium did not show any significant differences.

Table 13

Mean, Standard Deviation and 'F' ratio for the scores on Emotional Maturity with respect to the Medium of Instruction

Emotional Maturity and its dimensions	Malayalam Mean	Malayalam SD	English Mean	English SD	t-value	Level of significance
Emotional Unstability	26.60	7.47	25.03	6.20	1.985	P<0.05
Emotional Regression	22.34	6.90	22.83	6.08	-0.657	P>0.05
Social Malajustment	23.14	6.31	21.59	5.26	2.315	P<0.05
Personality Disintegration	21.64	5.38	18.86	5.37	4.293	P<0.05
Lack of Independence	19.06	4.74	18.80	4.79	0.472	P>0.05
Total Emotional Maturity	112.78	24.52	107.11	21.18	2.145	P<0.05

(ix)Emotional Maturity with respect to type of management

The Mean, Standard Deviation and F ratio were calculated for the total Emotional Maturity and its dimensions of high school students with respect to the Type of Management and the results are given in table 14

Table - 14

Mean, Standard Deviation and 'F' ratio for the scores on Emotional Maturity with respect to the Type of Management of school

Self-Concept and its dimensions	Private (1) Mean	Private (1) SD	Aided (2) Mean	Aided (2) SD	Govt (3) Mean	Govt (3) SD	F ratio	L.S	Groups differed significantly
Emotional Unstability	26.57	5.79	22.4 1	6.24	28.46	7.20	23.118	P<0.05	(1,2) (2,3)
Emotional Regression	23.95	5.76	20.9 7	6.35	22.84	7.02	5.537	P<0.05	(1,2)
Social Maladjustment	20.77	5.16	21.6 4	5.39	24.68	6.27	13.315	P<0.05	(1,3) (2,3)
Personality Disintegration	18.08	5.31	20.0 8	5.44	22.59	5.69	16.982	P<0.05	(1,2) (1,3) (2,3)
Lack of Independence	19.03	4.07	18.0 5	5.20	19.71	4.84	3.118	P<0.05	(2,3)
Total Emotional Maturity	108.4 0	20.3 7	103. 15	21. 69	118.2 8	24.4 8	11.9 23	P<0.05	(1,3) (2,3)

From table 14, it is observed that the Total Emotional Maturity was less for the students coming from Government school (118.28) than those who come from Private and Aided school.

The F ratio calculated for the total Emotional Maturity and its dimensions with respect to the type of management revealed that the students studying in Government Schools differed significantly in the total Emotional Maturity and all its dimensions namely Emotional unstability, Emotional Regression, Social Maladjustment, personality disintegration and lack of independence.

Further analysis of differences between the different school Types revealed that in the total Emotional Maturity, the pupils from Government Schools differed significantly from those of Private and Aided schools.

The same was found to be true for Social Maladjustment.

With regard to emotional unstability, aided school students differed significantly from those who studied in private and government schools. Pupils from Government schools are found to possess more Emotional unstability.

In the case of Emotional regression the Private School students and aided school students differed significantly and the Private School students were found to have more Emotional regression than the other two groups.

With regard to personality disintegration, the pupils belong to all the Private, Aided and Government Schools differed significantly with each other and the Government School students possess more Personality Disintegration (22.59) when compared to the other two groups.

Regarding lack of independence, it is found that the students studying in Aided and Government Schools showed significant difference and the students studying in Government Schools are found to have more lack of independence.

(x)Emotional Maturity with respect to locality

The Mean Standard deviation and 't' value were calculated for the total Emotional Maturity and its dimensions of high school students with respect to the locality and the results are given in table 15.

From the table 15, it is observed that the Emotional Maturity scores is more for the pupils coming from rural area, indicating that they are having less Emotional Maturity than the pupils from Urban Area.

Table - 15

Mean, standard deviation and 't' value for the scores on Emotional Maturity with respect to locality of school

Emotional Maturity and its dimensions	Rural Mean	Rural SD	Urban Mean	Urban SD	t-value	Level of significance
Emotional Unstability	26.60	7.47	25.03	6.20	1.985	P<0.05
Emotional Regression	22.34	6.90	22.83	6.08	0.657	P>0.05
Social Maladjustment	23.14	6.31	21.59	5.26	2.315	P<0.05
Personality Disintegration	21.64	5.83	18.86	5.37	4.293	P<0.05
Lack of Independence	19.06	4.74	18.80	4.79	0.472	P>0.05
Total Emotional Maturity	112.78	24.52	21.18	21.18	2.145	P<0.05

The 't' value calculated for the Total Emotional Maturity and its dimensions with respect to Locality revealed that students coming from rural and Urban Areas, differed significantly in their total Emotional Maturity and its dimensions such as Emotional Unstability, Social Maladjustment and personality disintegration. In emotional regression and lack of Independence the students from Rural and Urban area did not differ significantly.

(xi)Emotional Maturity with respect to Type of Family.

The mean, Standard Deviation and t value were calculated for the total Emotional Maturity and its dimensions of high school students with respect to type of family and the results are given in table 16.

Table - 16

Mean, Standard Deviation and 't' value for the scores on Emotional Maturity with respect to Type of Family

Emotional Maturity and its dimensions	Nuclear Mean	Nuclear SD	Joint Mean	Joint SD	t-value	Level of significance
Emotional Unstability	26.07	6.86	22.43	6.65	2.412	P>0.05
Emotional Regression	22.78	6.45	20.05	6.71	1.802	P>0.05
Social Maladjustment	22.44	5.97	21.29	3.90	1.255	P>0.05
Personality Disintegration	20.35	5.86	18.90	4.32	1.437	P>0.05
Lack of Independence	19.07	4.82	17.05	3.38	2.553	P>0.05
Total Emotional Maturity	110.71	23.16	99.71	19.11	2.503	P>0.05

From the table 16, it is observed that the mean score of Emotional Maturity is more (110:71) for students coming from nuclear family which shows that they are having less Emotional Maturity than those who are coming from Joint Family.

The 't' value calculated for the total Emotional Maturity and its dimensions with respect to Type of Family, revealed that the students coming from nuclear and Joint Families did not differ significantly in their total Emotional Maturity and any of their dimensions such as Emotional Unstability, Emotional Regression, Social Maladjustment, Personality disintegration and lack of Independence.

(xii) Emotional Maturity with respect to Birth Order

The Mean, Standard Deviation and 'F' ratio were calculated for the total Emotional Maturity and its dimensions of High School students with respect to the Birth Order and the Results are given in table 17.

Table - 17

Mean, Standard Deviation and 'F' ratio for the score on Emotional Maturity with respect to the Birth Order of the students

Emotional Maturity and its dimensions	First (1)		Second (2)		Third and Above (3)		F value	L.S	Groups differed significantly
	Mean	SD	Mean	SD	Mean	SD			
Emotional Unstability	24.93	6.58	26.56	7.11	27.58	7.24	2.659	P>0.05	N.S
Emotional Regression	22.11	6.25	22.98	6.69	23.63	7.10	0.889	P>0.05	N.S
Social Maladjustment	21.56	5.62	22.84	5.93	25.37	6.07	4.456	P<0.05	(1,3)
Personality Disintegration	19.91	5.63	20.41	6.02	21.84	5.01	1.039	P>0.05	N.S
Lack of Independence	18.67	4.63	19.08	4.81	19.95	5.45		P>0.05	N.S
Total Emotional Maturity	107.17	21.45	111.86	24.00	118.37	26.08	2.843	P>0.05	N.S

From the table 17, it is found that the total Emotional Maturity score was high for the pupils whose birth order is 'third and above' which indicates that they have a less Emotional Maturity than the other two groups.

The F ratio calculated for the total Emotional Maturity and its dimensions with respect to the birth order revealed that the students belonging to different birth orders did not differ significantly in the total Emotional Maturity and its Dimensions such as Emotional Unstability, Emotional Regression, Personality Disintegration and Lack of Independence. The total Emotional Maturity score was high for the students whose Birth Order is third and above which shows that they show less Emotional Maturity.

With regard to Social Maladjustment, students whose Birth Order is first and 'third and above' differed significantly. The Children whose Birth Order is first was found to have less Social Maladjustment and Emotional Maturity.

Association Analysis

(i) Association between Self-Concept and the background variables

The significant association between the variable Self-Concept and the background variables have been assessed through chi-square test, the details of which are represented in the following table.

Table - 18

Showing the Chi-square Distribution to find out the Association between Self-Concept and background variables

Self-Concept & Variables	χ^2	df	L.S.	Contingency Coefficient
Gender	5.497	2	P>0.05	0.134
Medium of Instruction	32.972	2	P<0.01	0.315
Type of Management	38.511	4	P<0.01	0.337
Locale	32.972	2	P<0.01	0.315
Type of Family	1.464	2	P>0.05	0.070
Birth Order	3.003	4	P>0.05	0.100

From the above table it is observed that there is a Significant Association between Self-Concept and medium of instruction; Self-Concept and Type of Management; and Self-Concept and locality as seen from the χ^2 value.

Table - 19

Showing the Chi-Square distribution to find out the Association between Self-Concept and Background variables

Emotional Maturity Vs variables	χ^2	df	L.S.	Contingency Coefficient
Gender	0.005	2	P>0.05	0.036
Medium of Instruction	2.173	2	P>0.01	0.085
Type of Management	21.785	4	P<0.01	0.260
Locale	2.173	2	P>0.01	0.085
Type of Family	7.615	2	P<0.05	0.157
Birth Order	4.574	4	P>0.05	0.123

(ii) Association between Emotional Maturity and the back ground variables

The significant association between the Emotional Maturity and the back ground variables have been studied through Chi-Square test, the details of which are represented in the following table.

From the above table, it is observed that there is a significant association between Emotional Maturity and type of management; and Emotional Maturity and type of family as seen from the χ^2.

Correlation Analysis

Relationship between Self-Concept and Emotional Maturity

The correlation between Self-Concept and Emotional Maturity has been calculated and results are presented in table 20.

Table - 20

Table showing 'r'-value and level of significance for the variables, Self-Concept and Emotional Maturity

Variables compared	r - value	Level of significance
Self-Concept and Emotional Maturity	0.051	NS

From the above table, we can conclude that there is no significant correlation between Self-Concept and Emotional Maturity.

CONCLUSION

A brief report of the research study together with major findings and conclusions arrived at along with their educational implications have been presented in the succeeding chapter.

5

Summary, Findings & Conclusions

INTRODUCTION

The present chapter gives a brief summary of the various findings of the entire study and it also gives the statistical analysis of data presented in the previous chapter. The implications along with suggestions for replicating the study or for investigating of other closely related problems in other settings with different samples and tools are also presented.

STATEMENT OF THE PROBLEMS

The present study has been specifically inducted to study the relation between Self-Concept and Emotional Maturity of High School students. The relative contribution of personal variables (Gender, Locale, Type of family and Birth Order) school related variables (medium of instructions and type of management) and research variables (Self-Concept and Emotional Maturity) among high school students are investigated in this study.

The problem is stated as "A study of Self-Concept and Emotional Maturity among high school students".

KEYWORDS IN THE STATEMENT

Self-Concept

Self-Concept is the individual's way of looking at himself. It also signifies his way of thinking, feeling and behaving.

Self - Concept is the dominant element is the personality pattern, it governs the individual's characteristic reaction to people and situations and determines the quality of his behaviour.

Emotional Maturity

Emotional Maturity is a process in which the personality is continuously striving for greater sense of emotional health, both intra physically and intra personally.

If the emotional development of the individual is relatively complete his adaptability is high, his regressive tendencies are low, and his vulnerability is minimal.

OBJECTIVES OF THE STUDY

1. To find out the level of Self-Concept among high school students.
2. To find out the level of Emotional Maturity among high school students.
3. To find out whether there is significant difference in the total Self-Concept and its dimensions of high school students with respect to their.
    a. Gender
    b. Medium of instructions
    c. Type of Management
    d. Locality
    e. Type of family
    f. Birth Order
4. To find out whether there is significant difference in the total Emotional Maturity and its dimensions of high school students with respect to their.
    a. Gender
    b. Medium of instructions

c. Type of Management
d. Locality
e. Type of family
f. Birth Order

5. To find out whether there is any significant association between Self-Concept of high school students and the following variables.

    a. Gender
    b. Medium of instructions
    c. Type of Management
    d. Locality
    e. Type of family
    f. Birth Order

6. To find out whether there is any significant association between Emotional Maturity of high school students and the following variables.

    a. Gender
    b. Medium of instructions
    c. Type of Management
    d. Locality
    e. Type of family
    f. Birth Order

7. To find out the relationship between Self-Concept of high school students and their Emotional Maturity.

HYPOTHESES

1. The level of Self-Concept among high school students is moderate in nature.
2. The level of Emotional Maturity among high school students is low in nature.
3. There is no significant difference in the total Self-Concept and its dimensions of high school students with respect to their

    a) Gender
    b) Medium of instructions
    c) Type of management

   d) Locality
   e) Type of family
   f) Birth order

4. There is no significant difference in the Total Emotional Maturity and its dimensions of high school students with respect to their.
   a) Gender
   b) Medium of instructions
   c) Type of management
   d) Locality
   e) Type of family
   f) Birth order

5. There is significant association in Self-Concept between high school students and the following variables.
   a) Gender
   b) Medium of instructions
   c) Type of management
   d) Locality
   e) Type of family
   f) Birth order

6. There is significant association in Emotional Maturity between high school students and the following variables
   a) Gender
   b) Medium of instructions
   c) Type of management
   d) Locality
   e) Type of family
   f) Birth order

7. There is no significant relationship between Self-Concept of high school students and their Emotional Maturity.

TOOLS AND TECHNIQUES

The following tools have been used to verify the hypotheses.

i. Self-Concept questionnaire prepared by Dr.Rajkumar Saraswat.
ii. Emotional Maturity scale prepared by Dr.Yashvir Singh and Dr.Mahesh Bhargava.

SAMPLE

Stratified random sampling technique has been adopted to choose the sample. A representative sample of 300 students were drawn from different high schools in Thiruvananthapuram District of Kerala.

MAJOR FINDINGS OF THE STUDY

1. The level of Self-Concept among high school students is high in nature.
2. The level of Emotional Maturity among high school students is low in nature.
3. There is significant difference in the Self-Concept of high school students with respect to their
   a. Gender
   b. Medium of instruction
   c. Type of management
   d. Locality
4. There is significant difference in the Emotional Maturity of high school students with respect to thus
   a. Medium of instruction
   b. Type of management
   c. Locality
5. There is significant association between Self-Concept of high school students and the following variables.
   a. Medium of instruction
   b. Type of management
   c. Locality
6. There is significant association between Emotional Maturity of high school students and the following variables.

   a. Type of management
   b. Type of family

7. There is no significant relationship between Self-Concept of high school students and their Emotional Maturity.

EDUCATIONAL IMPLICATIONS

A persons concept of his self is one of the best predictions of his successful achievement. The relationship of Self-Concept to school achievement is very specific. The level of school success predicts the level of regard of self and one's own ability. Hence the teachers need to concentrate on the academic successes and failures of the students. It is the student's history of success and failures that gives them the information with which to assess themselves. Developing proper emotions and controlling them is another important objective of education during adolescence. Emotional Maturity is reflected in an individual's ability to be responsive to the entire hierarchy of emotions - as they are the communications that provides the basis for differentiation and discernment of just what our impact is. Emotional Maturity is a result of conscious choice, our conscious choice to be responsible for our impact. As Self-Concept and Emotional Maturity are both constructed by one's conscious reflections, the educators and parents should provide experiences that students can master rather than attempting to boost self esteem directly through other means. It is the responsibility of the teachers and school to facilitate adjustment and learning. In this research the findings of the study will be helpful for the teachers as well as curriculum planners to work out innovative strategies in improving the Self-Concept and Emotional Maturity of the students.

DELIMITATIONS OF THE STUDY

1. The study was limited to the schools located in Kerala.
2. The study was limited to high school students only.
3. The sample is restricted to 300 students.

SUGGESTIONS FOR FURTHER RESEARCH

Following are some of the suggestions put forward by the investigator for further research.

1. This study was confined only with the students of high school. To make the findings of this study more universal, a comprehensive study of this type involving different standards of students could be undertaken.
2. This study was conducted only in a few selected schools. It can be extended to many districts.
3. A comparitive study can be undertaken among primary, secondary and higher secondary school students.
4. Investigation may be made on identifying various ways to improve the Self-Concept and Emotional Maturity of the students.

BIBLIOGRAPHY

1. **Allan Brad Brake** (1997). *Emotion and its influence on problem solving. Dissertation abstract.*
2. **Allen Jaffe,** (1981). *A study of emotional maturity on the legislators of Illinois* state; *Dissertation abstract.*
3. **Arya - A,** (1984). *Emotional maturity and value of superior children in family. Buch,* 1327 IV (2).
4. **Barooh .S and Phukan M,** (1999). *Self concept of Orphan children and the children with natural parents.*
5. **Benge et al.,** (1996). *Understanding the emotional development of twice exceptional rural student.* Dissertation abstract.
6. **Bryman, Alan**, (2001), *Social Research Methods, Oxford University Press,* pp.28 - 30.
7. **Bush Kethryn,** (1989). *Studies of emotional maturity.* Dissertation abstract.
8. **Chanda, Sunanda,** (1990). *Study on self-concept parental influence of socio economic status and sex in education to carreer choice attitude among high school students.* Dissertation abstract
9. **Chauhan, Sarita,** (1992). *A study of valves, self - concept, creativity and anxiety among professional college students.* Journal of education and psychology.
10. **Connolly et al.,** (1994). *Peer self - concept of adolescence: Analysis of factor structure and association with peer experiences;* Journal of research on adolescence; V4n3, p.385-403.

11. **Creamer, Don .G:** *Using a developmental model of emotional maturity.* Dissertation abstract from, New Directions for community colleges; Vol.20, n3/p.73-82.

12. **Cross,** (1991). *A study of self - concept of middle school students,* Dissertation abstract.

13. **Dastoor, H.F.** (1982). *A study of different types of self concept prevalent among nurses,* Fifth survey of educational research. Dissertation abstract.

14. **Deo P et al.,** (1971). *A study of relationship of self - concept and anxiety, Fifth survey of educational research.*

15. **Dhami, G.S.** (1974). *Intelligence, emotional maturity and socio - economic status and factors indicative of success in scholastic Achievement*; Buch, V/II/P-1885.

16. **Kaisa Aunola, et al.,** (2002). *Developmental changes in reading skills and self - concept*; University of Finland.

17. **Karan, Patricia,** (1989). *Relationship of peer group and the self - concept of adolescence,* Dissertation abstract.

18. **Kellner et al.,** (1995). *A school based Anger Managmeent programme for developmentally and emotionally disabled high school students;* Adolescence; V30n120, p.813-25.

19. **Kloomok, et al.,** (1992). *Positive self - concept on academic difficulties; International*; Dissertation Abstract.

20. **Manral Bheema** (1988). *The input of emotional maturity and prolonged deprivation on indisciplined behaviour among university students in relation to their academic achievement.* Dissertation abstract.

21. **Mohan** (1975); *Self concept over years of adolescence:* Dissertation abstract.

22. **Narayanan and Ganesan**, (1978). *Self concept of scheduled tribes of Palamalai in Tamil Nadu,* Dissertation abstract.

23. **Pandit, I** (1985). *Self acceptance of sixth grade of adolescence; Journal of Psychology.*

24. **Paul Bruece** (1958). *Self concept of sixth grade students: Journal of Psychology.*

25. **Gerdes et al.,** (1994). *Emotional social and academic adjustment of college students. A longitudinal study of retention.* Journal of Counselling and Development, v.72n3/ p.281 - 88.

26. **Ghose P and Khurana** (1986). *A study of socio economic status and Self - Concept. Journal of education and psychology.*

27. **Gordon et al.,** (1995). *Self-Concept and motivational patterns of Resilient African American High School Students. Journal of black psychology;* v21 n3, p.239-55.

28. **Heyer and et al.,** (1993). *The relationship between parental marital status and development of identify and emotional autonomy in college students.* Journal of college student development. v. 34, n6, p.432 - 36.

29. **Jogawar, V.V.** (1983). *Self-Concept and family relation in India,* Fourth Survey of Research, Vol.27.

30. **Joseph Alexander E and Rajendran, K**. (1992). *Influence of self - concept, sex, area and parents education on adjustment problems;* Dissertation abstract.

31. **Prasad S,** (1982). *Important factors of stability of self - concept,* Dissertation abstract.

32. **Pyryt et al.,** (1994). *The multi dimensional Self-Concept:* A comparsion of gifted and average ability adolescents.

33. **Ramiah. L** (1990). *A relational study of parent involvement and self - concept of standard IX students in Devakottai Educational District* - Alagappa Univ. Fifth Survey of educational Research, Volume II, page 922.

34. **Sandhu, Daya Singh,** (1992). *A child's mind in the adult body.* Journal of Adult development Spec. Issue, p.23 - 35.

35. **Sax Linda,** (1994). *Development of Mathematical Self-Concept in college students,* Dissertation abstract international.

36. **Siddiqui M.M.** (1976). *Social pscyhological study of student behaviours with special reference to indiscipline,* Buch, 1327, iv/ 2.

37. **Walia, D,** (1973). *Gifted adolescent and their self concept;* India, Faculty of Education & Psychology.

PERSONAL DATA

1. Name of the Student :
2. Name of School :
3. Gender (Male / Female) :
4. Class :
5. Medium of Instruction :
6. Type of Management
   (Govt. / Aided / Private) :
7. Location of School
   (Rural / Urban) :
8. Type of Family
   (Nuclear / Joint) :
9. Birth Order of the Child
   (1st / 2nd / 3rd and above) :

APPENDIX – I

Instructions

On the following pages there are some questions and their probable answers given against them. You read them carefully and whichever suits, you, put a tick (✓) in the blank space given against it. You have to mark only one answer. An illustration is given below. There is no time limit for it but you should answer it as soon as possible.

1 Do your friends come to you for advice?

Always	( )
Usually	( )
Sometimes	( )
Usually Not	( )
Never	( )
Obtained R.S	

2 What do you think about your appearance?

V. beautiful	( )
Beautiful	( )
Satisfactory	( )
Not satisfactory	( )
Ugly	( )

3. What do you think about your appearance?
   Very Strong ( )
   Strong ( )
   Average ( )
   Delicate ( )
   Very Delicate ( )
4. How do you like school studies?
   Always cheerful ( )
   Cheerful ( )
   Normal ( )
   Sometimes unhappy ( )
   Always unhappy ( )
5. How do you like school studies
   Very good ( )
   Good ( )
   Average ( )
   Not good ( )
   Not good at all ( )
6. Do you believe in religious customs and traditions?
   Very much ( )
   Usually ( )
   Normally ( )
   Sometimes ( )
   Never ( )
7. Do you participate in criticizing others?
   Always ( )
   Mostly ( )
   Generally ( )
   Not usually ( )
   Never ( )
8. Do you express your ideas frankly in the presence of others?

Always ( )
Mostly ( )
Normally ( )
Some time ( )
Never ( )

9. How do you like your complexion?
V. beautiful ( )
Beautiful ( )
Normal ( )
Not so beautiful ( )
Ugly ( )

10. Do you think yourself one of the cheerful persons?
Always ( )
Mostly ( )
Normally ( )
No ( )
Never ( )

11. Do you behave abnormally also?
Always ( )
Mostly ( )
Sometimes ( )
Seldom ( )
Never ( )

12. Do you think yourself an experienced person?
High ( )
Usually ( )
Average ( )
Less experienced ( )
Without any experience ( )

13. Do you think about your teachers?
Always ( )
Mostly ( )

Normally ( )
Usually not ( )
Never ( )

14. Do you think yourself to be a cool-tempered man?
Very much ( )
Usually ( )
Average ( )
Some disturbed ( )
Much disturbed ( )
Obtained R.S.

15. Are you regular in doing your home-work assignments?
Always ( )
Mostly ( )
Normally ( )
Some times ( )
Never ( )

16. Do you insult others?
Never ( )
Not often ( )
Usually ( )
Mostly ( )
Always ( )

17. Do you have difficulty in understanding something when the teacher explains in the class?
Never ( )
Usually ( )
Generally ( )
Often feel difficulty ( )
Usually feel difficulty ( )

18. Do you think if you get an opportunity you can discover something new?
Definitely ( )
Most definitely ( )

Probably ( )
Doubtful ( )
Not at all ( )

19. Do you feel irritated if somebody finds fault with your work?
Never ( )
Usually not ( )
Sometimes ( )
Usually ( )
Always ( )

20. How do you find your personality?
Most attractive ( )
Attractive ( )
Normal ( )
Unattractive ( )
Totally unattractive ( )

21. How do you like the company of others?
Always good ( )
Mostly good ( )
Usually good ( )
Sometimes dislike ( )
Never like ( )

22. How much are you satisfied with your weight?
Fully satisfied ( )
Satisfied ( )
Usually satisfied ( )
Not so satisfied ( )
Unsatisfied ( )

23. Do you feel irritated while you face petty difficulties?
Never ( )
Mostly not ( )
Generally ( )
Sometimes ( )
Always ( )

24. Are you coward by nature?

Not at all ( )
Not much ( )
Normal ( )
Usually ( )
Very much ( )

25. How much are you satisfied with the present position of your studies in class?

Completely satisfied ( )
Somewhat satisfied ( )
Average ( )
Somewhat dissatisfied ( )
Totally dissatisfied ( )

26. How do you like school examination?

Like very much ( )
Mostly like ( )
Generally like ( )
Seldom like ( )
Never like ( )
Obtained R.S.

27. How is your voice?

Very good ( )
Good ( )
Normal ( )
Not good ( )
Unsatisfactory ( )

28. Are you curious to know the end while reading a novel or seeing a movie?

Always ( )
Usually ( )
Normally ( )
No ( )
Not at all ( )

29. How do you find your health?

Very good ( )
Good ( )
Average ( )
Week ( )
Feeble ( )

30. How is your attendance in the class?

Always present ( )
Usually present ( )
Average ( )
Generally absent ( )
Usually absent ( )

31 How much are you satisfied with your height?

Fully satisfied ( )
Satisfied ( )
Normal ( )
Somewhat ( )
Fully dissatisfied ( )

32. Do you try to get first position in the tests given in the class?

Always ( )
Usually ( )
Generally ( )
Often not ( )
Never ( )

33. Do you take care of the merits and demerits of a work before doing it?

Always ( )
Usually ( )
Generally ( )
Usually not ( )
Never ( )

34. Where do you place your self while speaking truth?

Always speak truth
Usually speak truth ( )
Generally speak truth ( )
Usually hesitate in speaking truth ( )
Always have to resort to false hood ( )

35. Where do you place yourself in obeying public rules e.g. rules ( ) pertaining to public places, like road, park, railway station etc.?
Always obey rules ( )
Usually obey rules ( )
Generally obey rules ( )
Usually do not obey rules ( )
Never care for rules ( )

36. Are you more intelligent than your colleagues?
Certainly more ( )
Usually ( )
Generally ( )
Less ( )
Not at all ( )

37. Do you taken part in organizing it when your classmates go to picnic?
Always ( )
Usually ( )
Generally ( )
Usually not ( )
Never ( )

38. Do you solve yourself the difficulties and problems of your studies?
Always solve ( )
Usually solve ( )
Generally solve ( )
Usually can't solve ( )

Always help to others ( )

Obtained R.S.

39. How much do you attend to artistic aspect of the photograph while seeing or making it?

Give very much attention ( )

Give much attention ( )

Give Average attention ( )

Give some attention ( )

Do not give any attention ( )

40. What will you do if you are doing some important work and your friends ask you to accompany them for a walk?

Will start immediately ( )

Will go after thinking for sometimes ( )

Will keep silent ( )

Will not go after thinking for sometime ( )

Will refuse at once ( )

41. While taking the examination you are not able to answer some question and a book of the same subject is lying near you, will you take help of the book?

Will never do such thing ( )

Do not have the courage to do inspire of will ( )

Generally do not do this ( )

Will use the book if get an opportunity ( )

Will immediately use the book ( )

42. If you get an opportunity to drink water in the house of so called low case persons, what will you do?

Shall take water ( )

Will take water after some consideration ( )

Will care for cleanliness ( )

Will take water but would tell nobody ( )

Will not take water ( )

43. Do you hesitate in mixing with persons of opposite sex?

Do not hesitate at all ( )

Sometimes hesitate ( )
Generally do not hesitate ( )
Usually hesitate ( )
Always hesitate ( )

44. You are standing in the bus queue for a longtime when bus comes, the conductor takes some passengers and stops at your turn because there is no space in the bus, what will you do in these circumstances?

Will wait for the next bus ( )
Will request the conductor ( )
Will run and try to board the bus ( )
Will push the other passengers and try to board the bus ( )
Will make a noise ( )

45. What will you do if you come to know of immoral character of your friend?

Will completely break the friendship ( )
Will lessen the friendship ( )
Will continue friendship but will try to make him understand ( )
Will continue friendship as it was ( )
Will strengthen the friendship ( )

46. You have to do four tasks – (a) you have to call the doctor to show your sick brother (b) you have to do the preparation for going out the next day (c) you have to read novel (d) the friend is going away, you have to go to see him. What will you do in the first place?Will call the doctor to show the sick brother

Will prepare for going out ( )
Will read novel ( )
Will go to see the friend ( )
Will not do any of the above mentioned work ( )

47. Your friend gives you one thousand rupees to keep and when you count they are eleven hundred what will you do?

Will return one hundred rupees to the friend at once ( )

Will tell the friend at once ( )

Will return 1100 rupees while returning them ( )

If the friend does not come to know, will take out one hundred rupees if possible ( )

Shall take out one hundred rupees ( )

48. Do you like to do the work keeping in mind the desire of other?

Always do the work keeping in mind the desire of others ( )

Usually do the work keeping in mind the desires of others ( )

Generally do the work keeping in mind the desires of others ( )

Sometimes do not care for the liking of other ( )

Always do according to one's own will ( )

APPENDIX -II

Questionnaire for Emotional Maturity

INSTRUCTIONS

In the following pages are given forty eight questions about yourself. Five possible modes of responses are provided, such as VM: Very Much; M: Much; UD: Undecided; P: Probably and N: Never, read each question carefully and mark tick (✓) in ANY ONE of the five alternative response modes to indicate your level of agreement with the particular content of the questions.

	Questions	Very much (VM)	Much (M)	Undecided (UD)	Probably (P)	Never (N)
A	1. Do you have any mental botherations?					
	2. Are you frightened of the coming situations?					
	3. Do you stop your work in the middle, before attaining the goal?					
	4. Do you take the help of others in completing your personal work?					
	5. Is there any difference between your desires and your objectives?					
	6. Do you think you are short tempered by					

nature?

7. Do you feel that you are very stubborn?
8. Do you feel jealous of other people?
9. Do you get wild due to anger?
10. Do you get lost in imagination and day-dream?

B 11. If you fail to achieve your goal, do you feel inferior?

12. Do you experience a sense of discomfort and lack of peace of mind?
13. Do you tease others?
14. Do you try to put the blame on others for your failures?
15. When you do not agree with others, do you quarrel with them?
16. Do you feel exhausted?
17. Are you more aggressive than your friends and others?
18. Do you get lost in the world of imaginations?
19. Do you feel that you are self centered?
20. Do you feel that you are dissatisfied with yourself?

C. 21. Do you have an uncomfortable companionship with your friends and colleagues?

22. Do you hate others?
23. Do you praise yourself?
24. Do you avoid joining in social gatherings?
25. Do you spend much of your time for your own sake?
26. Do you lie?
27. Do you bluff?
28. Do you like very much to be alone?
29. Are you a proud person by nature?
30. Do you shirk from work?

D. 31. Even though you know some work, do you pretend as if you do not know it?

32. Even if you do not know about some work, do you pose as if you know it?
33. Having known that you are wrong, instead

of accepting, do you try to establish that you were right?

34. Do you suffer from any kind of fear?
35. Do you lost your mental balance?
36. Do you have the habit of stealing anything?
37. Do you indulge freely without bothering about moral codes of conduct?
38. Are you pessimistic towards life?
39. Do you have a weak will?
40. Are you intolerant about the vicws of others?

E 41. Do people think that you are not dependable?
42. Do people disagree with your views?
43. Do you accept any one as your role model?
44. Do you disagree with the opinions of your groups?
45. Do people think of you, as an irresponsible person?
46. Do you show interest in others work?
47. Do people hesitate to take your help in any work?
48. Do you give more importance to your work than others work?

Index